SUPER GREEN SMOOTHIES

SUPER GREEN SMOOTHIES

Veggie-Based Recipes
to Boost Your Health and Well-Being

DANIELLE OMAR, RDN

photography by **MARIJA VIDAL**

**ROCKRIDGE
PRESS**

Interior and Cover Designer: Carlos Esparza
Art Producer: Sue Bischofberger
Editors: Nicky Montalvo and Crystal Nero
Production Editor: Andrew Yackira
Photography © 2019 Marija Vidal. Food styling by Elisabet der Nederlanden.

ISBN: Print 978-1-64611-001-8 | eBook 978-1-64611-002-5
R0

This book is for Norah.
You are the light, love, and joy of my life.

CONTENTS

INTRODUCTION

The truth is, I once was a raw foodie.

Yup, I dabbled in the raw food lifestyle. I went to raw food seminars and conferences for fun. I did weekend cleanses and read tons of books on the benefits of raw food. I watched all the documentaries. I even taught monthly raw food cooking classes and started a catering business, delivering raw meals each week to local clients. I fully immersed myself in the lifestyle and learned an enormous amount of information about the power of plants.

All that said, as a registered dietitian and lifelong vegetarian, I didn't need much convincing that plants are amazingly beneficial for our health. I just didn't fully appreciate all the nourishing power of leafy greens until I started to study them extensively.

I had been drinking fruit smoothies pretty regularly before, but I wasn't adding greens to them. And at first, I didn't know what to expect. I'll admit, I was a little nervous about the idea of blending pineapple and spinach in *the same drink*. But I tried it and was pleasantly surprised. I mean, who knew that if I added fresh mint and coconut milk to pineapple and spinach, it would taste shockingly similar to a virgin piña colada?

Here's the thing . . . I couldn't taste the spinach *at all*.

This led me to experiment with other leafy greens and vegetables, and before I knew it, I was hooked! Green smoothies had become my "thing." I started to drink one every day and was feeling better than ever. I was so excited about the incredible benefits I was noticing, like clearer skin, better digestion, and tons of energy, that I began talking to my clients about drinking green smoothies. Soon they started to see some great results, too. They were losing weight, sleeping better, having fewer aches and pains. It was pretty amazing.

To spread the news about green smoothies to as many people as possible, I decided to create an online nutrition program with green smoothies as its foundation. And just like that, my signature program, *Nourish: 21 Days of Clean Eating*, was born. Since then I've shared my passion for greens with so many people—thousands have gone through my program, and many do it up to three times per year!

I believe that the small changes we make every day toward living a healthier life build up our confidence and enable us to do more. Incorporating green smoothies into your diet can be that one small change. Not only will you start feeling better physically because you're keeping hydrated and absorbing more nutrients, but you'll start to feel better mentally, too. Why? Because greens keep your brain sharp! There's a growing body of evidence suggesting that greens contribute to better cognition as we age. In fact, consuming just one cup of raw leafy green vegetables every day can help slow decline in brain function, thanks to brain-boosting nutrients like lutein, vitamin K, nitrate, folate, beta-carotene, and kaempferol.

In the pages to come you'll find 80 delicious and easy-to-make, low-sugar, vegetable-heavy smoothie recipes organized by their health benefits, including weight loss, detox, heart and digestive health, antioxidant, anti-inflammatory, energy boosting, and healthy skin. You'll also learn everything you need to make successful smoothies, from the fundamentals on ingredients to expert tips on superfoods, to smoothie prep, information on equipment, and more.

In short, green smoothies can truly be the key that opens the door to more conscious, empowered eating. But if we take a moment to consider the big picture, this is about more than your daily diet. It's about living life to its fullest—and most delicious. So join me, and let's take the first step.

CHAPTER ONE

HEALTHY SMOOTHIE, HAPPY BODY

In a world of diet advice overload, it's easy to become confused about what to eat. Many of my clients come to me wanting a healthier lifestyle and a more balanced relationship with food, but they don't know where to start. I see this pattern all the time. Conflicting information leads to confusion and feeling overwhelmed, and they end up doing nothing at all.

Green smoothies are the answer! Starting the day with an infusion of nutrient-rich greens and powerful antioxidants is a natural energy booster and an easy way to supercharge your health. Green smoothies are not just convenient and super easy to prepare, they're also portable, making them a perfect choice for those days on the go.

This chapter will teach you all you need to know about the art of green smoothie making. You'll get step-by-step instructions for building the perfect smoothie, how to select the best produce, choosing liquid bases and add-ins, using herbs and spices, what equipment you need, and the flavors and health benefits of a wide range of fruits and veggies you might use. You'll also get the scoop on how to make your smoothies creamy and delicious with low-sugar, simple ingredients.

If you're already a green smoothie devotee, you may want to get superfood savvy—we'll get into that, too.

Let's get blending!

The Benefits of Going Green

One of the first things I teach my clients is that smoothie making is not difficult. In fact, whipping up a smoothie is one of the quickest (and simplest) ways you can upgrade your health.

Here's the thing. To start drinking green smoothies, you don't have to make drastic changes to your lifestyle, and you certainly don't need to acquire amazing cooking skills. Smoothies are easy to prepare and enjoy—no complicated equipment or special ingredients required.

Still not convinced? Let's dive in to all the reasons green smoothies are the fastest way to start improving your health.

Why go green? The nutrients we obtain from plants are abundant and remarkable. In fact, plant foods are some of the most nutritious foods you can eat. Leafy greens and vegetables are rich sources of antioxidants, vitamins A, C, and E, and important minerals like iron, potassium, calcium, and magnesium. They're also loaded with fiber. Dietary fiber feeds the good bacteria in your gut while helping reduce inflammation, improve digestion, and promote a healthy microbiome.

Cruciferous veggies are especially powerful and top the list of nutrition superstars. Kale, arugula, cauliflower, and broccoli are loaded with vital nutrients and powerful phytochemicals. Kale is a potent detoxifier, packed with compounds called glucosinolates that support detox at the cellular level, while broccoli is a natural bone booster, containing as much calcium per ounce as milk. Cauliflower is rich in sulforaphane, an antioxidant that helps fight against heart disease and diabetes. The various antioxidants and phytonutrients found in crucifers also lower inflammation in the body and have potent anticancer properties.

Adding these and other important nutrients to your smoothie is the perfect stepping-stone to a healthier body, especially if you're not currently eating a lot of vegetables. It takes almost no effort to pack your smoothie with these nutritious ingredients—and it's fun to experiment with different fruit and vegetable combinations.

While green smoothies can help you boost your intake of nutrient-rich fruits, veggies, and leafy greens, it's important to balance your ingredients. You want to avoid smoothies too high in fruit and fruit juices: These can actually cause a spike in your blood sugar and leave you feeling hungry shortly afterwards. The trick to creating a satisfying, nutrient-boosting smoothie is to balance the fruit with equal parts veggies and leafy greens, along with low-sugar base ingredients. This combination will keep you full and satiated for hours.

All the recipes in *Super Green Smoothies* are vegetable-forward, low in sugar, and wonderfully satisfying. Fruit is an important ingredient for adding flavor and balance, but it's not the main course. In fact, you won't find more than one cup of fruit in any of these recipes.

Your diet is a powerful player when it comes to staying healthy, so by consuming delicious, nutrient-rich smoothies, you take a first step in the right direction. Adding a green smoothie to your daily routine can make a huge difference in how you feel, without the need for fancy, hard-to-find ingredients, or tons of time spent in the kitchen. Better yet, your daily infusion of liquid green goodness is sure to inspire the rest of your meals, too.

Raw, Cooked, Fresh, Frozen

RAW VERSUS COOKED

It's a little-known fact that some veggies are better for you when eaten raw. It may sound strange, but the effect of heat on produce is not always good. In some cases, cooking your vegetables decreases the availability of important phytonutrients, especially enzymes.

Live enzymes are responsible for converting the nutrients inside plants into powerful antioxidant compounds. A great example of this effect occurs in broccoli. Raw broccoli has up to 20 times the sulforaphane than cooked broccoli does, thanks to the enzyme myrosinase, which is needed to activate it. Why does this matter? Well, sulforaphane is responsible for most of broccoli's cancer-fighting properties.

Another example is beets. Beets lose more than 25 percent of their folate content when cooked. And cooked kale loses almost half of its antioxidant power from lutein, beta-cryptoxanthin, and zeaxanthin.

So how can you have your veggie and cook it, too? To get the most nutrients from cooked vegetables, less is more. Lightly steam your veggies for about 4 minutes (you want them slightly crunchy) and when it comes to leafy greens, a nice sauté in olive oil (just enough to wilt them) is the best way to go.

(continued)

Profiles in Green

Now that we've established all the amazing benefits of going green, let's break down the best leafy greens for smoothies.

As already discussed, leafy greens are nutrition powerhouses. They're loaded with phyto-nutrients like antioxidants, flavonoids, and carotenoids, and they're a major source of vitamins, minerals, and fiber in the diet. That said, they're also unique in flavor, with distinct properties that affect our health. Looking to lower your blood pressure? Go with arugula and kale. Want to improve your vision? Spinach is on the job. Need liver support? Dandelion is king.

But before we go too much further into which greens are great for what, let's get one thing straight—what exactly is a leafy green?

For our purposes here, "greens" are what I refer to as leafy greens. A leafy green is basically a plant's leaves eaten as a vegetable. They are typically high in vitamins A and C, calcium, iron, fiber, and folic acid, and range in flavor from bitter and earthy to peppery and sweet. Leafy greens include lettuce greens (e.g., romaine and arugula) and cruciferous greens (e.g., cabbage and kale). Lettuce greens are typically milder and eaten raw, whereas cruciferous greens can be a bit more pungent and fibrous. I've chosen a few of my go-to favorite greens for the recipes in this book, but this is by no means an exhaustive list. I encourage you to experiment on your own and discover new flavors and combinations.

That said, I've noticed over the years that people are creatures of habit when it comes to adding greens to their smoothies, sticking mainly to what they know tastes good. Many are afraid to add new greens to the mix, for fear they will dislike the flavor. But fear not! Some of my most popular (and tasty) recipes were created just by becoming a little more brave in the kitchen and keeping an open mind. That's all I ask of you now. Open your mind and your heart and let the leafy greens in!

Leafy greens are the backbone of my recipes and provide the foundation for the smoothie recipes you'll find in this book. Each offers a unique health property and flavor, and their function is highlighted in each section.

If you're new to green smoothies, I suggest starting with mild greens, such as any of the "baby" varieties (baby spinach, kale, arugula, etc.). Microgreens can also be milder in flavor, and are especially rich in nutrients.

Baby greens are harvested earlier than their mature counterparts, which gives them a less intense flavor and more tender texture overall. Nutritionally speaking, they may also be more nutritious. Some studies show an increased level of vitamins and phytonutrients in baby greens compared to mature ones, but the research is limited.

When deciding which variety of leafy green to choose, I recommend experimenting, especially with greens like kale, which have several types to choose from. Curly kale has a tough stem (which you should remove before blending), whereas flat-leaf kale (aka lacinato, Tuscan, and dinosaur kale) are a bit more smoothie-friendly. Red kale (aka red Russian kale) also has a flat leaf and tends to have the sweetest flavor.

For easy reference, use the following chart to locate a recipe using your favorite greens. To learn more about the nutritional value of each green, check out the Vegetables, Leafy Greens, and Fruits chart on page 16.

Green	Recipe Reference
Arugula (also known as rocket)	Citrus Cilantro (p. 46) Orange Pepper (p. 100)
Broccoli	Deep Green (p. 48) Green Gazpacho (p. 58) Tropical Green (p. 83) Melon Ball (p. 104) Bee Wild (p. 109) Wild Watermelon Mint (p. 125)
Cabbage	Ginger Berry (p. 45) Drink Your Greens (p. 132)
Collard greens	Apple Cayenne (p. 41) Deep Green (p. 48) Green Gazpacho (p. 58) Reishi Pear (p. 119) Baby Face (p. 120)
Dandelion (also known as Lion's Tooth)	Lemon Cilantro (p. 42) Peachy Keen (p. 43) Turmeric Ginger (p. 49)

Green	Recipe Reference
Kale	Chamomile Pear (p. 44) Sweet Potato Chai (p. 54) Tropical Matcha Kale (p. 60) Probiotic Power (p. 64) Super Seed (p. 69) Ginger Pear (p. 71) Peaches 'n' Cream (p. 76) Green Grapefruit (p. 78) Wild Blueberry Power (p. 90) Mango Cauli Kale (p. 92) Almond Grape (p. 103) PB&J Smoothie (p. 105) Pineapple Matcha (p. 107) Red Minty Magic (p. 108) Kiwi Cucumber Kale (p. 114) Green Machine (p. 124) Blueberry Chaga (p. 126) Morning Dew (p. 121) Lemon Tart (p. 128) I Heart Berries (p. 129) Chlorella Kale (p. 131)
Microgreens (immature greens)	Berry Tart (p. 47) Smooth Sailin' (p. 67)

Green	Recipe Reference
Romaine Lettuce	Purify (p. 115) Skin Saver (p. 118) I Heart Berries (p. 129) Cranberry Orange (p. 130)
Spinach (baby)	Deep Green (p. 48) Wild Matcha (p. 52) Blackberry Chia (p. 57) Raspberrylicious (p. 61) Bloat Fighter (p. 65) Chocolate Almond (p. 66) Mango Tango (p. 70) Sweet Potato Apple Pie (p. 72) Licorice Dream (p. 73) Strawberry Mint (p. 77) Green Grapefruit (p. 78) Orange Delight (p. 79) Berries & Beets (p. 80) Morning Maca (p. 81) Mango Oats (p. 84) Cherry Blaster (p. 85) Chocolate Chai (p. 88) Green Tahini (p. 89) Queen of Green (p. 91) Orange Avocado (p. 94)

Green	Recipe Reference
Spinach (baby) *(continued)*	Almond Spice (p. 95) Happy Place (p. 97) Blue Coconut (p. 101) Raspberry Cream (p. 102) Pumpkin Spice (p. 106) Bee Wild (p. 109) Radiance (p. 112) Skin Rejuvenator (p. 113) Kiwi Cucumber Kale (p. 114) Sweet Basil (p. 116) Orange Crush (p. 127) Drink Your Greens (p. 132) Chocolate Mint (p. 133)
Swiss Chard	Cucumber Mint (p. 40) Raspberry Cacao (p. 53) Blueberry Muffin (p. 55) Spicy Sunrise Breakfast (p. 59) Swiss Chard My Heart (p. 68) Chocolate Cherry Almond (p. 82) Queen of Green (p. 91) Berry Berry Good (p. 96) Melon Ball (p. 104) Tangy Citrus (p. 117)

Is Organic Better?

There's no doubt about it—organic food is better both for the environment and for our bodies. I love that organic options are becoming more available and more affordable. But does that mean every single item you place in your shopping cart needs to be organic, all the time? Probably not. When considering this choice for myself, I go with one simple rule. If I eat it every day, or more than three times per week, I opt for organic. That means I go organic with my baby spinach, frozen berries, and Granny Smith apples, since these are my smoothie staples. For anything that's especially concentrated, like dehydrated-greens powder and spices, I also choose organic. That said, if I only eat plums three times a year, I'm not all that worried about my chemical exposure. Same rule applies if I'm not eating the skin of fruits like avocado or banana. When you do eat the skin of a fruit, be sure to wash it first.

Overall, why do I tend to choose organic? I'm a bit of a nutrient junkie, and while recent studies don't yet show conclusively that organic produce has significantly more vitamins and minerals than their conventionally grown counterparts, they DO contain higher levels of antioxidants. And for me, that's reason enough.

Smoothie Fundamentals

When I started making smoothies at home, I didn't realize how easily I could mess things up. And let me tell you, I made some serious screw-ups. From watery and flavorless to gritty, overly "healthy" mishaps, I've made every rookie mistake you can make. And there's nothing worse than wasting ingredients on a smoothie you simply can't drink.

So whether you're making a post-run protein shake, a tasty breakfast smoothie on the go, or a yummy midday snack, let's skip the disasters and get you blending like a pro!

To blend your green smoothie with ease, I suggest adding your ingredients to your blender in the following order:

Liquid + Powders + Nut butter/oil and seeds + Greens and soft veg/fruit + Hard veg/fruit and ice

1. Add your liquid base first, then your powders. This will help the powders dissolve fully.

2. Layer in your cooked or water-based veggies (cucumbers, zucchini, sweet potato) and greens.

3. Raw fruit and uncooked vegetables go next.

4. Last is frozen fruit (or ice), as it will push the other ingredients down toward the blade.

Tip: If you're using a blender that's inverted on the motor, then reverse the process.

Keep in mind: A smoothie should be cold. There's nothing worse than a lukewarm smoothie on a hot summer day—or any day. If you're using ice, be careful not to over-dilute your smoothie. Remember, a little goes a long way. Using frozen fruit is a great alternative to ice if you want to avoid a watered-down smoothie.

Smoothie Basics

Now that you have the order of operations down, let's talk about the primary components for making green smoothies that delight and satisfy.

The ingredients you'll find in most of the recipes in this cookbook include all types of liquid bases (mostly nondairy milks, but I use some kefir and Greek yogurt, too), tons of leafy greens and high-fiber veggies, and a variety of low-sugar fruits like berries, tart cherries, apple, pear, and avocado (yes, avocado is a fruit).

I also use superfoods like chia and hemp seed, protein and greens powders, matcha, and other fun add-ins in many of the recipes. These provide a source of healthy fats, protein, and fiber, and also enhance flavor and nutrition. You'll learn more about superfoods on page 28.

Smoothie Prep

A question I'm often asked is how to save time when it comes to smoothie prep.

Prepping your smoothie ingredients in advance is a great way to simplify the process and save time. I started making frozen smoothie packs for clients years ago in my catering business. I would stuff all the smoothie ingredients into plastic freezer bags, so all they had to do was pull one out, add their liquid of choice, and blend. Many reported back that this was a game changer for them on busy mornings, especially parents rushing to get their kids off to school.

What I love about freezer prep bags is that you can make an entire week's worth of smoothies in no time at all and have a beautiful green smoothie prepped and waiting for you every single day. Plus, you can mix and match your ingredients to create a different smoothie each day. After all, variety is the spice of life.

Here's how you do it:

STEP 1: Layer your frozen fruit, powders, nut butters, seeds, chopped veggies and chopped greens into quart-size freezer bags (you can also use frozen greens and veggies here).

STEP 2: Squeeze out the air in the bag, seal it, and freeze for up to three months.

STEP 3: To make your smoothie, pour the ingredients into your blender, add your liquid of choice, and blend until smooth.

Tip: If you don't want to use plastic bags (and you have lots of freezer space), you can prep your smoothie in Mason jars, too.

Another option is the pre-blend method, in which you pre-blend a big batch of smoothies in advance, and then freeze them in grab-and-go containers. Mason jars work well here; just make sure to leave at least an inch of room at the top for expansion when frozen. And don't forget to move the smoothie from the freezer to the refrigerator to thaw overnight.

Tools & Equipment

Smoothie making shouldn't be complicated, but it does require some basic equipment. You may have read that you don't need a high-powered blender to make a delicious smoothie, and that is absolutely true—until you start adding greens to the equation. I've found that once you introduce greens to the party, especially tougher varieties like kale, you'll want some extra oomph for a smooth and palatable finish.

That said, I would consider two factors before purchasing: how much space you have for a blender, and how much money you want to spend. You can find a quality blender for almost any budget, so deciding these straight away will help narrow things down.

Once you've settled on a budget, you can start comparing features and brands. The main features that differentiate one blender from another are the motor's speed, the blender controls, and the container size. Blenders range in power from 200 to 1200 watts. The lower the watts, the harder the blender will have to work to make your smoothie smooth; this will eventually shorten its lifespan, which you should consider when making an investment. If you plan on making green smoothies several times a week, I would go with a minimum of 600 watts.

You can either go with a more pricey, high-powered blender that will last for years and years (and likely have a warranty), or you can replace your cheaper blender each year because you've used it to death. After replacing my cheap blender once, I went with a more expensive, high-powered blender the second time around . . . and I haven't looked back. I've had it for almost 10 years with no issues, and I use it almost every day, sometimes twice.

When determining container size, consider your counter space and counter height. Other factors are whether you want to leave your blender out all the time (if you have space for it), and if it will fit under your countertop. When considering functionality, preset settings take the guesswork out of blending.

After deciding on a blender, you're pretty much set to go. Most likely, you have your other tools on hand; measuring cups, spoons, and a silicone spatula are all you'll need.

Superstar Smoothie Ingredients

Now that we've gone through the basics of prep and equipment, it's time to collect your ingredients and start whipping up some amazing green smoothies!

In the following section, I'll walk you through all the ingredients you'll need to make the delicious green smoothie recipes in the pages to come, including tips on selecting produce, facts about their nutritional value, and descriptions of their flavor profiles. I'll also discuss how to sweeten your smoothies naturally, and how to use superfoods to amp up their powerful benefits to the next level.

Choosing the Best Produce

Since the recipes you'll find in this book are all vegetable based, you'll want to seek out the freshest, most flavorful, and most nutrient-rich produce possible. This is important because the produce you're using is going to greatly impact the flavor of your smoothie, so you want it to be tasty and fresh.

That said, let's talk about a few of my tried and true tips for getting the most out of your produce.

Most produce is picked mature but not fully ripened, with the expectation that it will ripen in transit, at the grocery store, or maybe even in your fridge. This is fine for fruits like avocado and grapes, but it might not be optimal for produce that doesn't ripen after harvest, like cucumber and squash. Because of this, I like to find local, in-season produce whenever possible. You can find local produce at farmers' markets or cooperatives, and in your local grocery store. Local produce is typically labeled as such, and positioned separately near the front of the produce section, and may even display the distance it has traveled.

Buying local produce doesn't just point to a greater likelihood of freshness; you also know that it will be in season, which usually translates into more flavor and nutrients—and will likely be less expensive. If you have access to a local farmers' market, you might also find a greater variety of fresh produce to choose from and have the opportunity to experiment with new varieties of produce you've never tried. When choosing to support a local farmers' market or farm stand, you're also helping your own community, your local economy, and the environment.

THREE GOLDEN RULES OF PRODUCE SELECTION

To help you select the most nutrient-dense vegetables and leafy greens, you'll want to follow my three golden rules. These are the guidelines I use when seeking out the most nutrient-rich produce for my own green smoothies.

1. **The more color, the better:** Dark green, red, burgundy, brownish, and purple varieties are going to have more antioxidants and other phytonutrients than the lighter green varieties. Look for bright colors, tight heads, and surfaces that are clear of yellow or brown leaves, blemishes and brown spots, or traces of mold. For leafy greens, the leaves should stand up tall and not wilt. Beets and carrots should have their green stems attached. *Note: One exception to this is cauliflower, which is a super nutritious cruciferous veg, despite being white.*

2. **Choose whole instead of precut:** Whole versions of cauliflower, cabbage, broccoli, and leafy greens are going to be fresher and have more nutrients intact than their prepared, precut counterparts. They're also going to last longer and be less expensive.

3. **Bigger isn't better:** A rule of thumb with produce, and especially fruit, is that smaller is better when it comes to nutrient content. While some produce has been bred to produce larger varieties, research shows that bigger doesn't mean more nutrients. This is especially true for apples, tomatoes, carrots, beets, and strawberries.

To get the most out of your leafy greens, follow these steps when cleaning and storing:

1. Pull off the leaves, rinse, and soak in very cold water for 5 to 10 minutes. Then dry with a towel or spinner.
2. Roll up the leaves in a moistened paper towel.
3. Store inside an airtight, micro-perforated, resealable bag.

You can easily make your own bag by poking a plastic bag with a needle 10 to 20 times—these bags can be reused over and over. Keep your greens in the crisper drawer until ready to use.

Vegetables, Leafy Greens, and Fruits

While leafy greens provide the foundation for green smoothies, fruits and vegetables add flavor, texture, and creaminess. They also offer a boost of antioxidants, fiber, vitamins, and minerals.

Vegetable	Profile
Arugula	Cruciferous veg, high in glucosinolates, calcium, magnesium, and folate. Also a rich dietary source of nitrate, a compound that converts to nitric oxide in the body.
Beets	Slightly sweet, earthy flavor; high in fiber, nitrates, antioxidants, folate, vitamin C, potassium.

Vegetable	Profile
Bell Pepper (red)	Slightly sweet, spicy flavor; high in antioxidants, richest source of vitamin C.
Broccoli	Cruciferous veg, high in fiber and antioxidants, vitamins C & K, and folate.
Cabbage (red)	Cruciferous leafy green, high in fiber, antioxidants, vitamins C & K, and folate.
Carrots	Slightly sweet flavor; high in beta-carotene and pectin, a fiber that improves gut health.
Cauliflower	Mild flavor, adds creaminess; cruciferous veg, low in calories, high in antioxidants, vitamins C & K, folate, choline, and fiber.
Celery	Refreshing and hydrating; low in calories, rich in antioxidants.
Collard Greens	Leafy green, excellent source of manganese and calcium, good source of vitamins A, C & K; antioxidant, anti-inflammatory; aids in detoxification.

Vegetable	Profile
Cucumber	Crisp and refreshing flavor; low calorie and hydrating, high in antioxidants, good source of vitamins C & K and potassium.
Dandelion	Slightly bitter wild leafy green; stimulates the liver; supports body's natural detox pathways; rich in calcium, iron, magnesium, and potassium.
Fennel	Licorice flavor; low calorie; high in vitamin C, calcium, magnesium, potassium, and manganese. Rich source of antioxidants, including chlorogenic acid, limonene, and quercetin.
Kale	Superfood! Cruciferous leafy green veg, rich in vitamins A, C & K; high in calcium; as an antioxidant has heart-healthy, anti-inflammatory, anti-viral, anti-depressant, and anticancer properties.
Microgreens	Seedlings of leafy greens, vegetables, and herbs; concentrated nutrients; rich in potassium, iron, zinc, magnesium, and antioxidants.

Vegetable	Profile
Romaine Lettuce	Hydrating leafy green; rich in vitamins A & C, calcium.
Spinach (baby)	Mild-flavored leafy green; rich in lutein, folate, vitamins A & K.
Sweet Potato	Slightly sweet flavor; adds creamy texture; high in fiber and vitamins A, C & B_6, high in potassium.
Swiss Chard	Mild-flavored leafy green; rich in vitamins A, C, E & K; good source of calcium, magnesium, copper, zinc, sodium, phosphorus.
Tomato	Rich source of lycopene, vitamins C & K, potassium, and folate.
Zucchini	Adds creaminess; low calorie, high in vitamin A, hydrating.

Fruit	Profile
Apple	Rich in pectin, fiber; low-glycemic index.
Avocado	Creamy texture; high in fiber, lutein, and healthy fats.
Banana	Sweet flavor, creamy texture; high in vitamin B_6, fiber, and potassium.
Blackberries	High in fiber and antioxidants; low sugar, low calorie.
Cranberries	Tart flavor; rich in vitamin C; very high in powerful flavonol polyphenols, quercetin, myricetin, peonidin, ursolic acid, and A-type proanthocyanidins, which are believed to protect against urinary tract infections.
Grapefruit	Sweet and sour flavor; low calorie, high in vitamin C and fiber; low-glycemic index.
Grapes	Sweet and hydrating; cancer fighter, anti-inflammatory, and antioxidant.

Fruit	Profile
Kiwi	Supports digestion and boosts immunity; excellent source of vitamin C.
Lemon	Citrusy and tart; rich in vitamin C and other plant compounds that may promote heart health and aid in weight loss.
Lime	Tart flavor; rich in vitamin C and antioxidants.
Mango	Supports digestion and boosts immunity; high in magnesium, potassium, and the antioxidant mangiferin, which all support a healthy heart.
Orange	Sweet and sour flavor; rich in vitamin C and antioxidants that support heart health; low-glycemic index.
Papaya	Anti-inflammatory and anti-oxidant; high in lycopene and vitamin C for heart health.
Peach	Helps maintain moisture in skin and protects against sun damage; rich in immune-boosting nutrients and antioxidants.

Fruit	Profile
Pear	Rich in antioxidants; heart-healthy, high in fiber; helps with weight loss; low-glycemic index.
Pineapple	Sweet, tart flavor; rich in bromelain, a digestive enzyme that helps break down proteins, boost immunity, and suppress inflammation.
Raspberries	Tart, floral flavor; low calorie and low sugar; high in fiber; rich in vitamin C and manganese.
Strawberries	Rich in vitamin C, manganese, folate, and potassium; low-glycemic index.
Tart Cherries	Tart flavor; source of polyphenols and vitamin C for heart health, suppresses inflammation and oxidative stress; rich in melatonin to help regulate sleep; low-glycemic index.
Watermelon	Hydrating and low calorie; high in anti-inflammatory antioxidants, and carotenoids including beta-carotene and lycopene.
Wild Blueberries	Mild sweetness, unique flavor; rich in antioxidants, fiber, and nutrients for brain and heart health.

How to Freeze Bananas for Smoothies

Frozen bananas provide a creamy texture and bulk up a smoothie. They're also a great replacement for ice when you want to freeze things up without watering down your smoothie. I like to freeze my bananas before they get too ripe and any brown spots begin to appear. The riper your banana is, the higher the sugar content.

Simply peel and slice your banana, and place in a freezer-safe plastic bag or glass container. I like to freeze one banana per bag, so I can manage my portions. When ready to use, just toss into your smoothie straight from the freezer.

Sweeten It Up!

Let's face it, sometimes you want to sweeten the pot—or in our case, the smoothie—and that's totally fine. I like to use warming spices and real fruit whenever I can, as they work beautifully to provide a natural sweet taste.

But how much sugar is too much? It's a question I'm asked all the time. And it's one that doesn't have a simple answer. Yes, too much sugar in your diet is linked to chronic diseases like obesity, type 2 diabetes, and heart disease—so what is considered a reasonable amount? The Dietary Guidelines for Americans advise consuming less than 10 percent of your daily calorie intake from added sugar. That's a great place to start, but keep in mind that our body chemistries are unique in what we can tolerate, and our lifestyle as a whole matters just as much. Also remember that along with natural sugar, fruit brings with it an important array of vitamins, minerals, phytonutrients, and fiber. Added sugars are different than the natural sugars found in fruits and vegetables (yes, there's some sugar in veggies!), so the type of sugar you're consuming matters, too.

That said, store-bought smoothies definitely overdo it, sometimes packing in as much sugar as two cans of soda, and often leaving you feeling less than great. But not all smoothies are created equal. At home, there are several ways you can slash the sugar without sacrificing flavor.

HERE ARE MY GO-TO STRATEGIES:

- **Use spices** like ½ teaspoon cinnamon, ginger, or pumpkin spice, or add 1 teaspoon vanilla extract.
- **Add low-sugar fruits** like one serving (1 cup) berries, avocado, grapefruit, tart cherries, or apple. If you need a bit more, half a frozen banana will do the trick. I also think a little magic happens when you blend in a date or two. Just remember: Balance the extra fruit with another serving of greens or veggies to keep your blood sugar from spiking.
- **Add naturally sweet veggies.** Try ½ cup grated carrots, grated beets, sweet potato, or red bell pepper.

To keep the total sugar content low, make sure your liquid "milk" base is unsweetened as well, or opt for no-sugar options like brewed tea, matcha, and unsweetened coconut water. Also, be sure to choose add-ins and powders that are sugar-free. This includes yogurt, kefir, and protein or greens powder.

Liquid Base

I always use nondairy liquid base "milks" in my smoothie recipes because personally, I don't tolerate dairy well. Luckily, there are tons of nondairy options widely available. Almond milk and coconut milk tend to work well in any smoothie, but each type brings its own unique flavor and nutrition profile, so the choice is yours.

Below is a list of the milk bases you might use in your smoothie. This list includes dairy, nut-based, and nondairy milk options. I recommend choosing the unsweetened versions of these whenever possible:

- Almond Milk
- Cashew Milk
- Coconut Milk
- Coconut Water
- Dairy Milk

- Macadamia Nut Milk
- Oat Milk
- Pea Milk
- Rice Milk
- Soy Milk

The downside of using nut milks and some other nondairy milks in your smoothie is that most of them are low in protein. And while protein is not a necessary component for every smoothie, you may prefer to add it for a more satiating smoothie—you'll therefore find additional protein sources in many of my recipes. That said, feel free to experiment using both dairy and nondairy liquid bases, as tolerated. You really can't go wrong here.

If you prefer to avoid milk bases altogether, other options for liquid bases include brewed teas, water, or natural unsweetened juices.

Using brewed tea as your liquid base is a fun way to add interesting flavors (and superfood power!) to your smoothie. Green tea has anticarcinogenic, anti-inflammatory, antimicrobial, and antioxidant properties, and has been shown to positively affect cardiovascular disease, diabetes, obesity, and brain health. The compounds in green tea responsible for most of these benefits are called flavonoids. The most pertinent flavonoids are the catechins, specifically EGCG. Matcha is a more potent form of green tea, made by grinding up the entire tea leaf into a powder, resulting in higher levels of antioxidants and caffeine.

Herbal tea is actually not really "tea" at all. Considered a "tisane," it can be a blend of flowers, leaves, roots, spices, seeds, or tree bark belonging to any variety of edible, non-tea plant. Herbal tea is naturally decaffeinated, so it's a great choice if you want to avoid caffeine. I love to brew chai for smoothies, which adds warming spices like turmeric, ginger, and cinnamon. Chai is traditionally a black tea, but you can find herbal versions, too. Chamomile, another mild-flavored herbal tea, makes an excellent option for a green smoothie base as well.

Unsweetened juices can also be used as a liquid base. Just bear in mind that these juices will still contain natural sugars that are present in the fruit. If you're not sure how to identify an unsweetened juice, look for the phrase "100% fruit juice" on the nutrition facts label—I recommend 100 percent cranberry or cherry juice. If these juices still feel too sweet for you but you enjoy the boost of flavor, try diluting them with water.

Yogurt & Kefir

Yogurt and kefir present two more great possibilities for superfood additions. They make your smoothie extra creamy and smooth, while offering a natural protein boost (which is super for the kids, too).

While both yogurt and kefir are fermented and cultured, they differ in consistency, nutrient content, and how they're prepared. Both are available in a variety of plant- and dairy-based options and bring a serving of gut-healthy live cultures to the table.

Because of its thinner consistency, kefir can sometimes replace the liquid in your smoothie, depending on the other ingredients included. Kefir ferments at room temperature and is made using a "starter" grain, either from dairy milk or a nondairy milk like almond, coconut, or rice. You can even make it with coconut water. Kefir is said to be a better source of live cultures, as it contains twice the bacterial strains found in yogurt.

Yogurt is fermented with heat and has a thicker consistency. As mentioned above, it often contains fewer strains of bacteria than kefir and is less nutrient-dense.

Whichever you choose, I recommend using the unsweetened versions and avoiding the fat-free varieties; they don't provide the same consistency and lack creaminess and flavor.

Nuts & Seeds

Nuts, nut butters, and seeds are excellent add-ins for providing a healthy plant-based source of fat, fiber, and protein. Numerous varieties of nuts and nut butters work well in smoothies, and most are interchangeable.

You might be thinking, wait . . . aren't nuts high in fat? Yes—the good kind. Nuts and seeds are a great source of plant-based omega-3 and omega-6 fatty acids. These types of polyunsaturated fats are essential, which means you need to obtain them from your diet. Hemp, chia, and flaxseed all contain omega-3 fatty acids, so I use them quite frequently for this purpose, but they also have unique properties of their own. For example, hemp seed is also rich in protein, and flaxseed is high in heart-healthy fiber.

Nuts and seeds are also extremely nutrient-rich. They are low in carbs and sugar, and a great source of vitamin E, magnesium, and selenium. In addition, nuts contain polyphenols, antioxidants that may protect your cells from damage caused by free radicals.

Below is a list of the nuts, seeds, and nut/seed butters you'll find in my smoothie recipes.

Nuts & Seeds:

- Almonds
- Cashews
- Chia seeds
- Flaxseed
- Hemp seeds
- Sunflower seeds

Nut/Seed Butters:

- Almond butter
- Cashew butter
- Peanut butter
- Sunflower seed butter
- Tahini

Add-Ins & Superfoods

Superfoods are foods, herbs, and spices that are rich in nutrients shown to improve health or prevent disease. Technically, *all* the fruits, veggies, and leafy greens I use in my smoothie recipes are considered superfoods because they're loaded with antioxidants, anti-inflammatories, and phytochemicals like carotenoids and flavonoids.

That said, the following ingredients are considered "super" in that they offer a special benefit or upgrade in the recipe, whether it be the anti-inflammatory power of turmeric, the digestive prowess of ginger, or the immunity boost of mushroom powder. Feel free to experiment with these fun add-ins as you desire.

Add-In	Profile
Aloe Vera Juice	A hydrating juice made from the leaves of an aloe vera plant; acts as a natural laxative and skin soother.
Basil	Rich in vitamins A, C & K, magnesium, iron, potassium, and calcium.
Bee Pollen	A plant pollen made up of carbs, fat, protein, vitamins, minerals, and antioxidants.
Black Pepper	Spice made by grinding peppercorns; rich in piperidine, a potent antioxidant that protects against cell damage and improves gut health; enhances curcumin absorption from turmeric when taken together.

Add-In	Profile
Cacao Powder	A powder made by cold-pressing unroasted cacao beans; this process retains the living enzymes and removes the fat (cacao butter).
Cayenne Pepper	A hot and spicy pepper, rich in capsaicin, a substance that helps relieve pain and may also boost metabolism, reduce hunger, and slow cancer growth.
Chia Seeds	A super seed! An excellent source of essential omega-3 fatty acids, a complete source of plant-based protein, and a good source of calcium, potassium, and fiber.
Chlorella	A single-celled, green freshwater algae rich in protein, B_{12}, iron, vitamin C, and antioxidants.
Cilantro	A natural binding agent that helps rid the body of excess minerals, while protecting against oxidative stress.
Cinnamon	A spice made from the inner bark of a tropical evergreen tree. A home remedy for heartburn, indigestion, and nausea; anti-inflammatory and antioxidant effects; may improve insulin sensitivity.

Add-In	Profile
Flaxseed (ground)	A super seed! A good source of essential omega-3 fatty acids and fiber. Also rich in lignans, plant compounds with antioxidant properties that help lower risk of cancer and improve overall health.
Greens Powder	Dehydrated and freeze-dried greens ground into a powder; can help boost energy, help with digestion, and improve overall health.
Ginger Root	A close relative of turmeric, the root of a tropical flowering plant; has amazing anti-inflammatory properties, helps stimulate digestion, and lowers blood pressure.
Hemp Seed	A super seed! High in plant-based protein, a good source of fiber, essential omega-3 fatty acids, and trace minerals.
Maca	Also known as Peruvian ginseng, an adaptogenic herb native to South America; contains glucosinolates, plant compounds that may play a role in cancer prevention.

Add-In	Profile
Matcha Powder	The ground powder of green tea leaves; packed with powerful antioxidants, including EGCG.
MCT Oil	Short for medium chain tri-glycerides; an oil made from coconut oil, but more concentrated; may help boost metabolism and burn fat.
Mint	An herb rich in vitamin A and anti-oxidants, ¼ cup provides nearly half the daily value for vitamin A.
Mushroom Powder (cordyceps, reishi, chaga)	The ground powder of functional mushrooms; provides immune system support.
Parsley	A nutrient-rich herb, particularly high in vitamins A, C & K, plus many powerful antioxidants.
Protein Powder	A concentrated source of protein made from plant and animal foods, including pea, whey, egg, rice, soy, hemp, and more!

Add-In	Profile
Rolled Oats	A great source of vitamins, minerals, and antioxidants; high in soluble fiber called beta-glucan, which helps reduce cholesterol and blood sugar, promotes healthy gut bacteria, and increases satiety.
Spirulina	A type of blue-green algae, one of the most nutrient-dense foods on earth; a complete protein; powerful antioxidant and anti-inflammatory.
Tahini	A paste made from toasted and ground sesame seeds, rich in phosphorus, manganese, and B vitamins (B_1 & B_6) and a source of heart-healthy monounsaturated fat.
Tumeric	A medicinal herb and spice that gives curry its yellow color. Curcumin is the active ingredient responsible for its powerful anti-inflammatory and antioxidant health effects.
Vanilla Extract (pure)	A flavor enhancer made by steeping whole vanilla beans in a mixture of alcohol and water; has antimicrobial and antioxidant properties and can help soothe digestion.

When we think of herbs and spices, we usually think of the aromatic leaves of edible plants that enhance the taste of our food (or make a really pretty garnish). But herbs and spices have been used medicinally for thousands of years in almost every culture, and are core remedies in Ayurveda and Chinese medicine. Popular herbs and spices like ginger, cilantro, and turmeric are as well known for their healing properties and powerful health benefits as they are for their culinary prowess.

I love adding fresh herbs and spices to my green smoothies for both reasons: they add amazing flavors and offer an additional layer of support for my health and wellbeing.

I'm a peppermint junkie for sure, and I tend to reach for it the most for its fresh, cool flavor and soothing properties. You'll find fresh mint leaves in many of my recipes.

I could probably add fresh ginger to every smoothie, it adds a warm spicy flavor that pairs so well with most any fruit, especially pineapple. Turmeric and cinnamon are a great flavor pair, too!

Cilantro is my other go-to; I love its fragrant, citrusy flavor and versatility. Funny thing about cilantro, you likely either love it or hate it. And studies suggest this trait is genetic. That's right, if cilantro tastes more like soap to you than it does citrus, you likely have the gene that codes for the receptor that picks up the same chemical scent found in cilantro and soap. Interesting, right?

I also use basil and parsley in my green smoothies, but to a lesser degree. They're both great options for savory smoothies, and pair well with fresh tomatoes and celery. Basil actually belongs to the mint family and comes in many different varieties, while parsley has a milder flavor.

Using the Recipes

In the following chapters you'll find 80 healthy and delicious vegetable-forward green smoothie recipes organized by the following ingredient benefits:

- Detox
- Weight Loss

- Digestive Health
- Energy Boosting

- Anti-Inflammatory
- Antioxidant
- Healthy Skin
- Healthy Heart

Each recipe is labeled with a nutrient tag. These nutrient tags provide a quick, at-a-glance guideline, highlighting the recipe's main nutritional attributes. You'll find that many of the recipes will fall into several of these categories, including:

High Fiber: These recipes will have 5 grams or more of fiber.

High Protein: These recipes will contain 14 or more grams of protein.

Less Sugar: These recipes will contain 15 grams or less of sugar.

Low Calorie: These recipes will have 200 or fewer calories.

Meal Replacement: These recipes are great for replacing one of your meals, like breakfast.

Superfood Star: These recipes feature an important superfood.

To help make your smoothie-making experience truly hassle-free, I've included the following types of tips or strategies with each recipe:

Substitution tip: on swapping an ingredient for an alternative

Ingredient tip: for prepping and selecting ingredients

Flavor/Texture tip: for improving smoothie flavor or texture

Health Boost tip: for improving smoothie health factor

Time-saver tip: for faster smoothie prep

Variation tip: for making alternative versions of a recipe by adjusting prep or ingredients

Serving tip: for finishing touches—dishes and garnishes for serving

As an added resource, the nutritional information has been broken down for each recipe.

Your Smoothie, Your Way

If there's one thing I've learned after years and years of smoothie making, it's this: If it doesn't taste good, you won't want to drink it. Poetic, right? Maybe not, but it's the truth. You can't make a habit out of something you don't enjoy.

This book is not about forcing you to make smoothies *my* way; it's about you finding your own love of smoothies and fitting them to your unique lifestyle. I wholeheartedly encourage you to customize and personalize any of my recipes to make them your own. If you don't like kale, sub in collard greens or spinach. If apples aren't your thing, try blueberries. To make this process even easier, I've included an "Alterations" section with each recipe so you can keep track of your own changes as you go.

If you're new to green smoothies and are feeling a little overwhelmed, take a nice deep breath and relax. I'm going to help you every step of the way with a tip or strategy, and soon enough, you'll be blending like a pro!

Three-Day Reset

Having run my *Nourish* program since 2012, I've seen firsthand the transformational power of green smoothies. From the very beginning, a daily green smoothie was the backbone of my program, and it soon became an anchor for many of my participants going forward. It connected them to the feel-good vibes they had experienced during the program and the healthy habits they adopted during that 21-day period of clean eating.

Because it was so easy for past participants to sink back into old habits after the program ended, I created a gentle three-day protocol, centered around green smoothies, to use when they needed a little reset. I even use this protocol myself whenever I feel the need, whether it's post-holiday or after a vacation when I'm feeling bloated or off-balance, or those times I just want to get back to feeling great in my body. This Three-Day Reset can help you do the same. The program is simple. Here's the basic routine:

Day One: Enjoy a delicious and satisfying green smoothie for breakfast, lunch, and dinner. Choose a smoothie from any section of the cookbook, making sure each one is packed with fiber, protein, and

(continued)

healthy fats to keep you full and satisfied. The Lemon Cilantro, Peachy Keen, and Ginger Berry are my favorites.

If you get hungry between meals, try snacking on some almonds with an apple, or cut-up veggies with guacamole at midday.

Day Two: Replace one green smoothie with a healthy meal. I recommend having a big green salad with chopped vegetables, avocado, cooked quinoa, pumpkin seeds, and baked salmon for lunch, all tossed with olive oil and lemon.

Day Three: Replace another green smoothie with a healthy meal. This could either be breakfast, lunch, or dinner—you decide. If you choose to have a meal for dinner, I suggest a low-sodium vegetable or bean-based soup, or steamed vegetables with a 4- to 5-ounce portion of lean protein, like baked chicken or salmon.

To summarize, the three-day plan breaks down into the following smoothies and meals:

Day 1: 3 smoothies

Day 2: 2 smoothies, 1 meal

Day 3: 1 smoothie, 2 meals

That's it. When you wake up on day four, I promise you'll feel reset, refreshed in your body, and ready to take on your day!

DETOX

The smoothie recipes in the following pages are cleansing, nourishing, and support your body's natural detoxification systems. Featuring chlorophyll-rich, liver-purifying greens like kale, arugula, and dandelion greens, these smoothies are not only full of flavor, they're loaded with vitamins and antioxidants that will give you a leg up when eliminating toxins and waste from the body. These recipes' powerful leafy greens are paired with fresh herbs like mint and cilantro, along with additional appetizing ingredients that have amazing detox power, such as radishes, beets, grapefruit, and fresh ginger.

Of all the recipes in this book, the smoothies in this section are probably the most intense in flavor. If dandelion and arugula taste too bitter for you at first, try cutting back on the quantity you use, or combine them with baby spinach to tone it down. As always, feel free to mix up your greens and fresh herbs to create smoothies that suit your preferences and palate.

CUCUMBER MINT

Yield: 1 (16-ounce) serving | Prep time: 5 minutes

HIGH FIBER, LESS SUGAR, LOW CALORIE

Cilantro is a known detoxifier and potent binding agent, helping remove heavy metals and toxins from the body. The spicy flavor blends perfectly with cucumber and mint, making for an herb-infused smoothie that's refreshing and delicious!

¼ cup water

Juice of ½ lemon

4 fresh mint leaves, chopped

¼ cup chopped fresh cilantro

1 pear, roughly chopped

¾ cup diced cucumber

1½ cups chopped Swiss chard (about 5 leaves)

½ cup ice

Per Serving (16 ounce)

Calories: 105; Total fat: 0g; Sodium: 164mg; Cholesterol: 0mg; Total carbs: 25g; Fiber: 7g; Sugar: 15g; Protein: 3g

Alterations:

1. Pour the water and lemon juice into the blender, then add the mint and cilantro.

2. Layer in the pear, cucumber, and Swiss chard. Top with the ice.

3. Blend all the ingredients together until completely smooth, adding more ice or water as needed to reach desired consistency. Consume immediately.

Variation tip: No Swiss chard? Baby spinach or kale make equally good alternatives for a healthy, delicious smoothie.

APPLE CAYENNE

Yield: 1 (16-ounce) serving | Prep time: 5 minutes

HIGH FIBER, LOW CALORIE, SUPERFOOD STAR

The sweet and zesty blend of apple and cayenne is perfectly balanced by the warming spice of ginger. This smoothie is exhilarating, soothing, and cleansing, and a great breakfast choice to start your day.

½ cup water

Juice of ½ lemon

1½ teaspoons peeled and grated fresh ginger

Pinch cayenne pepper

1 small apple, cored and chopped

2 celery stalks, roughly chopped (about ½ cup)

1 cup chopped collard greens (4 to 5 leaves)

½ cup ice

1. Pour the water and lemon juice into the blender, then add the ginger and cayenne.

2. Layer in the apple, celery, and collard greens. Top with the ice.

3. Blend all the ingredients together until completely smooth, adding more ice or water as needed to reach desired consistency. Consume immediately.

Per Serving (16 ounce)

Calories: 124; Total fat: 1g; Sodium: 42mg; Cholesterol: 0mg; Total carbs: 31g; Fiber: 7g; Sugar: 20g; Protein: 2g

Alterations:

_____

_____

_____

_____

_____

_____

_____

Flavor tip: Use a Granny Smith apple for added sweetness.

LEMON CILANTRO

Yield: 1 (16-ounce) serving | Prep time: 5 minutes

LESS SUGAR, LOW CALORIE, SUPERFOOD STAR

Both the cilantro and dandelion greens are impressive detoxifiers and offer liver-cleansing power. The addition of pear lends just enough sweetness for the perfect detox smoothie.

¼ cup water

Juice of ½ lemon

¼ cup fresh chopped cilantro

1 tablespoon chia seeds

1 pear, roughly chopped

2 celery stalks, roughly chopped (about ½ cup)

1 cup chopped dandelion greens

½ cup ice

1. Pour the water and lemon juice into the blender, then add the cilantro and chia seeds.

2. Layer in the pear, celery, and dandelion greens. Top with the ice.

3. Blend all the ingredients together until completely smooth, adding more ice or water as needed to reach desired consistency. Consume immediately.

Per Serving (16 ounce)

Calories: 192; Total fat: 5g; Sodium: 84mg; Cholesterol: 0mg; Total carbs: 34g; Fiber: 12g; Sugar: 15g; Protein: 5g

Alterations:

Substitution tip: No chia? Use ground flaxseed instead.

PEACHY KEEN

Yield: 1 (16-ounce) serving | Prep time: 5 minutes

HIGH PROTEIN, MEAL REPLACEMENT, SUPERFOOD STAR

Loaded with iron and calcium, dandelion leaves are potent detoxifiers. They're extremely liver-supportive and high in vitamins A and K. They're also a bit strong in flavor, so I've paired them here with peaches and cherries to help balance the bitter with sweet.

1 cup coconut water

1 tablespoon ground flaxseed

1 scoop vanilla protein powder

½ cup frozen peaches

½ cup frozen tart cherries

1 cup chopped dandelion greens

1. Pour the coconut water into the blender, then add the flaxseed and protein powder.

2. Layer in the peaches, cherries, and dandelion greens.

3. Blend all the ingredients together until completely smooth, adding more coconut water as needed to reach desired consistency. Consume immediately.

Per Serving (16 ounce)

Calories: 296; Total fat: 7g; Sodium: 217mg; Cholesterol: 80mg; Total carbs: 45g; Fiber: 9g; Sugar: 18g; Protein: 32g

Alterations:

Substitution tip: No tart cherries? Frozen strawberries work here, too.

CHAMOMILE PEAR

Yield: 1 (16-ounce) serving | Prep time: 5 minutes

HIGH FIBER, LESS SUGAR, LOW CALORIE, SUPERFOOD STAR

The anti-inflammatory power of chamomile combined with the detox and liver-healing power of bee pollen make this the perfect cleansing drink.

½ cup brewed chamomile tea

1 teaspoon bee pollen

1 pear, roughly chopped

½ cup diced zucchini (steamed, frozen)

1½ cups chopped kale (stems removed, as needed)

½ cup ice

1. Pour the tea into the blender, then add the bee pollen.

2. Layer in the pear, zucchini, and kale leaves. Top with the ice.

3. Blend all the ingredients together until completely smooth, adding more ice or tea as needed to reach desired consistency. Consume immediately.

Per Serving (16 ounce)

Calories: 150; Total fat: 0g; Sodium: 52mg; Cholesterol: 0mg; Total carbs: 35g; Fiber: 6g; Sugar: 15g; Protein: 5g

Alterations:

_____

_____

_____

_____

_____

_____

_____

Variation tip: If you're not a chamomile tea drinker, this recipe also works using cooled peppermint tea as your liquid base.

GINGER BERRY

Yield: 1 (16-ounce) serving | Prep time: 5 minutes

Raspberries, beets, and cabbage bring the fiber and detox force to this super flavorful, nutrient-packed powerhouse.

½ cup water

1½ teaspoons peeled and grated fresh ginger

1 tablespoon chia seeds

¾ cup frozen raspberries

⅓ cup grated raw beets

1 cup shredded red cabbage

½ cup ice

1. Pour the water into the blender, then add the ginger and chia seeds.

2. Layer in the raspberries, beets, and red cabbage. Top with the ice.

3. Blend all the ingredients together until completely smooth, adding more ice or water as needed to reach desired consistency. Consume immediately.

Per Serving (16 ounce)

Calories: 158; Total fat: 5g; Sodium: 59mg; Cholesterol: 0mg; Total carbs: 27g; Fiber: 11g; Sugar: 12g; Protein: 6g

Alterations:

Health Boost tip: Add a scoop of greens powder for even more cleansing power.

CITRUS CILANTRO

Yield: 1 (16-ounce) serving | Prep time: 5 minutes

LESS SUGAR, LOW CALORIE, SUPERFOOD STAR

This citrus-inspired smoothie is a detoxifying superstar thanks to the inclusion of arugula and cilantro. Both act as chelators, helping remove toxins and heavy metals from your body. The grapefruit also brings a hit of antioxidant power to this refreshingly sweet and peppery smoothie.

½ cup water

Juice of ½ lemon

1 handful fresh cilantro leaves, chopped

1 grapefruit, peeled and segmented

½ cup diced celery

2 cups arugula

½ cup ice

1. Pour the water and lemon juice into the blender, then add the cilantro.

2. Layer in the grapefruit, celery, and arugula. Top with the ice.

3. Blend all the ingredients together until completely smooth, adding more ice or water as needed to reach desired consistency. Consume immediately.

Per Serving (16 ounce)

Calories: 75; Total fat: 1g; Sodium: 81mg; Cholesterol: 0mg; Total carbs: 16g; Fiber: 4g; Sugar: 12g; Protein: 3g

Alterations:

Substitution tip: Not a fan of arugula? Try dandelion instead.

BERRY TART

Yield: 1 (16-ounce) serving | Prep time: 5 minutes

LESS SUGAR, LOW CALORIE, SUPERFOOD STAR

This smoothie is a nutrient powerhouse thanks to the wild blueberries and cherries. Adding microgreens to the mix, as well, gives it antioxidant prowess that can't be beat.

½ cup water

Juice of ½ lime

1½ teaspoons peeled and grated fresh ginger

½ cup frozen wild blueberries

¼ cup frozen tart cherries

½ cup diced cucumber

1 cup chopped mixed microgreens

½ cup ice

Per Serving (16 ounce)

Calories: 99; Total fat: 0g; Sodium: 10mg; Cholesterol: 0mg; Total carbs: 23g; Fiber: 4g; Sugar: 15g; Protein: 2g

Alterations:

1. Pour the water and lime juice into the blender, then add the ginger.

2. Layer in the blueberries, cherries, cucumber, and microgreens. Top with the ice.

3. Blend all the ingredients together until completely smooth, adding more ice or water as needed to reach desired consistency. Consume immediately.

Health Boost tip: Add ⅓ cup hemp seeds for added protein.

DEEP GREEN

Yield: 1 (16-ounce) serving | Prep time: 5 minutes

HIGH FIBER, LOW CALORIE, SUPERFOOD STAR

This magical green smoothie is like a multivitamin in a glass. Rich in vitamins A, C, and K, it's detoxifying, bone-building, and a kick start to your immune system.

½ cup water

1 teaspoon spirulina powder

1 pear, roughly chopped

½ cup diced fresh or frozen broccoli florets

1 cup chopped spinach

½ cup collard greens (2 to 3 leaves, chopped)

½ cup ice

1. Pour the water and spirulina powder into the blender.

2. Layer in the pear, broccoli, spinach, and collard greens. Top with the ice.

3. Blend all the ingredients together until completely smooth, adding more ice or water as needed to reach desired consistency. Consume immediately.

Per Serving (16 ounce)

Calories: 124; Total fat: 1g; Sodium: 81mg; Cholesterol: 0mg; Total carbs: 30g; Fiber: 7g; Sugar: 19g; Protein: 4g

Alterations:

Substitution tip: No spirulina? Use ½ cup hemp seeds instead.

TURMERIC GINGER

Yield: 1 (16-ounce) serving | Prep time: 5 minutes

HIGH FIBER, LESS SUGAR, LOW CALORIE, SUPERFOOD STAR

A powerful mix of dandelion and turmeric, this detox drink is great for optimizing digestion, providing the body with a gentle cleanse.

½ cup water

1 teaspoon ground turmeric

1½ teaspoons fresh peeled and grated ginger

Pinch black pepper

½ small orange, peeled and segmented

¼ cup frozen pineapple chunks

½ cup diced cucumber

1 cup chopped dandelion greens

½ cup ice

1. Pour the water into the blender, then add the turmeric, ginger, and black pepper.

2. Layer in the orange, pineapple, cucumber, and dandelion greens. Top with the ice.

3. Blend all the ingredients together until completely smooth, adding more ice or water as needed to reach desired consistency. Consume immediately.

Per Serving (16 ounce)

Calories: 90; Total fat: 1g; Sodium: 44mg; Cholesterol: 0mg; Total carbs: 15g; Fiber: 5g; Sugar: 15g; Protein: 3g

Alterations:

_____

_____

_____

_____

_____

_____

Variation tip: If pineapple isn't your thing, try swapping with frozen mango, peaches, or bananas for tasty alternatives.

WEIGHT LOSS

In this chapter you'll find 10 light and refreshing smoothie recipes that will boost your energy and keep you feeling full for hours. Packed with greens and berries, these smoothies are high in fiber, lower in sugar, and packed with powerful antioxidants like anthocyanin, which boosts metabolism and improves blood sugar and insulin response. These smoothies make the perfect meal replacement or post-workout drink, too. Ingredients like green tea and bell peppers (containing capsaicin) rev up your metabolism, while Greek yogurt provides protein, and hemp seeds increase satiety and decrease appetite. These green smoothies will help curb your cravings and provide a healthy way to satisfy your sweet tooth at the same time!

WILD MATCHA

Yield: 1 (16-ounce) serving | Prep time: 5 minutes

HIGH FIBER, LESS SUGAR, LOW CALORIE, SUPERFOOD STAR

I love to add matcha to my smoothies. It pairs deliciously well with coconut and wild blueberries, and because it's a concentrated form of green tea, you get a super dose of the antioxidant EGCG, which has been shown to aid in weight loss.

1 cup unsweetened coconut milk

1 teaspoon matcha powder

½ teaspoon cinnamon

1 cup chopped baby spinach

1 cup frozen wild blueberries

1. Pour the coconut milk into the blender, then add the matcha and cinnamon.

2. Layer in the spinach and blueberries.

3. Blend all the ingredients together until completely smooth, adding more coconut milk as needed to reach desired consistency. Consume immediately.

Per Serving (16 ounce)

Calories: 130; Total fat: 3g; Sodium: 194mg; Cholesterol: 0mg; Total carbs: 21g; Fiber: 6g; Sugar: 13g; Protein: 5g

Alterations:

Variation tip: No wild blueberries? Frozen raspberries or blackberries make flavorful alternate versions.

RASPBERRY CACAO

Yield: 1 (16-ounce) serving | Prep time: 5 minutes

HIGH FIBER, HIGH PROTEIN, LESS SUGAR, MEAL REPLACEMENT, SUPERFOOD STAR

Rich in antioxidants and naturally occurring nitrates, beets are the star in this ruby-red beauty. Drink before your morning workout for a boost of oxygen to your cells.

¼ cup water

½ cup plain kefir

1 tablespoon cacao powder

1 tablespoon hemp seeds

¾ cup frozen raspberries

½ cup diced cooked beets

1½ cups chopped Swiss chard (about 5 leaves)

½ cup ice

1. Pour the water and kefir into the blender, then add the cacao powder and hemp seeds.

2. Layer in the raspberries, beets, and Swiss chard. Top with the ice.

3. Blend all the ingredients together until completely smooth, adding more ice or water as needed to reach desired consistency. Consume immediately.

Per Serving (16 ounce)

Calories: 247; Total fat: 11g; Sodium: 226mg; Cholesterol: 5mg; Total carbs: 38g; Fiber: 14g; Sugar: 15g; Protein: 14g

Alterations:

Time-saver tip: Buy pre-steamed beets to speed up your prep.

SWEET POTATO CHAI

Yield: 1 (16-ounce) serving | Prep time: 5 minutes

HIGH FIBER, HIGH PROTEIN, MEAL REPLACEMENT, SUPERFOOD STAR

High in fiber and protein, this creamy chai smoothie will keep you full, satisfied, and energized all morning long.

½ cup chilled, brewed chai

¼ teaspoon cinnamon

1 scoop unsweetened protein powder

1 pear, roughly chopped

¼ cup grated sweet potato

1½ cups chopped kale (stems removed, as needed)

½ cup ice

1. Pour the brewed chai into the blender, then add the cinnamon and protein powder.

2. Layer in the pear, sweet potato, and kale. Top with the ice.

3. Blend all the ingredients together until completely smooth, adding more ice or chai as needed to reach desired consistency. Consume immediately.

Per Serving (16 ounce)

Calories: 286; Total fat: 1g; Sodium: 313mg; Cholesterol: 0mg; Total carbs: 43g; Fiber: 8g; Sugar: 17g; Protein: 29g

Alterations:

Time-saver tip: No sweet potato? Use canned pumpkin instead.

BLUEBERRY MUFFIN

Yield: 1 (16-ounce) serving | Prep time: 5 minutes

HIGH FIBER, LESS SUGAR, LOW CALORIE

Trade in that high-calorie, sugar-laden muffin for this tasty low-calorie, blueberry muffin–inspired smoothie instead. It's the perfect breakfast for those busy mornings on the go!

½ cup unsweetened vanilla almond milk

2 tablespoons quick-cooking rolled oats

¾ cup frozen wild blueberries

½ cup diced zucchini (steamed, frozen)

1½ cups chopped Swiss chard (about 5 leaves)

½ cup ice

1. Pour the almond milk into the blender, then add the oats.

2. Layer in the blueberries, zucchini, and Swiss chard. Top with the ice.

3. Blend all the ingredients together until completely smooth, adding more ice or almond milk as needed to reach desired consistency. Consume immediately.

Per Serving (16 ounce)

Calories: 138; Total fat: 2g; Sodium: 219mg; Cholesterol: 0mg; Total carbs: 26g; Fiber: 6g; Sugar: 12g; Protein: 4g

Alterations:

Variation tip: No chard? Kale and baby spinach make good variations.

PROTEIN REFRESHER

Yield: 1 (16-ounce) serving | Prep time: 5 minutes

HIGH FIBER, HIGH PROTEIN, MEAL REPLACEMENT

This hydrating smoothie is super refreshing, satisfying, and full of fresh flavor. I love this one for a Saturday afternoon when I need an on-the-go lunch.

½ cup water

1 scoop unsweetened protein powder

½ apple, cored and chopped

½ cup peeled and segmented orange

½ cup diced cucumber

1 celery stalk, roughly chopped (about ¼ cup)

2 cups chopped romaine lettuce (about 6 large leaves)

½ cup ice

1. Pour the water into the blender, then add the protein powder.

2. Layer in the apple, orange, cucumber, celery, and romaine lettuce. Top with the ice.

3. Blend all the ingredients together until completely smooth, adding more ice or water as needed to reach desired consistency. Consume immediately.

Per Serving (16 ounce)

Calories: 213; Total fat: 2g; Sodium: 62mg; Cholesterol: 20mg; Total carbs: 33g; Fiber: 6g; Sugar: 23g; Protein: 20g

Alterations:

_____

_____

_____

_____

_____

_____

Flavor tip: Add a dash of cinnamon for a twist of fall-inspired flavor.

BLACKBERRY CHIA

Yield: 1 (16-ounce) serving | Prep time: 5 minutes

HIGH FIBER, LESS SUGAR

Blackberries are one of my favorite varieties of berry—and they're loaded with nutrients. Thanks to the avocado, this creamy smoothie is incredibly satisfying and keeps me full for hours. Avocados add fiber and healthy monounsaturated fats, which are great for your heart, too.

½ cup water

1 teaspoon chia seeds

¼ cup plain Greek yogurt

1 cup frozen blackberries

⅓ avocado, pit and skin removed

½ cup diced cucumber

2 cups chopped baby spinach

½ cup ice

1. Pour the water, chia seeds, and Greek yogurt into the blender.

2. Layer in the blackberries, avocado, cucumber, and spinach. Top with the ice.

3. Blend all the ingredients together until completely smooth, adding more ice or water as needed to reach desired consistency. Consume immediately.

Per Serving (16 ounce)

Calories: 252; Total fat: 14g; Sodium: 93mg; Cholesterol: 13mg; Total carbs: 29g; Fiber: 14g; Sugar: 12g; Protein: 8g

Alterations:

Substitution tip: No blackberries? Use blueberries instead.

GREEN GAZPACHO

Yield: 1 (16-ounce) serving | Prep time: 5 minutes

HIGH FIBER, LESS SUGAR, LOW CALORIE

Ever tried a savory smoothie? This tasty vegetable drink is loaded with vitamins C and K, while the garlic serves as a natural cleansing agent.

½ cup water

Juice of ½ lemon

¼ cup chopped fresh cilantro

1 garlic clove

½ cup diced fresh tomatoes

½ cup frozen broccoli florets

¼ cup diced red bell pepper

1 cup chopped collard greens (about 5 to 6 leaves)

½ cup ice

1. Pour the water and lemon juice into the blender, then add the cilantro and garlic.

2. Layer in the tomatoes, broccoli, bell pepper, and collard greens. Top with the ice.

3. Blend all the ingredients together until completely smooth, adding more ice or water as needed to reach desired consistency. Consume immediately.

Per Serving (16 ounce)

Calories: 70; Total fat: 1g; Sodium: 39mg; Cholesterol: 0mg; Total carbs: 13g; Fiber: 5g; Sugar: 6g; Protein: 4g

Alterations:

Serving tip: Serve in a bowl and top with chopped avocado and scallions.

SPICY SUNRISE BREAKFAST

Yield: 1 (16-ounce) serving | Prep time: 5 minutes

HIGH FIBER, HIGH PROTEIN, MEAL REPLACEMENT

Get your blood pumping in the morning with this sweet and spicy smoothie that's loaded with protein and fiber. Perfect either before or after a workout.

½ cup water

Pinch cayenne pepper

1 scoop unflavored protein powder

1 small orange, peeled and roughly chopped

¼ cup diced avocado, pit and skin removed

2 celery stalks, chopped (about ½ cup)

1½ cups chopped Swiss chard (about 5 leaves)

½ cup ice

1. Pour the water into the blender, then add the cayenne and protein powder.

2. Layer in the orange, avocado, celery, and Swiss chard. Top with the ice.

3. Blend all the ingredients together until completely smooth, adding more ice or water as needed to reach desired consistency. Consume immediately.

Per Serving (16 ounce)

Calories: 278; Total fat: 9g; Sodium: 206mg; Cholesterol: 0mg; Total carbs: 28g; Fiber: 8g; Sugar: 19g; Protein: 26g

Alterations:

Flavor tip: Add some ginger to kick up the heat another notch or two.

TROPICAL MATCHA KALE

Yield: 1 (16-ounce) serving | Prep time: 5 minutes

LESS SUGAR, LOW CALORIE

Channel the tropic sun (and fun!) with this energizing matcha green smoothie. While extremely satisfying, it's also chock-full of antioxidants and EGCG, which helps boost your metabolism.

¼ cup cold water

½ cup plain kefir

1 teaspoon matcha powder

½ cup diced frozen mango

1 cup chopped kale (stems removed, as needed)

½ cup ice

1. Pour the water and kefir into the blender, then add the matcha.

2. Layer in the mango and kale leaves. Top with the ice.

3. Blend all the ingredients together until completely smooth, adding more ice or water as needed to reach desired consistency. Consume immediately.

Per Serving (16 ounce)

Calories: 126; Total fat: 2g; Sodium: 74mg; Cholesterol: 5mg; Total carbs: 23g; Fiber: 4g; Sugar: 14g; Protein: 6g

Alterations:

Substitution tip: No kefir? Swap for plain Greek yogurt.

RASPBERRYLICIOUS

Yield: 1 (16-ounce) serving | Prep time: 5 minutes

HIGH FIBER, MEAL REPLACEMENT

When it comes to losing weight, it's important to stay full and satisfied while eating less, and this protein-rich smoothie does the trick. Packed with antioxidants, fiber, and omega-3 fatty acids, this will curb your appetite all morning long.

⅓ cup water

1 cup plain Greek yogurt

1 teaspoon cinnamon

1 tablespoon ground chia seeds

1 cup frozen raspberries

1 cup chopped baby spinach

½ cup ice

1. Pour the water and Greek yogurt into the blender, then add the cinnamon and chia seeds.

2. Layer in the raspberries and spinach. Top with the ice.

3. Blend all the ingredients together until completely smooth, adding more ice or water as needed to reach desired consistency. Consume immediately.

Per Serving (16 ounce)

Calories: 308; Total fat: 15g; Sodium: 175mg; Cholesterol: 50mg; Total carbs: 37g; Fiber: 9g; Sugar: 21g; Protein: 12g

Alterations:

Ingredient tip: For a nondairy protein choice, add a scoop of plant-based protein powder or ¼ cup hemp seeds

DIGESTIVE HEALTH

Packed with prebiotic-rich veggies, gut-supportive soluble fiber, soothing fats, and the restorative power of protein, these green smoothies can help heal and repair the gut. Prebiotics are carbohydrates that act as food for the gut's good bacteria. Warming spices like ginger also work to relieve gas and indigestion; when combined with a little cayenne pepper, these wake up your digestive system to really get things moving.

The fruit featured in these smoothie recipes play a dual role, adding both flavor and fiber to promote digestive health. Bananas feed the healthy bacteria in your gut and promote regularity, pineapple contains natural digestive enzymes that break down protein in the gut, and pears and apples provide a natural digestive healer.

Fresh herbs like mint offer natural digestive soothers, too. I've also included a few superfood add-ins like probiotic powder and ground flaxseed to help feed your good bacteria, promoting a healthy gut flora.

PROBIOTIC POWER

Yield: 1 (16-ounce) serving | Prep time: 5 minutes

HIGH FIBER, MEAL REPLACEMENT

Mangos are great for digestion because they contain amylase, a digestive enzyme that helps break down carbs into sugars. They're also rich in fiber and other compounds that support digestive health. Combining mango with the gut-soothing power of ginger and kefir makes this smoothie a digestion superstar.

1 cup unsweetened almond milk

1 cup plain kefir

1½ teaspoons peeled and grated fresh ginger

4 fresh mint leaves, chopped

2 cups chopped kale (stems removed, as needed)

½ cup frozen mango

1. Pour the almond milk and kefir into the blender, then add the ginger and mint.

2. Layer in the kale and mango.

3. Blend all the ingredients together until completely smooth, adding more almond milk as needed to reach desired consistency. Consume immediately.

Per Serving(16 ounce)

Calories: 255; Total fat: 8g; Sodium: 333mg; Cholesterol: 10mg; Total carbs: 40g; Fiber: 5g; Sugar: 20g; Protein: 13g

Alterations:

Flavor tip: Try mango-flavored kefir for more intense mango flavor.

BLOAT FIGHTER

Yield: 1 (16-ounce) serving | Prep time: 5 minutes

HIGH FIBER, SUPERFOOD STAR

Rich in natural digestive enzymes such as bromelain, this mix of kiwi, pineapple, and mint is the perfect blend for naturally enhancing digestion while decreasing bloat.

½ cup water

1 tablespoon chia seeds

5 to 6 leaves fresh mint, chopped

1 scoop greens powder

½ cup diced cucumber

1½ cups chopped baby spinach

1 kiwi, peeled and diced

½ cup frozen pineapple

1. Pour the water into the blender, then add the chia seeds, mint, and greens powder.

2. Layer in the cucumber, spinach, kiwi, and pineapple.

3. Blend all the ingredients together until completely smooth, adding more water as needed to reach desired consistency. Consume immediately.

Per Serving (16 ounce)

Calories: 262; Total fat: 6g; Sodium: 179mg; Cholesterol: 0mg; Total carbs: 42g; Fiber: 14g; Sugar: 17g; Protein: 10g

Alterations:

_____

_____

_____

_____

_____

_____

Substitution tip: No greens powder? Use ½ cup plain, low-fat kefir instead.

CHOCOLATE ALMOND

Yield: 1 (16-ounce) serving | Prep time: 5 minutes

HIGH FIBER, HIGH PROTEIN, LESS SUGAR, MEAL REPLACEMENT

Collagen powder and omega-3 fatty acids from flax are powerful gut healers in this creamy smoothie that helps repair the gut lining and lower inflammation. Meanwhile its nutty, chocolate flavor makes it a popular favorite.

1 cup unsweetened almond milk

1 tablespoon ground flaxseed

1 scoop collagen protein powder

2 tablespoons cacao powder

1 tablespoon almond butter

½ cup frozen strawberries

½ frozen banana

¼ cup fresh or frozen cauliflower florets

1 cup chopped baby spinach

½ cup ice

1. Pour the almond milk into the blender, then add the flaxseed, collagen powder, cacao powder, and almond butter.

2. Layer in the strawberries, banana, cauliflower, and spinach. Top with the ice.

3. Blend all the ingredients together until completely smooth, adding more ice or almond milk as needed to reach desired consistency. Consume immediately.

Per Serving (16 ounce)

Calories: 357; Total fat: 21g; Sodium: 258mg; Cholesterol: 0mg; Total carbs: 47g; Fiber: 19g; Sugar: 13g; Protein: 21g

Alterations:

Time-saver tip: Freeze ingredients together in a zip-top bag the night before for easy morning prep.

SMOOTH SAILIN'

Yield: 1 (16-ounce) serving | Prep time: 5 minutes

LOW CALORIE

This sweet and spicy smoothie will keep your digestive juices flowing. Rich in natural probiotics, concentrated antioxidants, and soothing spice, it's deliciously smooth and packed with health benefits.

½ cup almond milk

½ cup plain kefir

Dash cinnamon

1½ teaspoons peeled and grated fresh ginger

1 cup red grapes

3 celery stalks, chopped

1 cup chopped microgreens

½ cup ice

1. Pour the almond milk and kefir into the blender, then add the cinnamon and ginger.

2. Layer in the grapes, celery, and microgreens. Top with the ice.

3. Blend all the ingredients together until completely smooth, adding more ice or almond milk as needed to reach desired consistency. Consume immediately.

Per Serving (16 ounces)

Calories: 125; Total fat: 2g; Sodium: 91mg; Cholesterol: 5mg; Total carbs: 24g; Fiber: 2g; Sugar: 19g; Protein: 4g

Alterations:

Substitution tip: No microgreens? Use any green you have on hand.

SWISS CHARD MY HEART

Yield: 1 (16-ounce) serving | Prep time: 5 minutes

HIGH FIBER, LESS SUGAR

Swiss chard works hard in this smoothie to keep your gut healthy. Packed with flavonol antioxidants like quercetin, kaempferol, rutin, and vitexin, Swiss chard demonstrates its potential here as a powerful anti-inflammatory and gut healer.

½ cup unsweetened coconut milk

1½ teaspoons peeled and grated fresh ginger

½ cup diced cucumber

2 celery stalks, chopped

1½ cups chopped Swiss chard (about 5 leaves)

⅓ avocado, pit and skin removed

¾ cup frozen pineapple

1. Pour the coconut milk into the blender first, then add the ginger.

2. Layer in the cucumber, celery, Swiss chard, avocado, and pineapple.

3. Blend all the ingredients together until completely smooth, adding more coconut milk as needed to reach desired consistency. Consume immediately.

Per Serving (16 ounce)

Calories: 200; Total fat: 11g; Sodium: 230mg; Cholesterol: 0mg; Total carbs: 27g; Fiber: 8g; Sugar: 13g; Protein: 4g

Alterations:

_____

_____

_____

_____

_____

_____

_____

Flavor tip: Leave out the chard stems to decrease bitterness.

SUPER SEED

Yield: 1 (16-ounce) serving | Prep time: 5 minutes

HIGH FIBER, HIGH PROTEIN, MEAL REPLACEMENT, SUPERFOOD STAR

This hearty three-seed smoothie is packed with healthy plant-based protein and prebiotic fiber for digestive health, plus omega-3 fatty acids for satiety and anti-inflammatory power.

1 cup unsweetened coconut milk

1 teaspoon vanilla extract

1 tablespoon chia seeds

1 tablespoon ground flaxseed

⅓ cup hemp seeds

1 cup chopped kale (stems removed, as needed)

⅓ avocado, pit and skin removed

½ cup frozen pineapple

1 frozen banana

1. Pour the coconut milk into the blender, then add the vanilla extract, chia seeds, flaxseed, and hemp seeds.

2. Layer in the kale, avocado, pineapple, and banana.

3. Blend all the ingredients together until completely smooth, adding more coconut milk as needed to reach desired consistency. Consume immediately.

Per Serving (16 ounce)

Calories: 491; Total fat: 24g; Sodium: 42mg; Cholesterol: 0mg; Total carbs: 64g; Fiber: 19g; Sugar: 24g; Protein: 14g

Alterations:

Ingredient tip: Store your seeds in the freezer to preserve them for longer and retain their nutrients.

MANGO TANGO

Yield: 1 (16-ounce) serving | Prep time: 5 minutes

HIGH FIBER, LOW CALORIE, SUPERFOOD STAR

High in vitamin C and beta-carotene, mango is a prebiotic fiber that helps feed the good bacteria in your gut. Aloe vera juice is also particularly gut supportive, healing, and great for keeping you regular.

½ cup water

2 tablespoons aloe vera juice

1 tablespoon hemp seeds

1½ teaspoons peeled and grated fresh ginger

½ cup frozen mango

½ cup diced zucchini (steamed, frozen)

1½ cups chopped baby spinach

½ cup ice

1. Pour the water and aloe vera juice into the blender, then add the hemp seeds and ginger.

2. Layer in the mango, zucchini, and spinach. Top with the ice.

3. Blend all the ingredients together until completely smooth, adding more ice or water as needed to reach desired consistency. Consume immediately.

Per Serving (16 ounce)

Calories: 122; Total fat: 3g; Sodium: 110mg; Cholesterol: 0mg; Total carbs: 25g; Fiber: 1g; Sugar: 15g; Protein: 7g

Alterations:

Variation tip: No mango available? Try adding frozen pineapple or ½ banana.

GINGER PEAR

Yield: 1 (16-ounce) serving | Prep time: 5 minutes

Refreshingly sweet and spicy, this smoothie is soothing to the gut and super hydrating. Including Greek yogurt here adds a dose of good bacteria for maintaining gut health and digestion.

½ cup unsweetened almond milk

Juice of ½ lemon

½ cup plain Greek yogurt

1 tablespoon ground flaxseed

1½ teaspoons peeled and grated fresh ginger

1 pear, roughly chopped

½ cucumber, diced

1 cup chopped kale (stems removed, as needed)

½ cup ice

Per Serving (16 ounce)

Calories: 339; Total fat: 10g; Sodium: 183mg; Cholesterol: 10mg; Total carbs: 46g; Fiber: 11g; Sugar: 23g; Protein: 22g

Alterations:

1. Pour the almond milk, lemon juice, and yogurt into the blender, then add the flaxseed and ginger.

2. Layer in the pear, cucumber, and kale. Top with the ice.

3. Blend all the ingredients together until completely smooth, adding more ice or almond milk as needed to reach desired consistency. Consume immediately.

Ingredient tip: Pear not quite ripe? Grate it for easier blending.

SWEET POTATO APPLE PIE

Yield: 1 (16-ounce) serving | Prep time: 5 minutes

HIGH FIBER, HIGH PROTEIN, MEAL REPLACEMENT

This sweet and creamy smoothie provides beta-carotene and the healing power of pectin, making it a tempting, gut-healthy treat for any time of day.

½ cup unsweetened almond milk

¾ teaspoon cinnamon

1 tablespoon almond butter

1 scoop vanilla protein powder

2 tablespoons quick-cooking rolled oats

1 small apple, cored and chopped

¼ cup diced sweet potato

1½ cups chopped baby spinach

½ cup ice

1. Pour the almond milk into the blender, then add the cinnamon, almond butter, protein powder, and oats.

2. Layer in the apple, sweet potato, and spinach. Top with the ice.

3. Blend all the ingredients together until completely smooth, adding more ice or almond milk as needed to reach desired consistency. Consume immediately.

Per Serving (16 ounce)

Calories: 453; Total fat: 14g; Sodium: 360mg; Cholesterol: 80mg; Total carbs: 52g; Fiber: 13g; Sugar: 20g; Protein: 36g

Alterations:

Substitution tip: No sweet potato? Use shredded carrots instead.

LICORICE DREAM

Yield: 1 (16-ounce) serving | Prep time: 5 minutes

HIGH FIBER, LESS SUGAR, LOW CALORIE

Often used to ease gas and bloating, fennel is the star in this digestive dynamo. A particularly versatile ingredient, fennel can double as a vegetable and a spice (fennel seed). The stems taste a bit sweet, while the bulb has a strong licorice flavor. Combined with ginger and soothing coconut milk, this smoothie may become your belly's best friend.

1 cup unsweetened coconut milk

5 fresh mint leaves, chopped

1½ teaspoons peeled and grated fresh ginger

½ bulb fennel, chopped

1 cup chopped baby spinach

½ grapefruit, peeled and segmented

½ cup ice

1. Pour the coconut milk into the blender, then add the mint and ginger.

2. Layer in the fennel, spinach, and grapefruit. Top with the ice.

3. Blend all the ingredients together until completely smooth, adding more ice or coconut milk as needed to reach desired consistency. Consume immediately.

Per Serving (16 ounce)

Calories: 115; Total fat: 5g; Sodium: 88mg; Cholesterol: 0mg; Total carbs: 18g; Fiber: 7g; Sugar: 5g; Protein: 3g

Alterations:

Ingredient tip: To prep the fennel, trim off the stalks and cut the bulb in half, removing any rough edges. Cut straight down through the root of the fennel bulb, then slice the halves into quarters, and chop into small pieces.

ENERGY BOOSTERS

Need an energy boost in the morning? And I don't mean that jittery caffeine-induced buzz inevitably produced by too much coffee. Don't get me wrong, I love my coffee, but it doesn't give me the kind of long-lasting energy that I'm talking about . . . The type of get-up-and-go vitality that only a green smoothie can bring.

Balanced with the energy-boosting combination of protein, healthy fats, and filling fiber, the green smoothies in this chapter will get your blood pumping and your cells ignited! Loaded with powerful antioxidant nutrients, superfood add-ins, and essential vitamins and minerals, these delectable smoothies will fuel you through even the most hectic mornings, leaving you energized and satisfied for hours.

PEACHES 'N' CREAM

Yield: 1 (16-ounce) serving | Prep time: 5 minutes

HIGH FIBER, MEAL REPLACEMENT, SUPERFOOD STAR

This peach smoothie is super tasty, and thanks to frozen peaches, can be enjoyed all year round—not just when peaches are in season. I always like to add a pinch of black pepper when I use turmeric, because the combination increases absorption of turmeric's active compounds.

¾ cup unsweetened coconut milk

½ cup plain kefir

2 tablespoons ground flaxseed

½ teaspoon ground turmeric

Pinch black pepper

1 cup chopped kale (stems removed, as needed)

¾ cup frozen peaches

1. Pour the coconut milk and kefir into the blender, then add the flaxseed, turmeric, and black pepper.

2. Layer in the kale and peaches.

3. Blend all the ingredients together until completely smooth, adding more coconut milk as needed to reach desired consistency. Consume immediately.

Per Serving (16 ounce)

Calories: 300; Total fat: 15g; Sodium: 74mg; Cholesterol: 5mg; Total carbs: 27g; Fiber: 10g; Sugar: 15g; Protein: 13g

Alterations:

Flavor tip: For an even more pronounced peachy flavor, use peach-flavored kefir.

STRAWBERRY MINT

Yield: 1 (16-ounce) serving | Prep time: 5 minutes

HIGH FIBER, LESS SUGAR, SUPERFOOD STAR

This refreshing smoothie is rich in vitamin C and medium-chain fatty acids for long-lasting energy all morning long.

½ cup unsweetened cashew milk

1 tablespoon coconut or MCT oil

6 mint leaves, chopped

1 cup frozen strawberries

½ cucumber, diced

1 cup chopped baby spinach

½ cup ice

1. Pour the cashew milk and MCT oil into the blender, then add the mint.

2. Layer in the strawberries, cucumber, and spinach. Top with the ice.

3. Blend all the ingredients together until completely smooth, adding more ice or cashew milk as needed to reach desired consistency. Consume immediately.

Per Serving (16 ounce)

Calories: 214; Total fat: 15g; Sodium: 110mg; Cholesterol: 0mg; Total carbs: 21g; Fiber: 5g; Sugar: 12g; Protein: 2g

Alterations:

Substitution tip: No cashew milk? Use almond milk instead.

GREEN GRAPEFRUIT

Yield: 1 (16-ounce) serving | Prep time: 5 minutes

HIGH FIBER, LESS SUGAR, LOW CALORIE, SUPERFOOD STAR

This zesty, energizing smoothie is jam-packed with nutrients like antioxidants, fiber, and vitamin C. It's the perfect jump start to a busy day ahead.

½ cup water

1 tablespoon freshly squeezed lime juice

1½ teaspoons peeled and grated fresh ginger

1 pink grapefruit, peeled and segmented

⅓ avocado, pit and skin removed

1 cup chopped baby spinach

1 cup chopped kale (stems removed, as needed)

½ cup ice

1. Pour the water and lime juice into the blender, then add the ginger.

2. Layer in the grapefruit, avocado, spinach, and kale. Top with the ice.

3. Blend all the ingredients together until completely smooth, adding more ice or water as needed to reach desired consistency. Consume immediately.

Per Serving (16 ounces)

Calories: 200; Total fat: 9g; Sodium: 58mg; Cholesterol: 0mg; Total carbs: 30g; Fiber: 8g; Sugar: 10g; Protein: 5g

Alterations:

Flavor tip: No ginger? Use a dash of cinnamon for spice instead.

ORANGE DELIGHT

Yield: 1 (16-ounce) serving | Prep time: 5 minutes

Rev up your morning from the inside out with this energizing smoothie. Rich in natural protein, vitamin C, and beta-carotene, it's a delicious way to kick off the day!

1 cup unsweetened macadamia nut milk

1 tablespoon hemp seeds

¼ teaspoon cinnamon, or to taste

1½ teaspoons peeled and grated fresh ginger

1 small orange, peeled and segmented

½ cup grated carrots

1 cup chopped baby spinach

½ cup ice (optional)

1. Pour the macadamia milk into the blender, then add the hemp seeds, cinnamon, and ginger.

2. Layer in the orange, carrots, and spinach.

3. Blend all the ingredients together until completely smooth, adding ice or more macadamia milk as needed to reach desired consistency. Consume immediately.

Per Serving (16 ounce)

Calories: 145; Total fat: 4g; Sodium: 223mg; Cholesterol: 0mg; Total carbs: 27g; Fiber: 6g; Sugar: 17g; Protein: 4g

Alterations:

_____

_____

_____

_____

_____

_____

_____

Health Boost tip: Add ½ teaspoon turmeric for added anti-inflammatory effects.

BERRIES & BEETS

Yield: 1 (16-ounce) serving | Prep time: 5 minutes

HIGH FIBER, LESS SUGAR, LOW CALORIE, SUPERFOOD STAR

This refreshing dose of natural energy will keep you motivated all afternoon. Blackberries and beets combined with lime and fresh mint provide all the antioxidant-rich energy you need to feel focused and invigorated.

½ cup unsweetened coconut milk

1 tablespoon freshly squeezed lime juice

1 tablespoon chia seeds

3 to 4 mint leaves, chopped

1 cup frozen blackberries

½ cup grated beets

1 cup chopped baby spinach

½ cup ice

1. Pour the coconut milk and lime juice into the blender, then add the chia seeds and mint.

2. Layer in the blackberries, beets, and spinach. Top with the ice.

3. Blend all the ingredients together until completely smooth, adding more ice or coconut milk as needed to reach desired consistency. Consume immediately.

Per Serving (16 ounce)

Calories: 240; Total fat: 8g; Sodium: 94mg; Cholesterol: 0mg; Total carbs: 34g; Fiber: 16g; Sugar: 15g; Protein: 7g

Alterations:

Variation tip: Herbs are wonderful sources of natural flavor. This recipe is delicious with mint, but it also works with parsley or cilantro.

MORNING MACA

Yield: 1 (16-ounce) serving | Prep time: 5 minutes

HIGH FIBER, HIGH PROTEIN, MEAL REPLACEMENT

Start your day off right with this high-power smoothie. Maca powder is rich in minerals like magnesium and calcium, and has been shown to balance hormones, increase vitality, and improve mood.

½ cup unsweetened almond milk

½ cup plain Greek yogurt

1 teaspoon maca root powder

1 tablespoon peanut butter

1 scoop chocolate protein powder

1 cup chopped frozen baby spinach

½ cup ice

1. Pour the almond milk and yogurt into the blender, then add the maca, peanut butter, and protein powder.

2. Layer in the spinach. Top with the ice.

3. Blend all the ingredients together until completely smooth, adding more ice or almond milk as needed to reach desired consistency. Consume immediately.

Per Serving (16 ounces)

Calories: 314; Total fat: 18g; Sodium: 287mg; Cholesterol: 45mg; Total carbs: 21g; Fiber: 5g; Sugar: 12g; Protein: 25g

Alterations:

_____

_____

_____

_____

_____

_____

_____

Substitution tip: No maca powder? Use cinnamon instead.

CHOCOLATE CHERRY ALMOND

Yield: 1 (16-ounce) serving | Prep time: 5 minutes

HIGH FIBER, HIGH PROTEIN, MEAL REPLACEMENT

This chocolate cherry smoothie is decadently rich and delicious. The cauliflower adds fiber and B vitamins for energy, providing extra bulk to your smoothie that keeps you fuller for longer.

1 cup unsweetened almond milk

1 tablespoon almond butter

2 tablespoons chia seeds

1 scoop chocolate protein powder

1½ cups chopped Swiss chard (about 5 leaves)

½ cup frozen cauliflower florets

½ frozen banana

½ cup frozen tart cherries

1. Pour the almond milk into the blender, then add the almond butter, chia seeds, and protein powder.

2. Layer in the Swiss chard, cauliflower, banana, and cherries.

3. Blend all the ingredients together until completely smooth, adding more almond milk as needed to reach desired consistency. Consume immediately.

Per Serving (16 ounce)

Calories: 448; Total fat: 22g; Sodium: 259mg; Cholesterol: 20mg; Total carbs: 47g; Fiber: 18g; Sugar: 20g; Protein: 22g

Alterations:

_____

_____

_____

_____

_____

_____

_____

Variation tip: Make it a mocha! Replace half the almond milk with chilled coffee.

TROPICAL GREEN

Yield: 1 (16-ounce) serving | Prep time: 5 minutes

HIGH PROTEIN, LESS SUGAR, MEAL REPLACEMENT

This energizing smoothie is packed with MCT oil, a type of fat that helps boost the absorption of antioxidants and vitamin C. Upgrade your morning coffee to this protein-packed energy booster.

1 cup unsweetened almond milk

1 tablespoon MCT oil

1 scoop vanilla protein powder

½ cup frozen pineapple

½ cup frozen cauliflower florets

¼ cup frozen broccoli florets

1. Pour the almond milk and MCT oil into the blender, then add the protein powder.

2. Layer in the pineapple, cauliflower, and broccoli.

3. Blend all the ingredients together until completely smooth, adding more almond milk as needed to reach desired consistency. Consume immediately.

Per Serving (16 ounce)

Calories: 410; Total fat: 22g; Sodium: 350mg; Cholesterol: 120mg; Total carbs: 30g; Fiber: 4g; Sugar: 13g; Protein: 23g

Alterations:

_____

_____

_____

_____

_____

_____

_____

Substitution tip: No MCT oil? Use coconut oil instead for a similar effect.

MANGO OATS

Yield: 1 (16-ounce) serving | Prep time: 5 minutes

HIGH FIBER, HIGH PROTEIN, MEAL REPLACEMENT

Naturally sweetened and chock-full of fiber, this smoothie provides the perfect breakfast fuel to power you through your day.

1 cup vanilla oat milk

1 teaspoon cinnamon

1 scoop unsweetened protein powder

¼ cup quick-cooking rolled oats

1½ cups chopped baby spinach

⅓ avocado, pit and skin removed

½ cup frozen mango chunks

1. Pour the oat milk into the blender, then add the cinnamon, protein powder, and oats.

2. Layer in the spinach, avocado, and mango.

3. Blend all the ingredients together until completely smooth, adding more oat milk as needed to reach desired consistency. Consume immediately.

Per Serving (16 ounces)

Calories: 503; Total fat: 17g; Sodium: 253mg; Cholesterol: 20mg; Total carbs: 65g; Fiber: 15g; Sugar: 18g; Protein: 29g

Alterations:

Serving tip: Serve in a bowl, topped with chia seeds and sliced banana.

CHERRY BLASTER

Yield: 1 (16-ounce) serving | Prep time: 5 minutes

HIGH FIBER, HIGH PROTEIN, MEAL REPLACEMENT

This is my favorite smoothie when I have an afternoon jam-packed with appointments. It provides long-lasting energy, tons of antioxidants and fiber, and is always a treat.

1½ cups unsweetened coconut milk
1 scoop vanilla protein powder
¼ cup quick-cooking rolled oats
1 teaspoon bee pollen
1 tablespoon peanut butter
2 cups chopped baby spinach
½ cup frozen tart cherries

1. Pour the coconut milk into the blender, then add the protein powder, oats, bee pollen, and peanut butter.

2. Layer in the spinach and cherries.

3. Blend all the ingredients together until completely smooth, adding more coconut milk as needed to reach desired consistency. Consume immediately.

Per Serving (16 ounce)

Calories: 444; Total fat: 17g; Sodium: 175mg; Cholesterol: 2mg; Total carbs: 44g; Fiber: 8g; Sugar: 17g; Protein: 37g

Alterations:

_____

_____

_____

_____

_____

_____

_____

Ingredient tip: Instead of peanut butter, try peanut butter powder to reduce total calories and fat.

ANTI-INFLAMMATORY

Inflammation is a natural part of our immune system and we love it for fighting off foreign invaders and healing injuries fast. But, like anything else, too much of a good thing can be bad for you. And when inflammation becomes chronic (or doesn't ever turn off), it can cause serious health problems, such as arthritis, heart disease, cancer, and diabetes.

Luckily for us, drinking green smoothies on a regular basis can make a difference. A diet rich in vitamins, minerals, and anti-inflammatory foods like leafy greens, nuts, wild blueberries, cherries, beets, ginger, and turmeric helps lower chronic inflammation and prevent disease. The delicious green smoothies found in this chapter are loaded with antioxidant ingredients and superfoods known for their anti-inflammatory properties. As such, consuming these is an excellent first step in being healthy from the inside out.

CHOCOLATE CHAI

Yield: 1 (16-ounce) serving | Prep time: 5 minutes

HIGH FIBER, LESS SUGAR, MEAL REPLACEMENT

Cacao is one of the richest sources of polyphenols and has potent anti-inflammatory effects. I love treating myself to this chocolate chai smoothie after an early yoga class to maintain my zen state of mind all morning long.

½ cup cooled, brewed chai

1 tablespoon unsweetened cacao powder

½ teaspoon cinnamon

3 tablespoons quick-cooking rolled oats

1 tablespoon cashew butter

1 cup chopped baby spinach

1 frozen banana

1. Pour the brewed chai into the blender, then add the cacao powder, cinnamon, oats, and cashew butter.

2. Layer in the spinach and banana.

3. Blend all the ingredients together until completely smooth, adding more chai as needed to reach desired consistency. Consume immediately.

Per Serving (16 ounce)

Calories: 317; Total fat: 13g; Sodium: 29mg; Cholesterol: 0mg; Total carbs: 54g; Fiber: 12g; Sugar: 15g; Protein: 11g

Alterations:

Flavor tip: For more chai flavor, use chai spice (cardamom, allspice, nutmeg, cinnamon, cloves, ginger) instead of just cinnamon.

GREEN TAHINI

Yield: 1 (16-ounce) serving | Prep time: 5 minutes

HIGH FIBER, MEAL REPLACEMENT, SUPERFOOD STAR

Adding tahini is a particularly tasty way to enhance your green smoothie with a little Middle Eastern flavor. Made by grinding sesame seeds into a thick paste, tahini is the perfect nut butter substitute. It provides a nice silky texture along with adding a dose of anti-inflammatory monounsaturated fat to any smoothie.

1 cup water

1½ teaspoons peeled and grated fresh ginger

1 tablespoon chia seeds

1 tablespoon tahini

½ cup diced zucchini (steamed, frozen)

1½ cups chopped baby spinach

⅓ avocado, pit and skin removed

1 frozen banana

1. Pour the water into the blender, then add the ginger, chia seeds, and tahini.

2. Layer in the zucchini, spinach, avocado, and banana.

3. Blend all the ingredients together until completely smooth, adding more water as needed to reach desired consistency. Consume immediately.

Per Serving (16 ounce)

Calories: 390; Total fat: 22g; Sodium: 69mg; Cholesterol: 0mg; Total carbs: 47g; Fiber: 15g; Sugar: 16g; Protein: 10g

Alterations:

Substitution tip: No tahini? Use sunflower butter instead.

WILD BLUEBERRY POWER

Yield: 1 (16-ounce) serving | Prep time: 5 minutes

HIGH FIBER, SUPERFOOD STAR

Wild blueberries are rich in anthocyanin, a powerful antioxidant flavonoid that works to fight inflammation (and also gives them their gorgeous deep-blue color). In this smoothie they are mixed with blackberries—also high in fiber and anti-oxidants—giving your body an instant super boost!

1 cup coconut water

1 tablespoon ground flaxseed

1 tablespoon almond butter

1½ cups chopped kale (stems removed, as needed)

½ cup frozen wild blueberries

½ cup fresh or frozen blackberries

1. Pour the coconut water into the blender, then add the flaxseed and almond butter.

2. Layer in the kale, blueberries, and blackberries.

3. Blend all the ingredients together until completely smooth, adding more coconut water as needed to reach desired consistency. Consume immediately.

Per Serving (16 ounce)

Calories: 313; Total fat: 14g; Sodium: 210mg; Cholesterol: 0mg; Total carbs: 34g; Fiber: 13g; Sugar: 20g; Protein: 11g

Alterations:

Health Boost tip: Add 3 tablespoons hemp seeds for an additional boost of protein.

QUEEN OF GREEN

Yield: 1 (16-ounce) serving | Prep time: 5 minutes

HIGH FIBER, HIGH PROTEIN, MEAL REPLACEMENT, SUPERFOOD STAR

This smoothie is a tall glass of creamy anti-inflammatory goodness, thanks to the fiber, zinc, magnesium, and essential fatty acids (EFAs) omega-3 and 6.

1 cup unsweetened coconut milk

¼ cup hemp seeds

1 cup chopped baby spinach

1½ cups chopped Swiss chard (about 5 leaves)

¾ cup frozen tart cherries

1. Pour the coconut milk into the blender, then add the hemp seeds.

2. Layer in the spinach, Swiss chard, and cherries.

3. Blend all the ingredients together until completely smooth, adding more coconut milk as needed to reach desired consistency. Consume immediately.

Per Serving (16 ounce)

Calories: 380; Total fat: 25g; Sodium: 139mg; Cholesterol: 0mg; Total carbs: 26g; Fiber: 1g; Sugar: 15g; Protein: 18g

Alterations:

Substitution tip: No hemp seeds? Use 1 scoop of protein powder instead.

MANGO CAULI KALE

Yield: 1 (16-ounce) serving | Prep time: 5 minutes

HIGH FIBER, SUPERFOOD STAR

This smoothie is a rich and delicious source of omega-3 fatty acids that help decrease inflammation and improve brain function. Rich in fiber and vitamins C and B6, it's also a natural stress reducer.

1 cup unsweetened coconut milk

2 tablespoons ground flaxseed

½ cup frozen mango

1 cup frozen cauliflower florets

1 cup chopped kale (stems removed, as needed)

½ cup ice

1. Pour the coconut milk into the blender, then add the flaxseed.

2. Layer in the mango, cauliflower, and kale, and top with the ice.

3. Blend all the ingredients together until completely smooth, adding more ice or coconut milk as needed to reach desired consistency. Consume immediately.

Per Serving (16 ounce)

Calories: 231; Total fat: 10g; Sodium: 66mg; Cholesterol: 0mg; Total carbs: 33g; Fiber: 10g; Sugar: 15g; Protein: 8g

Alterations:

Flavor tip: Add dashes of cinnamon and mint for a tropical flair.

TROPICAL REFRESHER

Yield: 1 (16-ounce) serving | Prep time: 5 minutes

HIGH FIBER, SUPERFOOD STAR

Spicy and sweet, this is one of my favorite smoothies. I use a greens powder here, made from dried leafy greens and cruciferous veggies, berries, and herbs. It's another convenient way to get in some green goodness when you don't have fresh greens available.

1 cup unsweetened coconut milk

1 scoop greens powder

1½ teaspoons peeled and grated fresh ginger

¼ teaspoon ground turmeric

Pinch black pepper

¼ teaspoon cinnamon

1 cup chopped fresh carrots

½ cup frozen pineapple

1. Pour the coconut milk into the blender, then add the greens powder, ginger, turmeric, black pepper, and cinnamon.

2. Layer in the carrots and pineapple.

3. Blend all the ingredients together until completely smooth, adding more coconut milk as needed to reach desired consistency. Consume immediately.

Per Serving (16 ounce)

Calories: 193; Total fat: 5g; Sodium: 132mg; Cholesterol: 0mg; Total carbs: 32g; Fiber: 11g; Sugar: 20g; Protein: 5g

Alterations:

_____

_____

_____

_____

_____

_____

_____

Serving tip: Garnish with shredded coconut flakes for added texture.

ORANGE AVOCADO

Yield: 1 (16-ounce) serving | Prep time: 5 minutes

HIGH FIBER, SUPERFOOD STAR

Cashew milk gives this tasty smoothie its unique flavor. If you don't have cashew milk on hand, it's simple to make some yourself. Just soak 1 cup cashews in water for at least 30 minutes (or leave overnight). Once soaked, drain and rinse the cashews, then blend with 4 cups of water until smooth and creamy. Voila!

1 cup unsweetened cashew milk

1 tablespoon ground flaxseed

½ teaspoon cinnamon

1 teaspoon vanilla extract

½ avocado, pit and skin removed

1 small orange, peeled and segmented

1 cup chopped baby spinach

½ cup ice

1. Pour the cashew milk into the blender, then add the flaxseed, cinnamon, and vanilla extract.

2. Layer in the avocado, orange, and spinach. Top with the ice.

3. Blend all the ingredients together until completely smooth, adding more ice or cashew milk as needed to reach desired consistency. Consume immediately.

Per Serving (16 ounce)

Calories: 291; Total fat: 18g; Sodium: 191mg; Cholesterol: 0mg; Total carbs: 30g; Fiber: 13g; Sugar: 15g; Protein: 6g

Alterations:

Texture tip: Want it creamier? Add ⅓ more avocado.

ALMOND SPICE

Yield: 1 (16-ounce) serving | Prep time: 5 minutes

HIGH FIBER, LESS SUGAR, SUPERFOOD STAR

Almond butter gives this smoothie its thick, velvety texture and is a great source of healthy fats. Blend it with cinnamon, vanilla, and a dash of turmeric for a cozy, anti-inflammatory delight.

1 cup unsweetened almond milk

½ teaspoon ground cinnamon

1 teaspoon vanilla powder or extract

¼ teaspoon turmeric

Pinch black pepper

1 tablespoon chia seeds

1 tablespoon almond butter

1½ cups chopped baby spinach

1 frozen banana

1. Pour the almond milk into the blender, then add the cinnamon, vanilla, turmeric, black pepper, chia seeds, and almond butter.

2. Layer in the spinach and banana.

3. Blend all the ingredients together until completely smooth, adding more almond milk as needed to reach desired consistency. Consume immediately.

Per Serving (16 ounce)

Calories: 339; Total fat: 18g; Sodium: 221mg; Cholesterol: 0mg; Total carbs: 41g; Fiber: 12g; Sugar: 15g; Protein: 9g

Alterations:

Flavor tip: Want some extra spice? Add fresh or powdered ginger.

BERRY BERRY GOOD

Yield: 1 (16-ounce) serving | Prep time: 5 minutes

HIGH FIBER, LOW CALORIE, SUPERFOOD STAR

This smoothie is a triple threat to inflammation. Loaded with phytonutrients from cranberry juice, fresh ginger, and beets, it's the perfect shot of anti-inflammatory muscle before a workout.

½ cup water
¼ cup pure unsweetened cranberry juice
1½ teaspoons peeled and grated fresh ginger
Pinch cinnamon
½ cup cooked or grated beets
1 cup frozen strawberries
1½ cups chopped Swiss chard (about 5 leaves)
½ cup ice

1. Pour the water and cranberry juice into the blender, then add the ginger and cinnamon.

2. Layer in the beets, strawberries, and Swiss chard. Top with the ice.

3. Blend all the ingredients together until completely smooth, adding more ice or water as needed to reach desired consistency. Consume immediately.

Per Serving (16 ounce)

Calories: 124; Total fat: 0g; Sodium: 190mg; Cholesterol: 0mg; Total carbs: 29g; Fiber: 7g; Sugar: 16g; Protein: 3g

Alterations:

_____

_____

_____

_____

_____

_____

Time-saver tip: Buy your beets precooked for easy prep.

HAPPY PLACE

Yield: 1 (16-ounce) serving | Prep time: 5 minutes

HIGH FIBER, MEAL REPLACEMENT, SUPERFOOD STAR

Turmeric, cauliflower, and ginger are potent superfoods with proven anti-inflammatory powers. Turmeric is actually so powerful, it matches the effectiveness of some anti-inflammatory drugs—without the side effects.

1 cup unsweetened almond milk

½ teaspoon ground cinnamon

1½ teaspoons peeled and grated fresh ginger

½ teaspoon ground turmeric

1 teaspoon chia seeds

1 tablespoon ground flaxseed

1 frozen banana

1 cup baby spinach

⅓ cup frozen cauliflower florets

1. Pour the almond milk into the blender, then add the cinnamon, ginger, turmeric, chia seeds, and flaxseed.

2. Layer in the banana, spinach, and cauliflower.

3. Blend all the ingredients together until completely smooth, adding more almond milk as needed to reach desired consistency. Consume immediately.

Per Serving (16 ounce)

Calories: 231; Total fat: 8g; Sodium: 219mg; Cholesterol: 0mg; Total carbs: 38g; Fiber: 10g; Sugar: 16g; Protein: 6g

Alterations:

_____

_____

_____

_____

_____

_____

_____

Ingredient tip: No frozen cauliflower? Use fresh instead.

CHAPTER SEVEN
ANTIOXIDANTS

I bring up antioxidants a lot in describing the health benefits of green smoothies—and for good reason. They are powerful workhorses in our bodies that play a major role in our overall health and wellness. Antioxidants act as fighter molecules in our cells, neutralizing free radicals while preventing oxidation.

Green smoothies offer us a great vehicle for packing in ingredients with high levels of antioxidant nutrients. From the polyphenols in grapes to the vitamin C in oranges, to the bioactive compounds in ginger and turmeric, you'll find antioxidant prowess across the board in the smoothies here. They can help lower systemic inflammation and blood pressure, as well as boost our immune system.

Superfoods are fun to play with here, too. A teaspoon or two of cacao powder doesn't just provide a dose of chocolate flavor; it's also one of the richest sources of polyphenols, which contain potent antioxidant power. You'll find other superfoods in the recipes to follow, but it's always optional to include them or not.

ORANGE PEPPER

Yield: 1 (16-ounce) serving | Prep time: 5 minutes

HIGH FIBER, MEAL REPLACEMENT

I love the peppery taste of arugula in this recipe. An antioxidant powerhouse, arugula is rich in vitamin K, pro-vitamin A carotenoids, folate, and calcium—in fact, more calcium per serving than spinach.

½ cup coconut water

¼ cup plain kefir

5 mint leaves, chopped

1 tablespoon almond butter

1 small orange, peeled and segmented

1 cup chopped arugula

½ cup frozen cauliflower florets

1. Pour the coconut water and kefir into the blender, then add the mint and almond butter.

2. Layer in the orange, arugula, and cauliflower.

3. Blend all the ingredients together until completely smooth, adding more coconut water as needed to reach desired consistency. Consume immediately.

Per Serving (16 ounce)

Calories: 225; Total fat: 10g; Sodium: 124mg; Cholesterol: 3mg; Total carbs: 26g; Fiber: 7g; Sugar: 23g; Protein: 8g

Alterations:

_____

_____

_____

_____

_____

_____

Health Boost tip: For an extra dose of antioxidants, try papaya instead of orange.

BLUE COCONUT

Yield: 1 (16-ounce) serving | Prep time: 5 minutes

HIGH FIBER, HIGH PROTEIN, SUPERFOOD STAR

This velvety smoothie is especially rich in vitamin C and antioxidants, making it heart healthy and a boost to your immune system. Meanwhile, turmeric and black pepper complement one another, intensifying the antioxidant effects.

½ cup coconut milk

½ cup plain Greek yogurt

1 teaspoon cinnamon

½ teaspoon turmeric

Pinch black pepper

1 tablespoon grated orange peel

1 cup chopped baby spinach

1 cup frozen wild blueberries

1. Pour the coconut milk and Greek yogurt into the blender, then add the cinnamon, turmeric, and black pepper.

2. Layer in the orange peel, spinach, and blueberries.

3. Blend all the ingredients together until completely smooth, adding more coconut milk as needed to reach desired consistency. Consume immediately.

Per Serving (16 ounce)

Calories: 210; Total fat: 3g; Sodium: 102mg; Cholesterol: 0mg; Total carbs: 31g; Fiber: 7g; Sugar: 20g; Protein: 19g

Alterations:

Substitution tip: No orange peel? Use ¼ teaspoon orange extract instead.

RASPBERRY CREAM

Yield: 1 (16-ounce) serving | Prep time: 5 minutes

HIGH FIBER, MEAL REPLACEMENT

This simple, raspberry-flavored smoothie is perfect for any time of day. Its high protein and fiber content will keep you full all morning long. It also makes the perfect midday snack or post-workout meal.

½ cup unsweetened coconut milk

1 cup raspberry-flavored kefir

1 tablespoon almond butter

½ cup frozen raspberries

½ cup diced zucchini (steamed, frozen)

1 cup chopped baby spinach

¼ cup ice

1. Pour the coconut milk and kefir into the blender, then add the almond butter.

2. Layer in the raspberries, zucchini, and spinach. Top with the ice.

3. Blend all the ingredients together until completely smooth, adding more ice or coconut milk as needed to reach desired consistency. Consume immediately.

Per Serving (16 ounce)

Calories: 306; Total fat: 15g; Sodium: 105mg; Cholesterol: 10mg; Total carbs: 39g; Fiber: 6g; Sugar: 26g; Protein: 11g

Alterations:

_____

_____

_____

_____

_____

_____

_____

Health Boost tip: For a lower-sugar option, use plain kefir and 1½ cups more frozen raspberries.

ALMOND GRAPE

Yield: 1 (16-ounce) serving | Prep time: 5 minutes

HIGH FIBER, LESS SUGAR

Using cacao powder is a great way to add some intense chocolate flavor to any smoothie. At the same time, it gives you a dose of powerhouse antioxidants that boost blood flow to the brain and increase energy—their anti-inflammatory effect may help protect against heart disease and cancer, too.

1 cup unsweetened almond milk

1 tablespoon almond butter

1 teaspoon cacao powder

¾ cup frozen grapes

1 cup chopped kale (stems removed, as needed)

1 cup frozen cauliflower florets

Per Serving (16 ounce)

Calories: 259; Total fat: 14g; Sodium: 242mg; Cholesterol: 0mg; Total carbs: 32g; Fiber: 9g; Sugar: 14g; Protein: 10g

Alterations:

1. Pour the almond milk into the blender, then add the almond butter and cacao powder.

2. Layer in the grapes, kale, and cauliflower.

3. Blend all the ingredients together until completely smooth, adding more almond milk as needed to reach desired consistency. Consume immediately.

Health Boost tip: For a higher protein content, use 1 scoop chocolate protein powder instead of cacao powder.

MELON BALL

Yield: 1 (16-ounce) serving | Prep time: 5 minutes

LESS SUGAR, LOW CALORIE

This minty-fresh smoothie is perfect on a hot summer day. It's refreshing and sweet, but still bursting with nutrients, thanks to the broccoli and chard.

½ cup water

1 tablespoon freshly squeezed lime juice

5 fresh mint leaves, chopped

¾ cup cubed honeydew melon

½ cup broccoli florets

1½ cups chopped Swiss chard (about 5 leaves)

½ cup ice

1. Pour the water and lime juice into the blender, then add the mint.

2. Layer in the honeydew, broccoli, and Swiss chard. Top with the ice.

3. Blend all the ingredients together until completely smooth, adding more ice or water as needed to reach desired consistency. Consume immediately.

Per Serving (16 ounce)

Calories: 86; Total fat: 1g; Sodium: 145mg; Cholesterol: 0mg; Total carbs: 21g; Fiber: 4g; Sugar: 14g; Protein: 3g

Alterations:

Texture tip: For a creamier texture, add ⅓ of an avocado.

PB&J SMOOTHIE

Yield: 1 (16-ounce) serving | Prep time: 5 minutes

HIGH FIBER, LESS SUGAR

I've never met a peanut butter–flavored smoothie I didn't like, and this PB&J is no exception. Take a time machine back to grade school with this antioxidant-rich smoothie, inspired by everyone's favorite sandwich. If you have a peanut allergy, try almond butter or sunflower butter instead.

1 cup unsweetened coconut milk

1 tablespoon peanut butter

¼ teaspoon ground cinnamon

1 cup red grapes

1 cup torn kale (stems removed, as needed)

½ cup frozen cauliflower florets

1. Pour the coconut milk into the blender, then add the peanut butter and cinnamon.

2. Layer in the grapes, kale, and cauliflower.

3. Blend all the ingredients together until completely smooth, adding more coconut milk as needed to reach desired consistency. Consume immediately.

Per Serving (16 ounce)

Calories: 246; Total fat: 13g; Sodium: 118mg; Cholesterol: 0mg; Total carbs: 29g; Fiber: 6g; Sugar: 15g; Protein: 8g

Alterations:

Serving tip: Garnish with a drizzle of creamy peanut butter for even more peanuty flavor.

PUMPKIN SPICE

Yield: 1 (16-ounce) serving | Prep time: 5 minutes

HIGH FIBER, HIGH PROTEIN, LESS SUGAR, MEAL REPLACEMENT

Pumpkin, carrot, and turmeric join forces in this sweet and soothing smoothie that's loaded with potassium and antioxidants like beta-carotene.

½ cup unsweetened almond milk

½ cup plain kefir

¼ cup canned pumpkin

1 scoop vanilla protein powder

1½ teaspoons peeled and grated fresh ginger

½ teaspoon turmeric

2 carrots, grated

1½ cups chopped baby spinach

½ cup ice

1. Pour the almond milk and kefir into the blender, then add the pumpkin, protein powder, ginger, and turmeric.

2. Layer in the carrots and spinach. Top with the ice.

3. Blend all the ingredients together until completely smooth, adding more ice or almond milk as needed to reach desired consistency. Consume immediately.

Per Serving (16 ounce)

Calories: 298; Total fat: 6g; Sodium: 309mg; Cholesterol: 85mg; Total carbs: 33g; Fiber: 7g; Sugar: 13g; Protein: 32g

Alterations:

Substitution tip: No kefir? Use Greek yogurt instead.

PINEAPPLE MATCHA

Yield: 1 (16-ounce) serving | Prep time: 5 minutes

HIGH FIBER, SUPERFOOD STAR

This chlorophyll-rich smoothie combines the tropical taste of pineapple with the antioxidant power of matcha green tea. Add a mini-umbrella to your glass and let this smoothie transport you to the beach!

1 cup unsweetened coconut milk

2 tablespoons freshly squeezed lemon juice

1 tablespoon matcha (green tea powder)

1 cup chopped kale (stems removed, as needed)

⅓ avocado, pit and skin removed

¾ cup frozen pineapple chunks

1. Pour the coconut milk and lemon juice into the blender, then add the matcha powder.

2. Layer in the kale, avocado, and pineapple.

3. Blend all the ingredients together until completely smooth, adding more coconut milk as needed to reach desired consistency. Consume immediately.

Per Serving (16 ounce)

Calories: 269; Total fat: 14g; Sodium: 42mg; Cholesterol: 0mg; Total carbs: 40g; Fiber: 10g; Sugar: 19g; Protein: 4g

Alterations:

_____

_____

_____

_____

_____

_____

Health Boost tip: Want more protein? Add ½ cup plain Greek yogurt.

RED MINTY MAGIC

Yield: 1 (16-ounce) serving | Prep time: 5 minutes

HIGH FIBER, LESS SUGAR, SUPERFOOD STAR

Beets are an antioxidant powerhouse. They are true liver healers with natural anti-aging properties. The betaine in beets also helps reduce overall inflammation in the body. This tasty smoothie is perfect for a crisp autumn morning.

1 cup unsweetened almond milk

2 tablespoons freshly squeezed lime juice

1 tablespoon ground chia seeds

6 to 9 fresh mint leaves, chopped

1 teaspoon pomegranate powder

¼ cup grated beet (about 1 small beet)

1 cup chopped kale (stems removed, as needed)

1 cup frozen raspberries

1. Pour the almond milk and lime juice into the blender, then add the chia seeds, mint, and pomegranate powder.

2. Layer in the beet, kale, and raspberries.

3. Blend all the ingredients together until completely smooth, adding more almond milk as needed to reach desired consistency. Consume immediately.

Per Serving (16 ounce)

Calories: 278; Total fat: 9g; Sodium: 202mg; Cholesterol: 0mg; Total carbs: 48g; Fiber: 17g; Sugar: 15g; Protein: 9g

Alterations:

_____

_____

_____

_____

_____

_____

Ingredient tip: Pomegranate is another star ingredient: If you don't have it in powder form, ¼ cup juice works just as well.

BEE WILD

Yield: 1 (16-ounce) serving | Prep time: 5 minutes

HIGH FIBER, LESS SUGAR, LOW CALORIE

Rich in anthocyanin, wild blueberries are one of the most potent antioxidant fruits you can eat. The addition of bee pollen here boosts the antioxidant content of this smoothie even further, bringing along with it an impressive array of nutrients (over 250, to be exact).

1 cup unsweetened soy milk

1 teaspoon bee pollen

½ cup broccoli florets

1 cup baby spinach

¾ cup frozen wild blueberries

1. Pour the soy milk into the blender, then add the bee pollen.

2. Layer in the broccoli, spinach, and blueberries.

3. Blend all the ingredients together until completely smooth, adding more soy milk as needed to reach desired consistency. Consume immediately.

Per Serving (16 ounce)

Calories: 182; Total fat: 5g; Sodium: 61mg; Cholesterol: 0mg; Total carbs: 23g; Fiber: 7g; Sugar: 13g; Protein: 13g

Alterations:

_____

_____

_____

_____

_____

_____

_____

Health Boost tip: Add a scoop of greens powder for even more antioxidant goodness.

HEALTHY SKIN

I'm a total skin care junkie, and I love incorporating superfoods, herbs, and natural skin smoothers into my diet whenever possible—especially into my smoothies!

Antioxidants, collagen, fiber, and protein are my go-to tools for maintaining skin elasticity, healing inflammation, and rehydrating my skin. I also love adding sea buckthorn powder to my smoothies. Sea buckthorn offers a unique fatty-acid blend known for its ability to regenerate and repair the skin, while improving circulation and oxygenation.

In this chapter, you'll find green smoothie recipes using a wide variety of berries, mostly for their antioxidant content. Antioxidants help boost collagen production and act as natural sunscreen, protecting your skin against the sun's harmful rays from the inside out. These recipes are among my very favorites, so I hope you love them as much as I do!

RADIANCE

Yield: 1 (16-ounce) serving | Prep time: 5 minutes

HIGH FIBER, MEAL REPLACEMENT

The skin-loving power of cucumber and kiwi will make this vitamin C–rich smoothie your new best friend. Replenish dull skin with this powerful, hydrating elixir.

1 cup water

1 teaspoon freshly squeezed lime juice (or to taste)

1 scoop collagen protein powder

⅓ avocado, pit and skin removed

2 kiwis, peeled

½ cucumber, diced

1 cup chopped baby spinach

½ cup ice

1. Pour the water and lime juice into the blender, then add the collagen powder.

2. Layer in the avocado, kiwis, cucumber, and spinach. Top with the ice.

3. Blend all the ingredients together until completely smooth, adding more ice or water as needed to reach desired consistency. Consume immediately.

Per Serving (16 ounce)

Calories: 248; Total fat: 9g; Sodium: 42mg; Cholesterol: 0mg; Total carbs: 29g; Fiber: 7g; Sugar: 20g; Protein: 10g

Alterations:

Flavor tip: Not a fan of kiwi? Try ½ cup of frozen mango for a tropical twist.

SKIN REJUVENATOR

Yield: 1 (16-ounce) serving | Prep time: 5 minutes

LESS SUGAR, LOW CALORIE

The skin regenerating, antioxidant power of cucumber and mango make this vitamin A–rich smoothie a welcome gift to your skin. It's hydrating, too—sure to replenish any dull or dry complexion.

1 cup water

Juice of ½ lemon

Juice of ½ lime

½ cup frozen mango chunks

½ cucumber, diced

2 cups chopped baby spinach

½ cup ice

1. Pour the water, lemon juice, and lime juice into the blender.

2. Layer in the mango, cucumber, and spinach. Top with the ice.

3. Blend all the ingredients together until completely smooth, adding more ice or water as needed to reach desired consistency. Consume immediately.

Per Serving (16 ounce)

Calories: 103; Total fat: 1g; Sodium: 57mg; Cholesterol: 0mg; Total carbs: 24g; Fiber: 4g; Sugar: 15g; Protein: 4g

Alterations:

Ingredient tip: Choose organic cucumbers and leave the skin on.

KIWI CUCUMBER KALE

Yield: 1 (16-ounce) serving | Prep time: 5 minutes

HIGH FIBER, SUPERFOOD STAR

Loaded with vitamin C, omega-3 fatty acids, powerful antioxidants, and anti-inflammatory nutrients, this kiwi-cucumber smoothie tastes light and refreshing, while hydrating and nourishing the skin.

1 cup unsweetened cashew milk

1 tablespoon freshly squeezed lime juice

1 tablespoon chia seeds

½ cucumber, diced

½ small green apple, cored and chopped

1 kiwi, peeled

1 cup chopped baby kale

1 cup chopped baby spinach

½ cup ice

1. Pour the cashew milk and lime juice into the blender, then add the chia seeds.

2. Layer in the cucumber, apple, kiwi, kale, and spinach. Top with the ice.

3. Blend all the ingredients together until completely smooth, adding more ice or cashew milk as needed to reach desired consistency. Consume immediately.

Per Serving (16 ounce)

Calories: 254; Total fat: 7g; Sodium: 222mg; Cholesterol: 0mg; Total carbs: 47g; Fiber: 12g; Sugar: 18g; Protein: 8g

Alterations:

_____

_____

_____

_____

_____

_____

_____

Flavor tip: Add fresh or powdered ginger for a warmer flavor.

PURIFY

Yield: 1 (16-ounce) serving | Prep time: 5 minutes

HIGH FIBER, HIGH PROTEIN

This skin-purifying smoothie features the addition of collagen protein powder. The amino acids found in collagen peptides are easy to digest and highly bio-available, while improving skin hydration, fine lines, and the overall appearance of skin.

1 cup water

2 tablespoons freshly squeezed lemon juice

5 mint leaves, chopped

1 scoop collagen protein powder

1 small Granny Smith apple, cored and chopped

½ cup chopped red bell pepper

½ cucumber, diced

5 large leaves romaine lettuce

½ cup ice

1. Pour the water and lemon juice into the blender, then add the mint and collagen powder.

2. Layer in the apple, bell pepper, cucumber, and romaine lettuce. Top with the ice.

3. Blend all the ingredients together until completely smooth, adding more ice or water as needed to reach desired consistency. Consume immediately.

Per Serving (16 ounce)

Calories: 182; Total fat: 1g; Sodium: 228mg; Cholesterol: 0mg; Total carbs: 29g; Fiber: 6g; Sugar: 19g; Protein: 20g

Alterations:

_____

_____

_____

_____

_____

_____

Serving tip: Garnish with some pomegranate seeds for antioxidants and a pop of color.

SWEET BASIL

Yield: 1 (16-ounce) serving | Prep time: 5 minutes

LESS SUGAR, LOW CALORIE

Honeydew is a great source of vitamin C, a powerful antioxidant that may protect your skin against sun damage. This recipe calls for spinach, but this smoothie would be just as delicious using arugula or kale, so feel free to experiment with whatever greens you have on hand.

1 cup water

Juice of ½ lime

1½ teaspoons peeled and grated fresh ginger

1 handful basil leaves

¾ cup honeydew melon cubes

½ cucumber, diced

1 cup chopped baby spinach

½ cup ice

1. Pour the water and lime juice into the blender, then add the ginger and basil.

2. Layer in the honeydew, cucumber, and spinach. Top with the ice.

3. Blend all the ingredients together until completely smooth, adding more ice or water as needed to reach desired consistency. Consume immediately.

Per Serving (16 ounces)

Calories: 91; Total fat: 1g; Sodium: 50mg; Cholesterol: 0mg; Total carbs: 22g; Fiber: 3g; Sugar: 14g; Protein: 3g

Alterations:

_____

_____

_____

_____

_____

_____

Substitution tip: No honeydew? Use cantaloupe instead.

TANGY CITRUS

Yield: 1 (16-ounce) serving | Prep time: 5 minutes

HIGH FIBER, LOW CALORIE

Opposites unite in the best way when tangy grapefruit marries cooling mint. Chard pipes in here, too, adding a dose of detoxifying greens and making this smoothie a potent antioxidant, anti-inflammatory delight.

1 cup water

5 mint leaves, chopped

1 scoop collagen protein powder

½ small apple, cored and chopped

½ grapefruit, peeled and segmented

½ cucumber, diced

1½ cups chopped Swiss chard (about 5 leaves)

½ cup ice

1. Pour the water into the blender, then add the mint and collagen powder.

2. Layer in the apple, grapefruit, cucumber, and Swiss chard. Top with the ice.

3. Blend all the ingredients together until completely smooth, adding more ice or water as needed to reach desired consistency. Consume immediately.

Per Serving (16 ounce)

Calories: 122; Total fat: 1g; Sodium: 165mg; Cholesterol: 0mg; Total carbs: 24g; Fiber: 4g; Sugar: 15g; Protein: 10g

Alterations:

Substitution tip: No apple? Use half a pear instead.

SKIN SAVER

Yield: 1 (16-ounce) serving | Prep time: 5 minutes

HIGH FIBER, LESS SUGAR, LOW CALORIE

This light and refreshing smoothie features the antioxidant power of beta-carotene and vitamin C. These nutrients help protect your skin from within, providing much needed hydration and rejuvenation.

½ cup water

1 orange, peeled and segmented

1 carrot, shredded

3 celery stalks, chopped

½ cucumber, diced

5 large leaves romaine lettuce

½ cup ice

1. Pour the water into the blender.
2. Layer in the orange, carrot, celery, cucumber, and romaine lettuce. Top with the ice.
3. Blend all the ingredients together until completely smooth, adding more ice or water as needed to reach desired consistency. Consume immediately.

Per Serving (16 ounce)

Calories: 143; Total fat: 1g; Sodium: 167mg; Cholesterol: 0mg; Total carbs: 30g; Fiber: 7g; Sugar: 18g; Protein: 4g

Alterations:

Texture tip: Want to make it creamy? Add ⅓ of an avocado.

REISHI PEAR

Yield: 1 (16-ounce) serving | Prep time: 5 minutes

LESS SUGAR, SUPERFOOD STAR

Chronic stress can affect your skin as much as your mental health. Reishi mushroom is considered an adaptogen in herbal medicine, which means it helps your body "adapt" to stress. While its grounding effect helps you relax, this nutrient-packed food contains additional benefits, too: Its antioxidant properties and beta-glucan help with skin health and immune function.

1 cup unsweetened cashew milk

1 teaspoon reishi mushroom powder

¼ cup raw cashews

1 pear, roughly chopped

1 cup chopped collard greens

½ cup ice

1. Pour the cashew milk into the blender, then add the mushroom powder and cashews.

2. Layer in the pear and collard greens. Top with the ice.

3. Blend all the ingredients together until completely smooth, adding more ice or cashew milk as needed to reach desired consistency. Consume immediately.

Per Serving (16 ounce)

Calories: 298; Total fat: 19g; Sodium: 175mg; Cholesterol: 0mg; Total carbs: 30g; Fiber: 4g; Sugar: 14g; Protein: 8g

Alterations:

Substitution tip: No cashew milk? Use almond milk instead.

BABY FACE

Yield: 1 (16-ounce) serving | Prep time: 5 minutes

HIGH FIBER, LESS SUGAR, LOW CALORIE

This smoothie is packed with the power of vitamin C, one of the best nutrients for skin health. Protecting against UV-related damage, it's also essential for collagen production and may even help reduce the appearance of wrinkles.

½ cup water

1 tablespoon freshly squeezed lime juice

1 tablespoon freshly squeezed lemon juice

1 scoop collagen protein powder

¼ cup chopped fresh flat-leaf parsley

½ teaspoon peeled and minced fresh ginger

3 celery stalks, chopped

1 cup chopped collard greens

½ cup diced, seeded cucumber

½ cup chopped red bell pepper

1 cup frozen berries

1. Pour the water, lime juice, and lemon juice into the blender, then add the collagen powder, parsley, and ginger.

2. Layer in the celery, collard greens, cucumber, bell pepper, and berries.

3. Blend all ingredients together until completely smooth, adding more water as needed to reach desired consistency. Consume immediately.

Per Serving (16 ounce)

Calories: 145; Total fat: 1g; Sodium: 108mg; Cholesterol: 0mg; Total carbs: 28g; Fiber: 7g; Sugar: 14g; Protein: 10g

Alterations:

Health Boost tip: Use freshly squeezed lemon and lime juice instead of bottled to get the most vitamin C.

MORNING DEW

Yield: 1 (16-ounce) serving | Prep time: 5 minutes

HIGH FIBER, LESS SUGAR, LOW CALORIE

Packed with vitamin C, antioxidants, and collagen, this smoothie offers food for your skin. We know that collagen is best consumed through hydrolyzed collagen peptide/protein powder—one of the ingredients. The term "hydrolyzed" means the amino acids in the collagen powder have already been broken down, making it easier for your body to digest.

½ cup water

Juice of ½ lemon

Pinch cayenne

1 scoop collagen protein powder

1 large kiwi, peeled

1 large red bell pepper, diced

1 cup chopped kale (stems removed, as needed)

½ cup ice

1. Pour the water and the lemon juice into the blender, then add the cayenne and collagen powder.

2. Layer in the kiwi, bell pepper, and kale. Top with the ice.

3. Blend all the ingredients together until completely smooth, adding more ice or water as needed to reach desired consistency. Consume immediately.

Per Serving (16 ounce)

Calories: 157; Total fat: 1g; Sodium: 89mg; Cholesterol: 0mg; Total carbs: 28g; Fiber: 5g; Sugar: 14g; Protein: 12g

Alterations:

Ingredient tip: For easy removal, slice the kiwi in half and scoop out the flesh with a spoon.

HEALTHY HEART

The superfood ingredients in these green smoothie recipes work like magic elixirs for your heart, combining antioxidant powerhouses like matcha green tea with superfoods like wild blueberries, mushroom powder, flaxseed, and greens.

Remember, when it comes to heart health, fiber is key. And the soluble fiber you get from ingredients like oats, avocado, and flaxseed will help lower your cholesterol naturally and keep your gut healthy. Avocados are actually a fruit, but they're particularly low in sugar and rich in fiber; they also contain healthy monounsaturated fats. The fiber and fat combination is excellent for heart health because "good" fats help increase your "good" cholesterol level.

You'll also find plenty of antioxidants, healthy omega-3 fatty acids, and minerals like potassium and magnesium in these amazing smoothie recipes—all of which focus on keeping your heart healthy and happy.

GREEN MACHINE

Yield: 1 (16-ounce) serving | Prep time: 5 minutes

HIGH FIBER, LOW CALORIE

What do you get when you combine the cholesterol-lowering power of ginger, flavonoids like hesperidin from oranges, and soluble fiber from flaxseed? An amazing heart-protective super smoothie that also tastes delicious.

¾ cup water

1 tablespoon freshly squeezed lemon juice

1 tablespoon ground flaxseed

1½ teaspoons peeled and grated fresh ginger

1 orange, peeled and segmented

½ cucumber, diced

1 cup chopped kale (stems removed, as needed)

¼ cup ice

1. Pour the water and lemon juice into the blender, then add the flaxseed and ginger.

2. Layer in the orange, cucumber, and kale. Top with the ice.

3. Blend all the ingredients together until completely smooth, adding more ice or water as needed to reach desired consistency. Consume immediately.

Per Serving (16 ounce)

Calories: 184; Total fat: 3g; Sodium: 37mg; Cholesterol: 0mg; Total carbs: 37g; Fiber: 8g; Sugar: 20g; Protein: 6g

Alterations:

_____

_____

_____

_____

_____

_____

_____

Texture tip: For a creamier finish, use almond milk instead of water.

WILD WATERMELON MINT

Yield: 1 (16-ounce) serving | Prep time: 5 minutes

HIGH FIBER, LOW CALORIE, SUPERFOOD STAR

This is a delicious tart and tangy smoothie with gorgeous color and tons of heart-healthy antioxidants. Wild blueberries are rich in powerful phytochemicals like anthocyanins and contain twice the antioxidant power of cultivated blueberries.

½ cup water

Juice of ½ lemon

Juice of ½ lime

2 to 3 sprigs fresh mint

½ cup frozen wild blueberries

1 wedge fresh watermelon

½ cup fresh or frozen broccoli florets

1. Pour the water, lemon juice, and lime juice into the blender, then add the mint.

2. Layer in the blueberries, watermelon, and broccoli.

3. Blend all the ingredients together until completely smooth, adding more water as needed to reach desired consistency. Consume immediately.

Per Serving (16 ounce)

Calories: 164; Total fat: 1g; Sodium: 113mg; Cholesterol: 0mg; Total carbs: 34g; Fiber: 5 g; Sugar: 28g; Protein: 4g

Alterations:

Substitution tip: For added sweetness, use coconut water instead of plain water.

BLUEBERRY CHAGA

Yield: 1 (16-ounce) serving | Prep time: 5 minutes

HIGH FIBER, LESS SUGAR, LOW CALORIE, SUPERFOOD STAR

Chaga mushrooms are considered the "King of Mushrooms," and have potent antioxidant properties. The taste is similar to that of a medium-blend coffee and adds depth and richness to any smoothie.

1 cup unsweetened almond milk

½ teaspoon vanilla extract

1 teaspoon chaga mushroom powder

1 tablespoon ground flaxseed

Pinch cinnamon

1 cup chopped kale (stems removed, as needed)

½ cup frozen wild blueberries

½ cup frozen tart cherries

Per Serving (16 ounces)

Calories: 194; Total fat: 6g; Sodium: 213mg; Cholesterol: 0mg; Total carbs: 31g; Fiber: 7g; Sugar: 15g; Protein: 6g

Alterations:

1. Pour the almond milk into the blender, then add the vanilla, mushroom powder, flaxseed, and cinnamon.

2. Layer in the kale, blueberries, and cherries.

3. Blend all the ingredients together until completely smooth, adding more almond milk as needed to reach desired consistency. Consume immediately.

Substitution tip: No blueberries? Use any berry blend you prefer.

ORANGE CRUSH

Yield: 1 (16-ounce) serving | Prep time: 5 minutes

HIGH FIBER, MEAL REPLACEMENT

Sweet potato in a smoothie? Yes, please! Super creamy and naturally sweet, sweet potato is chock-full of fiber and bursting with beta-carotene. Turmeric and chia seeds punch up the benefits, making this smoothie a heart-healthy delight.

¼ cup unsweetened almond milk

¼ teaspoon ground turmeric

1 tablespoon chia seeds

¼ teaspoon cinnamon

1 tablespoon almond butter

1 small orange, peeled and segmented

¼ cup cooked sweet potato flesh

1 cup chopped baby spinach

½ cup ice

Per Serving (16 ounce)

Calories: 302; Total fat: 15g; Sodium: 90mg; Cholesterol: 0mg; Total carbs: 39g; Fiber: 13g; Sugar: 18g; Protein: 10g

Alterations:

1. Pour the almond milk into the blender, then add the turmeric, chia seeds, cinnamon, and almond butter.

2. Layer in the orange, sweet potato, and spinach. Top with the ice.

3. Blend all the ingredients together until completely smooth, adding more ice or almond milk as needed to reach desired consistency. Consume immediately.

Flavor tip: No fresh oranges on hand? Just use ¼ cup orange juice to give your smoothie that distinctive citrus flavor.

LEMON TART

Yield: 1 (16-ounce) serving | Prep time: 5 minutes

HIGH FIBER, HIGH PROTEIN, LESS SUGAR, MEAL REPLACEMENT

If you love lemon, this extra-tart smoothie may become your favorite morning energizer—the perfect way to saturate your cells with hydrating vitamin C. At once delicious and satisfying, this one will definitely wake up your taste buds!

1½ cups unsweetened coconut milk

Juice of 1 lemon

1 scoop vanilla protein powder

1 cup frozen cauliflower florets

1 cup chopped kale (stems removed, as needed)

½ cup ice

1. Pour the coconut milk and lemon juice into the blender, then add the protein powder.

2. Layer in the cauliflower and kale. Top with the ice.

3. Blend all the ingredients together until completely smooth, adding more ice or coconut milk as needed to reach desired consistency. Consume immediately.

Per Serving (16 ounces)

Calories: 289; Total fat: 10g; Sodium: 220mg; Cholesterol: 80mg; Total carbs: 23g; Fiber: 5g; Sugar: 6g; Protein: 31g

Alterations:

_____

_____

_____

_____

_____

_____

Health Boost tip: No protein powder? Use 3 tablespoons hemp seeds instead.

I HEART BERRIES

Yield: 1 (16-ounce) serving | Prep time: 5 minutes

HIGH FIBER

Berries tend to find their way into almost every smoothie I make. Low in sugar and high in fiber and antioxidants, they're a natural choice for heart health. I love mixing berries with a dash of pomegranate juice for an extra dose of intense berry flavor.

¾ cup unsweetened almond milk

¼ cup pomegranate juice

1 tablespoon ground flaxseed

¼ cup quick-cooking rolled oats

3 large leaves romaine lettuce

1 cup chopped kale (stems removed, as needed)

¾ cup frozen mixed-berry blend

Per Serving (16 ounces)

Calories: 275; Total fat: 7g; Sodium: 176mg; Cholesterol: 0mg; Total carbs: 50g; Fiber: 8g; Sugar: 16g; Protein: 8g

Alterations:

1. Pour the almond milk and pomegranate juice into the blender, then add the flaxseed and oats.

2. Layer in the romaine lettuce, kale, and mixed-berry blend.

3. Blend all the ingredients together until completely smooth, adding more almond milk as needed to reach desired consistency. Consume immediately.

Ingredient tip: Store your flaxseed in the freezer to maximize freshness.

CRANBERRY ORANGE

Yield: 1 (16-ounce) serving | Prep time: 5 minutes

HIGH FIBER, SUPERFOOD STAR

Some think cranberries are just for Thanksgiving, but I add a handful of fresh cranberries to my smoothies all year long for their deliciously tart flavor and health benefits. With the Greek yogurt for balance, this fun, heart-healthy smoothie is super delicious.

1 cup water

½ cup plain Greek yogurt

1½ teaspoons peeled and grated fresh ginger

¼ cup fresh cranberries

½ small orange, peeled and segmented

5 large leaves romaine lettuce

½ cup ice

1. Pour the water and yogurt into the blender, then add the ginger.

2. Layer in the cranberries, orange, and romaine lettuce. Top with the ice.

3. Blend all the ingredients together until completely smooth, adding more ice or water as needed to reach desired consistency. Consume immediately.

Per Serving (16 ounce)

Calories: 188; Total fat: 6g; Sodium: 65mg; Cholesterol: 10mg; Total carbs: 27g; Fiber:1g; Sugar: 20g; Protein: 5g

Alterations:

Ingredient tip: Store a bag of fresh cranberries in the freezer, so you can enjoy them year-round.

CHLORELLA KALE

Yield: 1 (16-ounce) serving | Prep time: 5 minutes

HIGH FIBER, LESS SUGAR, MEAL REPLACEMENT, SUPERFOOD STAR

This smoothie is a nutrient powerhouse, thanks to greens like kale and chlorella. Did you know that chlorella contains the highest quantity of chlorophyll of any known plant? It's also rich in beta-carotene, alpha-carotene, and lutein, and is an abundant source of many nutrients, including B vitamins, minerals, antioxidants, and omega-3 fatty acids.

½ cup unsweetened coconut milk

½ teaspoon chlorella powder

¼ cup raw cashews

1 pear, roughly chopped

1 cup chopped baby kale

½ cup ice

1. Pour the coconut milk into the blender, then add the chlorella powder and cashews.

2. Layer in the pear and kale. Top with the ice.

3. Blend all the ingredients together until completely smooth, adding more ice or coconut milk as needed to reach desired consistency. Consume immediately.

Per Serving (16 ounces)

Calories: 337; Total fat: 18g; Sodium: 36mg; Cholesterol: 0mg; Total carbs: 40g; Fiber: 7g; Sugar: 15g; Protein: 9g

Alterations:

Substitution tip: No chlorella? Use greens powder or spirulina instead.

DRINK YOUR GREENS

Yield: 1 (16-ounce) serving | Prep time: 5 minutes

HIGH FIBER, LOW CALORIE, SUPERFOOD STAR

Believe it or not, red cabbage is the superstar of this delicious, nutrient-dense smoothie. Packed with antioxidants and probiotics, it's just what the dietitian ordered for a healthy heart!

½ cup water
1 cup plain kefir
¾ cup frozen wild blueberries
1 cup chopped baby spinach
1½ cups chopped red cabbage
½ cup ice

1. Pour the water and kefir into the blender.

2. Layer in the blueberries, spinach, and red cabbage. Top with the ice.

3. Blend all the ingredients together until completely smooth, adding more ice or water as needed to reach desired consistency. Consume immediately.

Per Serving (16 ounces)

Calories: 203; Total fat: 4g; Sodium: 143mg; Cholesterol: 0mg; Total carbs: 34g; Fiber: 7g; Sugar: 22g; Protein: 9g

Alterations:

_____

_____

_____

_____

_____

_____

Time-saver tip: Buy your cabbage pre-shredded to save prep time.

CHOCOLATE MINT

Yield: 1 (16-ounce) serving | Prep time: 5 minutes

HIGH FIBER, HIGH PROTEIN, LESS SUGAR, MEAL REPLACEMENT

This tasty smoothie will make you think you're eating dessert, not a low-sugar, heart-smart smoothie. But due to the cauliflower and cacao powder, it's bursting with heart-protective antioxidants. It's also loaded with mint, a nutrition super-star in its own right, boasting an impressive load of antioxidants, phenolic acids, flavonoids, and carotenoids.

1½ cups unsweetened vanilla almond milk

1 tablespoon cacao powder

1 tablespoon almond butter

10 fresh mint leaves, chopped

1 scoop protein powder

1 cup chopped baby spinach

1 cup diced zucchini (steamed, frozen)

½ cup frozen cauliflower florets

1. Pour the almond milk into the blender, then add the cacao powder, almond butter, mint, and protein powder.

2. Layer in the spinach, zucchini, and cauliflower.

3. Blend all the ingredients together until completely smooth, adding more almond milk as needed to reach desired consistency. Consume immediately.

Per Serving (16 ounces)

Calories: 295; Total fat: 16g; Sodium: 261mg; Cholesterol: 20mg; Total carbs: 18g; Fiber: 7g; Sugar: 7g; Protein: 27g

Alterations:

_____

_____

_____

_____

_____

Ingredient tip: Choose a vanilla-flavored protein powder for more vanilla flavor.

RESOURCES

I recommend eating seasonally for the freshest produce at the best price, so head to your local grocery store or farmers' market for your greens, vegetables, and fresh fruit. You might also find it more budget-friendly to buy your greens and frozen fruit in bulk at Costco or other warehouse stores.

For the nuts, seeds, spices, add-ins, and superfoods mentioned in this book, shop online for the best price and availability. Most can be purchased at Amazon, Thrive Market, or Nuts.com.

Products may vary somewhat among brands, but here are a few that I use and recommend:

BRANDS:

McCann's Steel Cut Oats

Koyah Organic (greens powder)

Y.S. Eco Bee Farms (bee pollen)

Wild MCT Oil

Four Sigmatic (mushroom powder blends)

Jade Leaf Matcha

Numi teas

Vital Proteins collagen

ONLINE RESOURCES:

Amazon.com

ThriveMarket.com

PureEncapsulations.com (fiber, protein powder)

GROCERY STORES:

Whole Foods (house brand 365 Everyday Value)

Trader Joe's

Costco

BJ's

WEBSITES:

Nuts.com offers a great selection of nuts, seeds, nut butters, and nutmilks at whole-sale prices.

On my website I provide nutrition strategies, resources, and recipes for all things plant based. You can find me at **FoodConfidence.com**

THE DIRTY DOZEN AND THE CLEAN FIFTEEN™

A nonprofit environmental watchdog organization called Environmental Working Group (EWG) looks at data supplied by the US Department of Agriculture (USDA) and the Food and Drug Administration (FDA) about pesticide residues. Each year it compiles a list of the best and worst pesticide loads found in commercial crops. You can use these lists to decide which fruits and vegetables to buy organic to minimize your exposure to pesticides and which produce is considered safe enough to buy conventionally. This does not mean they are pesticide-free, though, so wash these fruits and vegetables thoroughly. The list is updated annually, and you can find it online at EWG.org/FoodNews.

DIRTY DOZEN™

1. strawberries
2. spinach
3. kale
4. nectarines
5. apples
6. grapes
7. peaches
8. cherries
9. pears
10. tomatoes
11. celery
12. potatoes

†Additionally, nearly three-quarters of hot pepper samples contained pesticide residues.

CLEAN FIFTEEN™

1. avocados
2. sweet corn*
3. pineapples
4. sweet peas (frozen)
5. onions
6. papayas*
7. eggplants
8. asparagus
9. kiwis
10. cabbages
11. cauliflower
12. cantaloupes
13. broccoli
14. mushrooms
15. honeydew melons

* A small amount of sweet corn, papaya, and summer squash sold in the United States is produced from genetically modified seeds. Buy organic varieties of these crops if you want to avoid genetically modified produce.

MEASUREMENT CONVERSIONS

	US Standard	US Standard (oz)	Metric (approx.)
Volume Equivalents (Liquid)	2 tablespoons	1 fl. oz.	30 mL
	¼ cup	2 fl. oz.	60 mL
	½ cup	4 fl. oz.	120 mL
	1 cup	8 fl. oz.	240 mL
	1½ cups	12 fl. oz.	355 mL
	2 cups or 1 pint	16 fl. oz.	475 mL
	4 cups or 1 quart	32 fl. oz.	1 L
	1 gallon	128 fl. oz.	4 L
Volume Equivalents (Dry)	⅛ teaspoon		0.5 mL
	¼ teaspoon		1 mL
	½ teaspoon		2 mL
	¾ teaspoon		4 mL
	1 teaspoon		5 mL
	1 tablespoon		15 mL
	¼ cup		59 mL
	⅓ cup		79 mL

	US Standard	US Standard (oz)	Metric (approx.)
Volume Equivalents (Dry, continued)	½ cup	——————	118 mL
	⅔ cup	——————	156 mL
	¾ cup	——————	177 mL
	1 cup	——————	235 mL
	2 cups or 1 pint	——————	475 mL
	3 cups	——————	700 mL
	4 cups or 1 quart	——————	1 L
	½ gallon	——————	2 L
	1 gallon	——————	4 L
Weight Equivalents	½ ounce	——————	15 g
	1 ounce	——————	30 g
	2 ounces	——————	60 g
	4 ounces	——————	115 g
	8 ounces	——————	225 g
	12 ounces	——————	340 g
	16 ounces or 1 pound	——————	455 g

	FAHRENHEIT (F)	CELSIUS (C) (APPROXIMATE)
	250°F	120°C
	300°F	150°C
	325°F	180°C
Oven Temperatures	375°F	190°C
	400°F	200°C
	425°F	220°C
	450°F	230°C

INDEX

RECIPE INDEX

ABOUT THE AUTHOR

Danielle Omar, RDN, is an Integrative Dietitian, founder of Food-Confidence.com, and creator of the Nourish 21-Day Clean Eating program and Food Confidence community. Through teaching, speaking, and writing, she has spent the past two decades helping thousands of women transform their health.

CPSIA information can be obtained
at www.ICGtesting.com
Printed in the USA
BVHW021958130220
571983BV00007B/10

GALLEONS AND GALLEYS

GALLEONS AND GALLEYS

John F. Guilmartin, Jr.

General Editor: John Keegan

CASSELL&CO

Cassell & Co
Wellington House, 125 Strand
London WC2R 0BB

First published 2002

British Library Cataloguing-in-Publication Data
A catalogue record for this book is available from the
British Library.
ISBN 0-304-35263-2

Cartography: Arcadia Editions
Picture research: Elaine Willis
Special photography: Martin Norris
Design: Martin Hendry

Typeset in Monotype Sabon

ACKNOWLEDGEMENTS

For many years my book-after-next was to be on Renaissance warfare at sea, but next books intruded: on Vietnam, on the 1991 Persian Gulf War, and on Vietnam again. Just when and how – or if – that book might have been written I cannot say... had Sir John Keegan not asked me to contribute to Cassell's History of Warfare series and suggested the title *Galleons and Galleys*. The idea implicit in the title, that I make the design evolution of two disparate but related types of warship a major theme, made this a very different book than it would otherwise have been and a better one. I am in Sir John's debt.

This book is about war and warriors. At the visceral level – and in war when all bets are down it is the visceral level that counts – I learned much of what I know about both from those with whom I served in South-east Asia as a US Air Force rescue helicopter pilot in 1956–66 and 1975. While the experience of modern war cannot be uncritically extrapolated to earlier eras, certain essential parameters are the same: knowing when to obey and when to disobey; remaining loyal to people and things that count; maintaining a sense of humour; understanding your equipment, the weather and your own limitations. I learned a lot about those things from those with whom I flew and fought and trust that understanding shows in the pages that follow. Thanks.

More immediately, Geoffrey Parker was generous with time and advice and saved me from embarrassment on numerous occasions. Chief Warrant Officer John Sims, US Army Reserve, led me to a new understanding of Lepanto. Rear Admiral Tiberio Moro, Italian Navy (Retired); Claudio Fogu; Christopher Reed; Peter Pierson; Bill Kelsey, Pararescueman extraordinaire; Douglas St. Pierre; Lieutenant Tom Schmidt, US Navy; Luis Filipe Marques de Sousa; David Wittner; Commander Duk-Hyun Cho, Korean Navy; Major Il-Song Park, Korean Army; and Matthew Keith all rendered invaluable assistance.

Penny Gardiner was my editor for Cassell and I cannot imagine a better one. Her awe-inspiring competence and good humour made my job easier... and more fun. It was a natural fit: we both like basilisks! Malcolm Swanston's cartography, Elaine Willis's art research and Martin Hendry's layout skills transformed the book into a thing of beauty.

Finally, I am indebted to my wife Hannelore, a good Prussian who understands war and warriors better than most ever will or would want to, for giving me the support and stability to see the thing through.

JOHN GUILMARTIN
Columbus, Ohio

War galleys under sail (upper left), caravels (upper right), and carracks (centre and bottom) from Barbarossa's heyday.

CONTENTS

KEY TO MAPS

General symbols

 site of battle

 fort or fortified settlement

 movement

Geographical symbols

 urban area

 urban area (3D maps)

——— river

— — — seasonal river

⊢⊢⊢⊢ canal

• town/city

— — — internal border

——— international border

MAP LIST

CHRONOLOGY

Dates after October 1582 new style.

1253–84	First Venetian–Genoese War.
1274, 1281	Unsuccessful invasions of Japan by China's Mongol Yüan dynasty.
1282–1302	War of the Sicilian Vespers; Aragon becomes a major sea power.
1284	Battle of Meloria; Genoa eliminates Pisa as a sea power.
1293–9	Second Venetian–Genoese War.
c. 1327	First European gunpowder weapons.
1337	Start of the Hundred Years War.
1340	24 June: English naval victory at Sluys.
1350–55	Third Venetian–Genoese War.
1368	Ming dynasty overthrows Yüan, consolidates control over China.
1368–9	Hanseatic League defeats Denmark–Norway.
1377–82	Fourth Venetian–Genoese War, the War of Chioggia.
1405–34	Chinese treasure fleets under the eunuch admiral Cheng Ho sail the Indian Ocean on seven occasions.
1435	Ming proscription on maritime trade; treasure fleets disbanded.
1453	29 May: Fall of Constantinople to Sultan Mehmed II, 'The Conqueror'.
1463–79	Ottoman–Venetian War; Venice loses Negroponte (1470) and most of her possessions in Greece.
1480	23 May–17 August: Unsuccessful Ottoman siege of Rhodes. 11 August: Ottoman seizure of Otranto on the heel of the Italian boot.
1481	3 May: Death of Mehmed II; succession contested between princes Bayezid and Cem. Defeated, Cem fled first to Egypt and then to Rhodes.
1492	Columbus reaches the New World; start of Spain's overseas empire.
1494	Charles VIII of France invades Italy prompting Spanish intervention; beginning of the Wars of Italy (1494–1559).
1498	Vasco da Gama reaches India, bypassing traditional spice route.
1499–1503	Ottoman–Venetian War; inconclusive fleet actions at Zonchio (12 August 1499 and again the following summer) cost Venice her remaining Greek bases.
1503	February: Vasco da Gama's victory over a Muslim fleet off the Malabar Coast leaves Portugal pre-eminent in the Indian Ocean.
1508–09	A Mameluke fleet reaches the west coast of India, defeating the Portuguese at Chaul in 1508 only to be destroyed at Diu the following year.
1508	League of Cambrai: the Holy Roman Empire, France and Aragon unite against Venice.
1510	Affonso d'Albuquerque seizes Goa, giving the Portuguese a permanent base in the Indian Ocean. Spanish seize Tripoli and the Peñon controlling the harbour of Algiers.
1511	Portuguese take Malacca.
1513	April: French defeat the English in Brest Roads; first decisive use of main centreline bow gun-armed galleys.
1515	Portuguese seize Ormuz.
1516	Charles I inherits the Spanish throne from Ferdinand of Aragon.
1517	Sultan Selim I conquers Egypt. Unsuccessful Portuguese attempt to seize Jiddah, the port of Mecca.
1519	Charles I of Spain elected Holy Roman Emperor Charles V.
1521	21 August: Fall of Tenochtitlán to Hernán Cortez, adding Mexico to Charles V's empire.
1522	25 June–21 Dec: Siege of Rhodes: Sultan Süleyman I expels the Knights of St John, depriving Christendom of its last outpost in the Levant.

1528	Andrea Doria transfers Genoa's allegiance from France to Spain.		the Turks the initiative at sea.		Siege of Malta; a major defensive victory for Christendom.
1529	23 Sept–14 Oct: Unsuccessful siege of Vienna by Süleyman I; the high point of Ottoman expansion into western Europe by land.	1540	Venetian–Ottoman peace treaty.	1567	Dutch resistance to Spanish rule and the Duke of Alba's suppression of Protestantism erupts into armed rebellion.
	27 May: Khaireddin Barbarossa takes the Peñon of Algiers.	1541	24–26 October: Charles V's expedition against Algiers wrecked by a violent storm.	1568	25 December: Revolt of Spanish Moriscos, not suppressed until September 1570.
1530	Charles V installs the Knights of St John in Malta and Tripoli.	1542–4	Barbarossa's fleet ravages the western Mediterranean, wintering at Toulon in 1543–44.	1570	April: Venice rejects Ottoman demands to cede Cyprus.
1532	Andrea Doria seizes Coron in southern Greece.	1543	First successful cast-iron cannon founded in England.		1 July: Turks invade Cyprus; Nicosia falls on 9 September.
	16 November: Capture of Emperor Atahualpa by Francisco Pizarro, leading to the overthrow of the Inca Empire and the addition of Peru to Charles V's domains.	1545	19 July: Inconclusive Anglo–French battle off Portsmouth; the largest fleet action until the Armada of 1588.		May: Philip II accedes to Venetian and Papal entreaties to join forces against the Turks.
1533	Barbarossa visits Constantinople to accept appointment as Kapudan Pasha, Ottoman high admiral.	1547	Discovery of massive silver deposits in Peru; the resulting gusher of specie sustained Habsburg strategic designs into the 1700s.		15 September: Turks lay siege to Famagusta, the last remaining Venetian position on Cyprus.
1534	Barbarossa retakes Coron.	1551	Turks take Tripoli.	1571	23 January: Venetian relief expedition reaches Famagusta.
1535	21 July: Tunis falls to a major Habsburg expedition under Charles V.	1555	Charles V abdicates, leaving his Spanish possessions to Philip II.		24 May: Spain, Venice and the Pope formally ratify the Holy League.
1537	April–May: Ottomans attack Venice and raid southern Italy; Spain and the Pope form a Holy League with Venice.	1559	3 April: Treaty of Câteau-Cambrésis ends the Wars of Italy and affirms Spanish hegemony over Italy.		1 August: Famagusta surrenders to the Turks.
	18 Aug–6 September: Unsuccessful siege of Corfu by Süleyman I.	1560	11 May: Battle of Djerba; Habsburg fleet under Gian Andrea Doria defeated by the Ottomans under Piali Pasha.		7 October: Battle of Lepanto; Turkish fleet under Müezzenzade Ali Pasha crushed by the Christians under Don Juan of Austria.
1538	28 September: Battle of Prevesa; Barbarossa defeats a Habsburg–Venetian fleet under Andrea Doria giving	1563–70	Northern Seven Years War; Sweden defeats Denmark and Lübeck to become the dominant power in the Baltic; first modern naval war.	1572	Apr–May: Expelled from English ports, Dutch privateers seize bases in Holland, reversing Alba's successes and giving the revolt a new lease on life.
		1565	18 May–11 Sept: Unsuccessful Ottoman		7–10 Aug: Inconclusive engagements off

Cerigo between the reconstituted Ottoman fleet under Uluj Ali Pasha and a partial allied fleet under Colonna and Foscarini.

17 Sept–7 October: Faced by the entire fleet of the Holy League under Don Juan, Uluj Ali takes shelter beneath the guns of Coron.

1573　5 March: Venetian–Ottoman peace treaty; dissolution of the Holy League.

October: Habsburg fleet under Don Juan seizes Tunis.

1574　24 Aug–13 Sept: A major Ottoman expedition from Constantinople under Uluj Ali recaptures Tunis and the outlying Spanish fortress of La Golleta.

1578　4 August: Moroccan victory over a Portuguese royal army at Alcazarquivir; the death of King Sebastian leaves the Portuguese throne to the aged Cardinal Henry.

1580　February: Death of Cardinal Henry makes Philip II heir to Portugal's throne.

18 July: Spanish forces under Alba take Lisbon, driving the pretender Dom Antonio into exile. All Portuguese possessions save the Azores accept Spanish rule.

August: Spanish–Ottoman truce.

1582　26 July: Battle of Punta

Delgada; Àlvaro de Bazán defeats a French fleet under Philip Strozzi giving Spain control of the Azores.

1583　23 July: Bazán conquers Terceira, defeating the last Franco-Portuguese holdouts in the Azores.

1585　May: Seizure of northern ships in Spanish ports gives Elizabeth of England *casus belli*.

1587　29 April–1 May: English fleet under Drake raids Cádiz, inflicting serious damage on Spanish provisions and shipping.

1588　30 May: The 'Invincible' Armada sails from Lisbon.

19–20 June: The Armada is dispersed by a storm and driven into Coruña where it remains until 21 July.

30 July: The Armada enters the Channel.

6 July: The Armada anchors off Calais, missing its rendezvous with the Duke of Parma; the following night it is dispersed by fire ships and driven north.

1591　Unification of Japan under Toyotomi Hideyoshi.

1592　23 May: Japanese seize Pusan; Hideyoshi's armies reach Seoul by 11 June and Pyongyang by 26 July.

3 June: First of a series of Japanese defeats by the Korean navy under Admiral Yi Sun-sin.

1 August: Battle of

Hansan Strait; Yi clears the coast of Japanese ships and by 21 October has blockaded the Japanese in Pusan.

1593　Ming army intervenes in Korea; with their supply lines cut and facing starvation, Hideyoshi's generals call a truce and by October have evacuated Korea save for a small garrison in Pusan.

1596　June–July: English fleet seizes Cádiz; galleons take the measure of heavily-armed war galleys on their home turf for the first time.

1597　August: Hideyoshi's forces re-invade Korea, defeating the Korean navy in Admiral Yi's absence.

October: Restored to power, Yi turns the tables; by year's end, he has the Japanese bottled up in Pusan.

1598　Philip III of Spain tightens the embargo on Dutch shipping; the Dutch respond by trading directly with the East Indies and the Americas.

September: Death of Hideyoshi; the Japanese negotiate withdrawal from Korea with the Chinese.

16 December: Battle of Noryang; the Korean fleet under Yi intercepts the Japanese evacuation convoy, inflicting enormous losses.

1602　Incorporation of the Vereeningde Ost-

Indische Compagnie, VOC or Dutch East India Company.

1604 England and Spain declare an end to hostilities.

1605 Dutch invade the Spice Islands.

1607 25 April: Battle of Gibraltar: Dutch destruction of the galleons of the Straits Guard… just after Dutch and Spanish envoys had negotiated a truce in the Netherlands.

1609 9 April: Start of the Twelve Years Truce between Spain and the Netherlands; Philip III ordered the Moriscos expelled from Spain the same day.

1615 17–18 July: Dutch victory at Canete off the Peruvian coast; first European fleet action in the Pacific.

1621 Expiration of the Twelve Years Truce; incorporation of the Dutch West Indies Company (WIC).

1622 In co-operation with the Shah of Persia, the English seize Ormuz from the Portuguese.

1624 May: The WIC takes Bahia, capital of Portuguese Brazil; a Habsburg expedition retakes the city the next year.

1628 8 September: A WIC fleet under Piet Heyn captures the entire Spanish treasure fleet at Matanzas Bay, Cuba.

1630 The WIC seizes the rich Brazilian sugar-growing province of Pernambuco.

1631 12 September: Battle of Abrolhos; the Spanish under Antonio de Oquendo defeat a WIC fleet off Brazil; first naval battle of consequence fought far from sight of land.

1635 France enters the Thirty Years War.

1638 22 August: French fleet victory over the Spanish at Guetaria on Spain's northern coast.

1639 15 September: The Dutch under Maarten Tromp fend off a much larger Spanish fleet under Oquendo off the Flemish coast demonstrating the potential of line-ahead tactics.

21 October: Battle of the Downs, a major Spanish defeat at the hands of the Dutch under Tromp.

1640 Catalonia and Portugal rise in rebellion against Spanish rule.

1641 The Dutch take Malacca by siege after an eight year blockade.

1643–45 Inconclusive Danish–Swedish naval war.

1645 24 June: Provoked by Christian pirates operating from Venetian ports, the Ottomans invade Crete.

1646 The Turks take Retimno and blockade Candia, the main Venetian position on Crete.

1647 First of a series of Venetian attempts to blockade the Dardanelles; yielding fleet victories in 1655, 1656 and 1657, these were the last major Mediterranean sea battles in which galleys played a major – albeit declining – role. The Turks ultimately prevailed by fortifying the straits and denying the Venetians access to fresh water.

1648–53 The Fronde; France plunged into turmoil by rebellious nobles.

1648 Companhia Geral do Comércio do Brasil (Brazilian Commerce Company) chartered in Lisbon to oppose the WIC.

January: Peace of Münster ends the Revolt of the Netherlands.

24 October: Treaty of Westphalia ends the Thirty Years War and effectively removes religion as the principal European cause of war.

1652–54 First Anglo-Dutch War; birth of a new era in warfare at sea dominated by the ship-of-the line and line-ahead tactics.

1654 Last Dutch planters in Brazil surrender.

1659 Peace of the Pyrenees; end of Franco-Spanish hostilities.

1668 Spain recognizes Portuguese independence.

1669 August: Venetians surrender Candia to the Ottomans, effectively ending the War of Crete.

THE AGE OF GALLEY, GALLEON AND EUROPEAN WORLD HEGEMONY

THE DETAIL ON THE LEFT, from a near-contemporary manuscript illumination depicting the 1340 battle of Sluys, vividly conveys the character of sea fights in the pre-gunpowder era: desperate contests with edged weapons, bows and crossbows, fought out behind the dubious protection of wooden bulwarks. The exaggerated size of the combatants and the prominence of armoured men-at-arms reflects the social and military dominance in Europe of chivalric élites who excelled in shock combat. The ships are cogs.

THE AGE OF GALLEY, GALLEON AND EUROPEAN WORLD HEGEMONY

THE TURN OF THE sixteenth century witnessed the beginning of a revolution in warfare at sea. It was a European revolution, although we must categorize the Ottoman Turks as European if the argument is to make sense; we must also consider Japan and Korea, although that is getting ahead of the story. It was a revolution long in the making, but one that unfolded with surprising speed once begun. The driving force was gunpowder. The principal agents were the galley and galleon. Beginning in the Mediterranean, then spreading with remarkable swiftness to the North Atlantic and the Baltic before spanning the globe, it produced a fundamental redistribution of military and economic power and laid the political foundations of the world we live in today.

A Greek fire-armed Byzantine dromon from a twelfth-century Sicilian manuscript. Greek fire had properties unlike those of any other incendiary. It ignited on contact with water and was all but impossible to extinguish.

The impact of that revolution was not limited to transient changes in the balance of power or, in the vocabulary of geopolitics, transfers of world hegemony. At the most basic level, the results can be seen on a linguistic map of the world. When our revolution began, Portuguese was spoken along the Atlantic fringe of Iberia, the Azores, Madeira and a handful of African trading posts; Spanish was spoken in central and southern Iberia and the Canary Islands; French was confined to France, the contiguous Netherlands and Switzerland; and English to the British Isles. Today, Portuguese is the language of Brazil, parts of southern Africa and several enclaves in Asia. Spanish is dominant in Mexico, Central and South America, and is, after Chinese and English, the world's most widely spoken first language. Beyond France, southern Belgium, Quebec in Canada, and parts of Louisiana in the USA, French is the language of government and higher education in much of Central Africa and is still spoken in former French Indo-China. As a native tongue, English ranks second only to Chinese. More importantly, English is the international language of commerce, aviation, popular culture and journalism, and is unchallenged as the world's second language.

To note that the languages listed above achieved their importance and geographic spread as a result of their speakers' success in warfare at sea is a statement of the obvious. To be sure, the fit is not perfect. The Dutch replaced the Iberians as global hegemons in the seventeenth century, but left only a slight linguistic imprint: street names in New York and Afrikaans in South Africa. The

One of the two earliest depictions of a gun, from a manuscript in the British Museum, De Secretis Secretorum Aristotelis, *dated to c. 1326; the other, in the Walter de Milimete manuscript in the Bodleian Library, shows a similar but smaller piece. Fired by a hot wire applied to the touch hole, the gun is expelling a projectile resembling an oversized crossbow bolt. The advantages of such pieces over mechanical artillery – if any – must have been slight, but gunpowder weapons were susceptible to further development in ways that counterpoise and tension weaponry was not.*

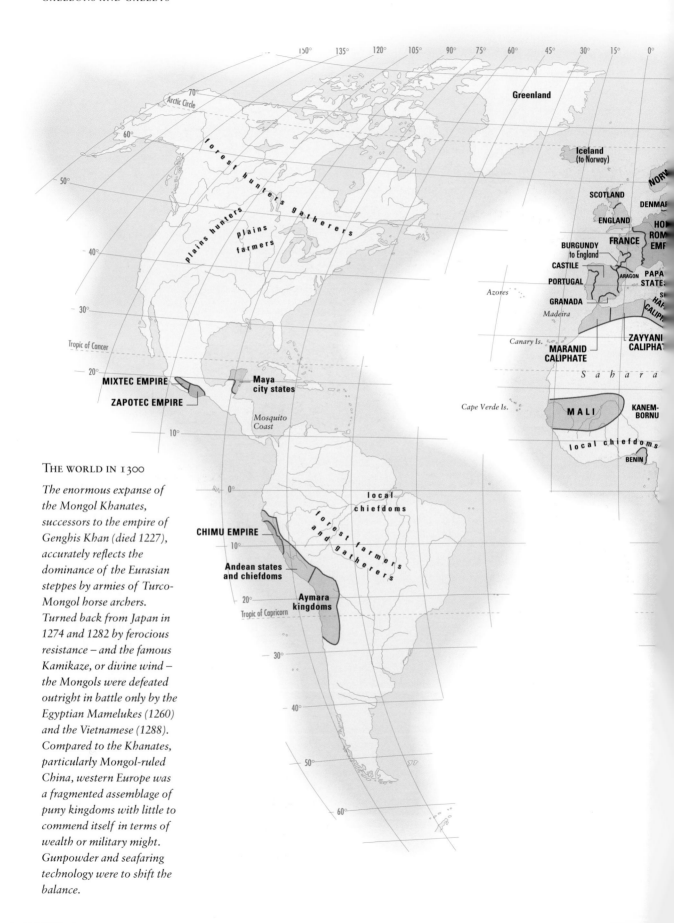

Greenland

Iceland
(to Norway)

NOR

SCOTLAND

DENMAR

ENGLAND

HO
ROM
EMF

BURGUNDY
to England

FRANCE

CASTILE

ARAGON

PAPA
STATE

PORTUGAL

S
HA
CALIPH

Azores

GRANADA

ZAYYANI
CALIPHAT

Madeira

Canary Is.

MARANID
CALIPHATE

S a h a r a

Cape Verde Is.

MALI

KANEM-
BORNU

l o c a l   c h i e f d o m s

BENIN

forest   hunters   gatherers

plains hunters

plains
farmers

MIXTEC EMPIRE

Maya
city states

ZAPOTEC EMPIRE

Mosquito
Coast

l o c a l
c h i e f d o m s

forest farmers
and gatherers

CHIMU EMPIRE

Andean states
and chiefdoms

Aymara
kingdoms

70°
Arctic Circle

60°

50°

40°

30°

Tropic of Cancer

20°

10°

0°

10°

20°
Tropic of Capricorn

30°

40°

50°

60°

150°   135°   120°   105°   90°   75°   60°   45°   30°   15°   0°

THE WORLD IN 1300

The enormous expanse of the Mongol Khanates, successors to the empire of Genghis Khan (died 1227), accurately reflects the dominance of the Eurasian steppes by armies of Turco-Mongol horse archers. Turned back from Japan in 1274 and 1282 by ferocious resistance – and the famous Kamikaze, or divine wind – the Mongols were defeated outright in battle only by the Egyptian Mamelukes (1260) and the Vietnamese (1288). Compared to the Khanates, particularly Mongol-ruled China, western Europe was a fragmented assemblage of puny kingdoms with little to commend itself in terms of wealth or military might. Gunpowder and seafaring technology were to shift the balance.

30° 45° 60° 75° 90° 105° 120° 135° 150° 165° 180° 165°

hunters

gatherers

h e r d e r s

NEDEN

NOVGOROD

UTONIC
HTS

• Moscow

LITH.

ID

**Russian
Principalities**

KHANATE OF THE GOLDEN HORDE

NG.

**BULGAR
KHANATE**

• Constantinople

**GREAT
KHANATE**

JAPAN

**CHAGATAI
KHANATE**

• Tatu

**BYZANTINE
EMPIRE**

**Seljuk
Turks**

• Kyoto

**KASHMIR
AND LADAKH**

ILKHANATE

TIBET

• Soochow

**MAMELUKE
SULTANATE**

**SULTANATE
OF DELHI**

• Mecca

PAGAN

• Canton

MUSCAT

**Minor Hindu
Kingdoms**

Hanoi

• Pagan

ANNAM

ORISSA

HADRAMAUT

SUKHOTHAI

CHAMPA

MAKKURA

**Chola
state**

LUVA

**KHMER
EMPIRE**

ALWA

YEMEN

**Panya
state**

Ceylon

ETHIOPIA

SHOA

e s t

Borneo

**Minor Hindu and
Buddhist Kingdoms**

m e r s

Celebes

**Islamic
trading towns**

Sumatra

KEDIRI

h e r d e r s   a n d   f a r m e r s

Java

Timor

The world
c. 1300

Mongol Empire

other imperial states

regional powers

19

French established linguistic toeholds in Asia and the Caribbean in the age of galley and galleon, but reached Africa only after the Industrial Revolution. The English language attained most of its spread after Britain's victory over France in the Seven Years War of 1756 to 1763.

Beyond that, our linguistic exercise suggests that warfare in European waters was incidental to the struggle for global hegemony, a struggle in which the winners were pre-ordained. Neither notion is sustainable. England resisted Spanish conquest between 1585 and 1603, then wrested global hegemony from the Dutch after three naval wars between 1652 and 1674. For their part, the Dutch achieved world hegemony only after winning their independence from Habsburg Spain in a bitter eighty-year struggle from 1567 to 1648, in which victory afloat was an essential component – arguably *the* essential component – of victory. When that struggle began, Spain was locked in an open-ended fight to halt Ottoman expansion in the Mediterranean, a fight won with the aid of Venice, the Pope and Spain's Italian dependencies. For her part, Venice was nearly throttled by Genoa between 1378 and 1381; survived Ottoman onslaughts from 1463 to 1479, 1499 to 1503 and from 1537 to 1540; and in 1509 weathered an assault on land by the combined forces of her Italian enemies: Spain, Habsburg Germany and Valois France.

All of these struggles were close-run things – the survival of Venice, in particular, was most improbable – and had other victors emerged our world would now be very different. Consider, too, that the Ottoman Turks absorbed an inordinate amount of Habsburg and Venetian resources that might well have been expended elsewhere, and if Ottoman is a dead language, Italian is very much alive although reduced geographically from its fifteenth-century apogee.

So we must consider losers as well as winners, not least because the latter benefited from hard lessons administered by the former. The Ottoman Turks loom large in this regard, for they used both gunpowder and galleys effectively and carved out an empire that stretched from Yemen to Morocco and threatened to overrun Europe. The Ottoman failure to contain the Portuguese in India and to overcome Spain in the Mediterranean has much to tell us about the capabilities and limitations of both galley and galleon.

Naval historians in the Anglo-American tradition have tended to view the galleon as an instrument of deep sea power projection and the principal agent of the galley's decline. The story is portrayed as a struggle between old and new – ramming and boarding versus broadside batteries and line-ahead tactics, conservatism against innovation – a struggle the galleon was destined to win. Like Athena the galleon emerges full blown from the brow of Zeus as an eighteenth-century ship-of-the-line in nascent form, and if it did not immediately sweep all before it, conservatism of mind and resistance to innovation were surely to blame. The reality was more complex. In fact, our revolution was sparked by the development of the Mediterranean war galley, the first warship capable of bringing heavy guns effectively to bear. Carracks, the prestigious sailing warships

European men-at-arms about to embark for a sea voyage, from a late fifteenth-century illuminated edition of Jean Froissart's Chronicles. *Their importance to the composition reflects the artist's social priorities, as does the accuracy with which their arms and equipment are depicted, and the clearly subservient position of the footmen. By contrast, the ships and harbour facilities are naïvely drawn. Note, however, the sheaves of gads – iron javelins – in the fighting tops, an accurate commentary on the nature of combat at sea.*

of the day, mounted more heavy guns, but could not stand up to cannon-armed galleys. Not until the 1590s did galleons successfully challenge galleys in stand-off artillery duels, and even then the galley retained its tactical viability.

In short, the story of galleon and galley is far more involved – and far more interesting – than traditional interpretations would have us believe. And the actors in the drama, when viewed through the lens of their own knowledge and experience rather than that of the age of Nelson, were a remarkably competent lot. We shall keep them in mind as we proceed: commanders, mariners and fighting men; and the smiths, shipwrights and gun-founders who constructed the tools of their trade.

To understand how our revolution played out we must start with gunpowder. Gunpowder reached Europe from China during the Mongol invasions of the thirteenth century, or so the evidence suggests. The earliest European formulae for gunpowder date from the mid 1200s (Roger Bacon's celebrated recipe dates from 1252), while the earliest evidence for European firearms dates from about 1300 or a bit later, roughly coincident with the first stirrings of the Italian Renaissance. Prior to 1300 innovation flowed from East to West: algebra, the zero, decimal notation, Arabic numerals, paper, the compass and gunpowder. The years around 1300 mark intellectual slack water. Thereafter, innovation flowed from West to East, gradually at first, with such seemingly trivial innovations as the steel crossbow and wrought-iron anchor shanks, and then with accelerating velocity and enormous consequences. The remarkably swift success of European smiths in harnessing gunpowder, long known in China but less effectively exploited, is symptomatic.

The earliest guns were feeble weapons, and their advantages over bows, crossbows and trebuchets were slight. Their most important advantages lay in their potential, for gunpowder weapons could be dramatically scaled up in size and power and, as it turned out, efficiency. But that was neither readily evident nor easily achieved, for the intellectual and physical barriers were formidable. In building to withstand extremes of stress, strain and temperature, the chambers of guns, particularly large guns, posed by far the most demanding challenge faced by the medieval smith … or by the modern engineer until the advent of high-pressure steam engines and the Bessemer steel process. To complicate matters, the design and use of gunpowder weapons at sea posed problems that were very different from those on land and less easily solved.

Challenged to combine the power of heavy gunpowder ordnance with the advantages of water transport, European shipwrights and gun-founders arrived at two solutions: first, the cannon-armed Mediterranean war galley that emerged shortly after 1500, and second, the fully developed galleon that came on the scene some three to four decades later. Given wooden hulls, canvas sails, wrought-iron fittings and heavy ordnance of cast bronze, the galley and the galleon represented optimum solutions. The pages that follow examine how that came to be, and with what consequences.

SLUYS, 1340

> This battle was right fierce and terrible, for the battles on the sea are more dangerous and fiercer than the battles by land, for on the sea there is no reculing nor fleeing, there is no remedy but to fight and to abide fortune, and every man show his prowess.   JEAN FROISSART

At the dawn of the gunpowder age, the waters of northern Europe were ferociously dangerous, and not just because of the narrow margin between survival and death in the ceaseless struggle against the sea. The king's writ

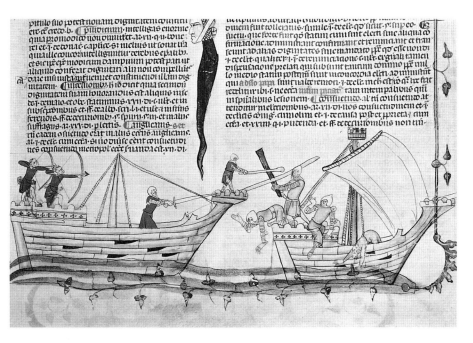

A remarkably realistic depiction of a sea fight between two cogs, dated to c. 1300–1320 by details of the armour and the ships' construction. The picture emphasizes the importance of shock combat as the ultimate arbiter of boarding fights, although the two archers, identifiable as English longbowmen by the size of their bows and their full draw to the ear, seem to be playing a major role in the fight.

stopped at the water's edge, and the only justice available to victims of piracy – those who survived – was that of retaliation. Unlike the Mediterranean, there was no market in slaves, and those robbed at sea were ordinarily murdered and tossed overboard. While raiders and invading armies were commonly transported by ship, sea battles proper were infrequent, and those that occurred were rarely decisive. This was due partly to resource limitations – war at sea was notoriously more expensive than war on land, particularly in terms of capital expenditure, and northern commercial economies were less developed than those of the Mediterranean – and partly a function of the limited weatherliness and manoeuvrability of northern ships. Of these, the dominant type was the cog, a beamy, high-sided vessel, with a single square sail and sternpost rudder, fitted with fighting castles at bow and stern when armed for war. Municipalities and monarchs built and operated sailing ships, but these were few in number; war fleets consisted mostly of impressed merchant vessels placed under royal orders and filled with fighting men.

Northern war fleets also included oared vessels, clinker-built barges (confusingly also called galleys) and true Mediterranean war galleys. Most of the latter were Genoese in the service of the French, although galleys were constructed for the French crown in the Clos des Gallée, the royal galley ships, in Rouen from 1294. The limited seaworthiness of these vessels generally restricted their use to the spring, the summer and the early autumn, but they were well suited for amphibious raids and were particularly useful in the Channel, where their oars provided solution to the swift tides and where short distances mitigated the effects of their limited stowage space for provisions and water.

The seal of Winchelsea with a nef, descended from lap-strake Viking ships and with the same basic construction and side rudder. The fore and aft fighting castles are probably temporary. The spars and rigging are accurately depicted, with powerful back stays to resist the forward thrust of the sail and braces (the lines hanging from the ends of the yard) to control it in the horizontal plane.

An English fleet landing at Lisbon during the time of the Hundred Years War, from a near-contemporary illuminated manuscript. A significant function of fleets at the time was to convey important persons and delegations to their destinations, though the vagaries of wind and weather made the business an uncertain one. As usual, the medieval artist's focus is on noble personages.

Strategic possibilities were constrained not only by the awkwardness of handling fleets of impressed ships of varying capabilities, but by the tendency of rulers to view ships and fleets purely as transport. Among the northern powers only the Hanseatic League (Hanse) and France – about which more below – could match the Mediterranean maritime city states in strategic sophistication. Exploiting a unity of purpose fuelled by common economic self-interest, and taking advantage of a ready supply of capable ships and skilled mariners, the Hanse could mobilize war fleets to considerable strategic effect, interdicting enemy shipping in conjunction with trade embargoes. This could be highly effective. Between 1368 and 1369, for example, in a war with Denmark and Norway over trading privileges, the Hanse sacked and burned Copenhagen and starved Norway into submission by cutting off her grain supply, forcing Denmark to sue for peace. A further example was the dispatch in 1374 of a fleet to ravage England's coast in response to Edward III's revocation of Hanseatic trading privileges. The nautical equivalent of a *chevauchée*, a mounted raid intended to destroy productive resources and discredit the enemy ruler, it had its desired effect: Edward caved in. In retrospect, coastal incursions of ships filled with heavily armed and rapacious seamen must have been every bit as frightening and destructive as similar onslaughts by mounted knights, archers and billmen on land, and with similar strategic results.

But before the advent of naval guns with hull-smashing potential, the Hanse did not commonly engage in sea battles, for the war of economic attrition at which they were masters was strategically far more effective. We must therefore look elsewhere for a case study of an early northern sea battle, and there is no more instructive example than Sluys. The most famous and best-documented naval engagement of the Hundred Years War (1337–1453), Sluys was fought on 24 June 1340 off the Flemish coast by a Franco-Genoese fleet attempting to prevent an English fleet under King Edward III from transporting his army to Flanders.

Following the outbreak of war between France and England in 1337, King Philip VI of France assembled a credible naval force, drawing on the resources of his Breton and Norman vassals and hiring galley squadrons from Monaco and Genoa. He pursued a co-ordinated strategy with his Scottish and Castilian allies, savaging the English coast and commerce. Edward, in turn, sought to exploit England's dynastic and commercial ties in Flanders where, in 1339, he fought an inconclusive land campaign, unsuccessfully laying siege to Cambrai. Meanwhile, Philip mobilized a sizeable fleet to invade England, with French and Genoese galley squadrons ravaging England's coasts. Adding insult to injury, Edward's two largest ships, *Cog Edward* and *Cristofer* were caught in French ports and captured. Fortunately for Edward, storms dispersed Philip's invasion fleet, and he lost most of his Genoese galleys to mutiny for non-payment.

SAILING VESSELS

From about 1300 the nef gave way to the cog as the dominant sailing vessel for trade and war in northern waters, save in Scandinavia and Scotland's Western Isles. Here, descendants of the nef fitted with sternpost rudders hung on into the sixteeenth century. Cogs could be built larger than nefs and were more efficient bulk carriers. The principal drawback of both nef and cog was reliance on a single sail, giving their crews little flexibility in working against adverse winds.

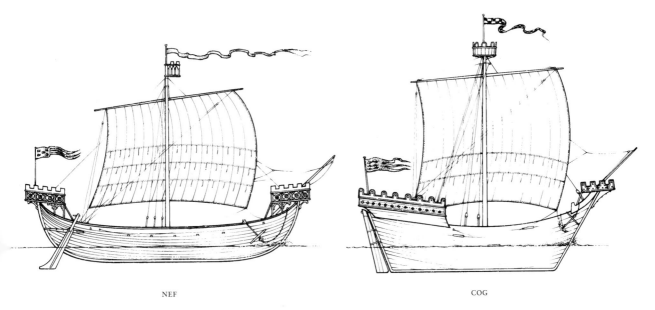

NEF   COG

Edward returned to England in February 1340 and by June had assembled a fleet of some 120 to 160 vessels, mostly cogs, which sailed on 22 June. Accurately perceiving his intentions, the French lay in wait, anchored off Sluys. The English sighted the Franco-Genoese fleet, of 202 sailing vessels, 6 galleys and 22 barges carrying some 40,000 men, the next afternoon. The English were outnumbered: Froissart says by four to one, which is probably as close as we can get, for comparing numbers of ships of heterogeneous types, many of them small, tells us

1 23 June: English fleet
sights French fleet in
late afternoon

2 English fleet work their way
around the French during
the night

3 24 June: English fleet attack in
the morning with the sun
behind them

4 French fleet lashed together at
anchor close in shore

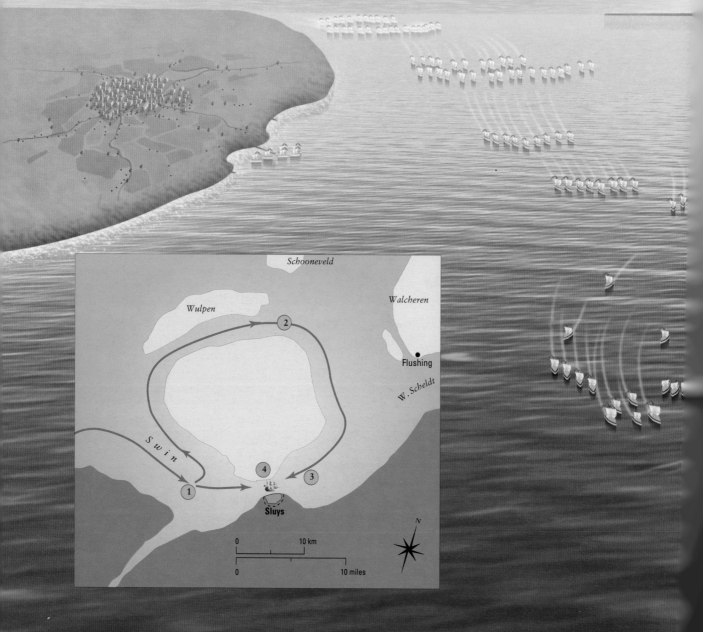

THE BATTLE OF SLUYS 1340

The sources for Sluys are frustratingly vague about the movements of the English. All we know for sure is that the two fleets sighted one another late in the afternoon of 23 June 1340 and that the English somehow managed to work their way around the French during the night to attack from the north-east at dawn. In this, they were aided by the nearness of the summer solstice – the date of the sun's northernmost ascent into the heavens – which allowed them to navigate by twilight throughout the evening. That advantage aside, King Edward's fleet was thoroughly heterogeneous and it is unlikely that all of his ships proceeded by the same route or arrived at the same time. What is clear is that the core of his war fleet attacked at dawn with the sun dead behind them, as shown below based on calculations from modern navigational tables. A last minute change of course was needed to extract full advantage from the sun's blinding rays. Edward, suitably advised, gave the appropriate orders and the rest is history.

Flushing

Sluys

3

4

little. The Genoese galley commander argued for an active pursuit, but the French admirals elected to chain their vessels together as a floating fortress, with *Cristofer*, filled with Genoese crossbowmen, in the forefront. The English worked their way around the French during the night, approaching them at dawn from the north-east with the wind on their starboard quarter. Edward marshalled his fleet with the largest ships in front, in groups of three – one ship filled with men-at-arms flanked by two filled with longbowmen – in imitation of the tactics that he had so successfully used against the Scots at Halidon Hill seven years earlier. Smaller ships filled with longbowmen followed as a mobile reserve. The vessels bearing the ladies of the court, with an archer escort, kept well to the rear.

On sighting the allies the English altered course, veering off to attack with the sun at their backs. Misunderstanding the purpose of the manoeuvre – to force the French and Genoese crossbowmen to fight with the sun in their eyes – the French concluded that the English were withdrawing, sounded their horns to signal the attack and were apparently in some disarray when the English struck. The ensuing battle resembled a siege, with the ships' castles and bulwarks substituting for siege towers and crenellated walls, albeit with the ferocity peculiar to sea battles noted by Froissart. Characteristically for medieval battles – and chronicles – the action revolved around the larger ships and most important personages. The English forced their way aboard *Cristofer*, killing her crew and thereafter using the vessel's height to good advantage. Although the English benefited enormously from the power of the longbow, the battle still went on until afternoon.

French losses were heavy: 190 ships and 16–18,000 men. Only the galleys and barges escaped. Tactically, Sluys was a brilliant English victory. Strategically, the results were equivocal. On the positive side, the heavy French losses of ships and men effectively ended the invasion threat, and English armies were able to move to and from France more or less unimpeded. Edward's Flemish strategy proved a failure, becoming bogged down in ineffectual sieges and the monetary demands of half-hearted allies. In 1341, the geographic focus of the war shifted when France and England intervened in a dynastic struggle in Normandy. Whether by accident, as historian Nicholas Rodger argues, or design, Edward invaded Normandy in 1346 and found a winning strategy of provoking decisive battle by launching *chevauchées* deep into French territory. For the balance of the war, English fleets served mainly to transport armies and their impedimenta to France, which was no mean feat, particularly where thousands of horses were involved, but was hardly decisive in a naval sense. French galleys continued to raid England's coast, but in the final analysis the decisive element of sea power in the Hundred Years War was the control of ports, an area in which French land power eventually prevailed.

Sluys is thus illustrative of the limits of fourteenth-century sea power in northern waters. It also shows a certain English facility with combat afloat, a confidence and competence in shiphandling and tactics that go far to bring victory under adverse circumstances. It is perhaps worth noting in this context that Edward III, whatever his abilities as a naval strategist, was one of the few medieval kings personally to command at sea. These considerations suggest, though they hardly prove, an English closeness to the sea that we shall encounter again.

Another depiction of Sluys, from a late fifteenth-century illuminated edition of Froissart's Chronicles. *Although the men-at-arms wear armour in a style of a century after the battle, it conveys essentials of the fight: the advantage of shooting from above enjoyed by men in the fighting tops, the threat of drowning for those who lost their footing leaping from ship to ship, and the incredibly crowded quarters with no room for retreat or escape. A critical aspect of the battle not adequately shown is the all-important fight for fire superiority between low-born English longbowmen and French and Genoese crossbowmen that went far to determine the battle's outcome.*

CHAPTER ONE

WARFARE AT SEA
1300–1453

THE PORT OF VENICE, here in a sixteenth-century perspective rendering, was Europe's most important commercial entrepôt from the high middle ages until the rise of Antwerp and Seville following the establishment of Spain's and Portugal's overseas empires. Venice's unique geographic situation, cut off from the mainland, rendered her safe from land invasion, while her republican form of government, although hardly egalitarian, gave all segments of society a stake in her survival and prosperity. The glut of shipping shown here is emblematic of Venice's economic importance and strategic resilience.

WARFARE AT SEA 1300–1453

Before the middle of the fifteenth century warfare at sea was waged within discrete regional spheres. There were strong commercial links between contiguous spheres, constituting a global trade network that extended from the Sea of Japan to Europe's Atlantic littoral. There was, however, little military interaction among them. Each sphere's geographic, economic and cultural peculiarities drove ship design along distinctive paths, and each had its characteristic technologies of war. Perhaps most importantly, the attitudes of ruling élites towards maritime commerce and warfare at sea fundamentally differed. These spheres were as follows.

The Indo-Arab sphere, encompassing the Indian Ocean, Persian Gulf and Red Sea, and extending from the east coast of Africa to the Straits of Malacca, was dominated commercially by princely emporia that served as transfer points

Depiction from an illuminated Arabic manuscript of a trading vessel, probably a dhow, bound from Basra to Oman. Arab seafarers were remarkable for their nautical skills and commercial acumen and in early medieval times traded directly with China. By the fifteenth century they had been largely replaced on eastern routes by Malay and Chinese mariners and seldom ventured further east than India and, rarely, Malacca.

between Chinese, Malay, Persian, Arab and African markets. Spices – cloves, nutmeg, mace, cinnamon and, above all, pepper – flowed from East to West, along with Chinese porcelain and silk. Much of this trade went to European markets, producing a flow of precious metals in return. In addition, bulk goods, such as rice, salt, aromatic woods, base metals, horses and cotton textiles, were traded internally. The dominant ships were the Arab dhows, lateen-rigged double-ended vessels of sewn, shell first construction, and junks built in imitation of Chinese practice, with flush-planked, nailed hulls and sails of bamboo matting. Maritime commerce was the province of the individual merchant, ship-owner and captain. Piracy was endemic, although more of an irritant than a serious threat to commerce. The idea of large-scale state-sponsored warfare at sea was alien to the region.

The Malay sphere encompassed the Indonesian archipelago and met the Indo-Arab and Chinese spheres in the Straits of Malacca. The western spice trade was entirely dependent on exports from the Spice Islands in eastern Indonesia – cinnamon, from Ceylon (Sri Lanka), was the only significant exception – and there was a substantial trade in pepper with China. Otherwise, trade patterns and commodities resembled those of the Indian Ocean. The princely states that dominated the region politically considered commercial profit an important element of power and on occasion launched invasion fleets against one another. That aside, state-sponsored warships were not used to project political power or to control trade in any systematic way. Chinese-style junks were used for long-distance bulk trade, but the dominant ship type was the relatively small, multi-hulled jukung. Merchants' tax revenues were appreciated and sailors accommodated, but they rarely benefited from state sponsorship or protection, except when in port.

The Chinese sphere stretched from the Sea of Japan to the Straits of Malacca. China was culturally and economically dominant in the region and had the potential for naval mastery, a potential that was actually realized under the southern Sung dynasty (1127–1279), although we know little about the details. By the thirteenth century, as travellers Marco Polo and ibn-Battutah attested and nautical archaeologists have confirmed, junks engaged in long-distance trade were as stoutly built and as seaworthy as any ocean-going vessel afloat. But with few exceptions, after the Sung dynasty, China's rulers focused their attention on terrestrial affairs. Of critical importance, the mandarins (the Confucian literati responsible for day-to-day governance) were at best ambivalent about overseas trade, particularly when conducted by Chinese. After overthrowing the Sung dynasty, the Mongol Yüan dynasty (1260–1368) mobilized Chinese and Korean shipyards and mariners to mount massive invasions of Japan in 1274 and 1281. Both invasions failed, and in the ensuing years the Yüan became

ARAB BAGHLA

Like dhows but larger, baghlas were built shell first with sewn planking and had lateen sails and stern rudders. Such vessels plied the Indian Ocean in early modern times, ranging as far west as Madagascar. Well suited for extended reaches on the same tack, their lateen rigs were not well suited for frequent tacking in constricted waters.

increasingly sinicized and turned their backs to the sea. Mandarin attitudes prevailed thereafter, save for a brief interlude under the first emperors of the Ming dynasty (1368–1644).

The Ming were an anomaly, a native dynasty founded by warrior kings who sought actively to expand China's boundaries by land and suzerainty by sea. They did so at sea by means of treasure fleets, so called because one of their main functions was to collect tribute in the form of ambassadors, precious metals, gems, exotic animals and other esoterica. Enormous in scope and competent in execution, these fleets sailed seven times between 1405 and 1434, under the eunuch admiral Cheng Ho, visiting Java and destinations as far afield as Ceylon, the Persian Gulf, the Red Sea and the Madagascar Channel. These fleets have acquired semi-legendary status and must therefore be put in perspective. The dimensions commonly given for the largest of Cheng Ho's ships, 450 feet long and 184 feet in breadth, are not only implausibly broad relative to length, but physically impossible, the result of erroneous interpolations by later Chinese authors and uncritical acceptance by western scholars. Still, they were impressive enough, sporting nine masts, measuring some 204 feet by 37 feet and displacing 1,000 to 1,100 tons. Some contemporary European vessels were larger, for example Henry V of England's 'great ships' *Jesus* (1,500 tons) and *Grace Dieu* (2,100 tons), but whereas these ships were exceptional, dozens of treasure ships were produced to a standardized design. The 1405 fleet consisted of 62 large and 255 small vessels and carried 27,870 men. Except for the smaller 1407 to 1409 expedition, the rest were of similar magnitude. The administrative and logistical competence required to outfit, man and provision such fleets speaks for itself. Moreover, the treasure fleets were not pure exercises in peaceful diplomacy, but suppressed piracy in the Straits of Malacca and intervened militarily in dynastic struggles in Java and Ceylon. We know little about the armament of Cheng Ho's ships, but Ming warships of the 1390s are known to have carried cannon that were at least equal in size and power to contemporary European naval ordnance. More importantly, seagoing junks, in contrast to Arab dhows and Malay jukungs, had hulls that could have been modified to support batteries of heavy ordnance.

The treasure fleets were successful in expanding Chinese suzerainty for a time, but behind their success lay a dark reality, for the Ming emperors who launched them proclaimed a ban on private seaborne trade that forced the vast majority of Chinese deep-sea mariners into poverty, smuggling or piracy. The last loophole was closed in 1435, when the treasure fleets were banned. The ban was partially lifted in 1567, but by then the design of large, ocean-going war junks had been lost, a victim of the mandarins' suspicion of outside cultural influence. The Ming war fleet had wasted away and Japanese *wako* pirates, sailing in ships that were far inferior to those of Cheng Ho's fleets, had filled the vacuum, turning China's coastal districts into a depopulated wasteland.

The European sphere, extending in 1300 from the eastern Mediterranean and the Black Sea to Iceland and Morocco, had expanded by the mid 1400s to

SOUTH-EAST ASIAN EXPLORATION

Ming China's brief flirtation with overseas expansion provides unequivocal evidence of the remarkable competence of Chinese shipwrights, navigators and sailors. Chinese mariners had long traded in the same waters without official sanction, but seafarers ranked low in the Confucian social hierarchy and received little attention from court historians and chroniclers. The inset shows an early sixteenth-century Portuguese nao silhouetted against a nine-masted Ming treasure ship.

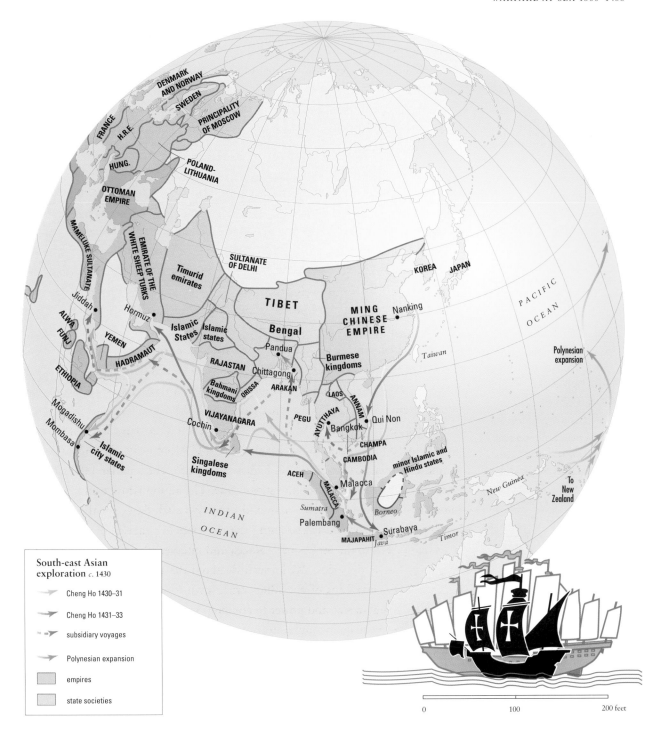

South-east Asian exploration *c.* 1430

→ Cheng Ho 1430–31

→ Cheng Ho 1431–33

⇢ subsidiary voyages

→ Polynesian expansion

☐ empires

☐ state societies

0   100   200 feet

encompass the Canaries, Madeira, the Azores and a thin chain of Portuguese factories along the western coast of Africa. In fact, the European sphere consisted of three subspheres: the Atlantic, Baltic and Mediterranean – four, if we consider the residual Viking sphere – each with its own distinctive technologies and customs and each largely self-contained. There was, however, a fundamental difference between their interrelationships and those that prevailed among the non-European spheres, in that there was recurrent military interaction among them. In part this was a function of geography, for Europe is not only a

SIZE AND TONNAGE

In assessing the capabilities of warships, the most basic parameter is size, usually given in tons. Unfortunately, pre-modern usage was inconsistent and modern authors all too frequently fail to specify which ton they are using and how. The ton has its origins in the English tun, a barrel with a capacity of 252 gallons used in the French wine trade that became the dominant unit of measure for shipping in medieval Britain and western Europe from Amsterdam south. The equivalent in northern waters was the last, roughly two tons, while the botte, about half a ton, prevailed in the Mediterranean. Capacity was at first given in terms of the number of tuns, lasts or botte that could actually be loaded into a ship's hold. Later, methods were developed for using hull dimensions to calculate precisely capacities in these units (and their local variants, of which there were many). The results were – and are – economically informative. The sizes of sailing warships were calculated in the same way, but the results are less helpful, for carrying capacity is a poor indicator of military potential. By contrast, war galleys were rated according to their number of rowing banks and oarsmen. In both cases, size *was* related to combat capability; the question is how best to measure and express it. Most modern authors use tonnage – by definition a measure of capacity – to express the size of medieval and early modern ships, but this can be misleading even when used correctly.

The modern solution is to rate warships in terms of the weight of water they displace, expressed for convenience in long tons of 2,240 pounds avoirdupois. Unlike medieval capacity calculations, the results are not exact, for a vessel's displacement varies with the load it carries. The results are, however, meaningful and apply to war galleys as well as sailing warships. We must obtain them ourselves, however, for in medieval times only Chinese shipwrights were able to calculate displacements, and their methods were lost with the Ming dynasty's ban on ocean-going vessels. European shipwrights began calculating displacements only in the late 1600s, and for another two centuries used the results only as part of the design process. Fortunately, medieval and early modern shipwrights – at least

successful ones – were systematic and their designs consistent. Knowing the dimensions of a few representatives of a given type, we can calculate the displacements of the rest with reasonable accuracy from one or two parameters: length, breadth and depth of hull or capacity in tons, lasts or botte. We are helped in this endeavour by naval historian Jan Glete who has calculated the displacements of an immense number of early modern warships and published the results in his trail-breaking *Navies and Nations: Warships, Navies and State Building in Europe and America, 1500–1860*.

A Spanish convoy departing Seville for America in 1498. On the right is the royal customs house, the famous Torre de Oro (Tower of Gold), so-called for its covering of golden ceramic tiles. Spanish shipping was closely regulated, based on the categorization of ships according to their capacity in toneladas, *equivalent in weight to about 62 per cent of a long ton.*

peninsula, and thus accessible by sea, but a peninsula of peninsulas: Scandinavian, Iberian, Italian, Greek and Anatolian, with the British Isles as an outlier. This geographic reality not only encouraged the development of seafaring, but accustomed Europeans to the movement of ships, men and ideas over long distances. The Vikings demonstrated the efficiency of northern ships and arms in Mediterranean waters during the Dark Ages; the Crusaders exported northern methods of warfare to the eastern Mediterranean; and in their heyday the Normans moved freely between the Atlantic and the Mediterranean. Interaction among these subspheres produced the technologies of warfare at sea that are the subject of this book. By 1300 the process was well under way.

In the far north, from Norway to Scotland's Western Isles, Viking methods of shipbuilding and warfare prevailed. Longships, built shell first of lapstrake construction, served as warships, while the *knarr*, of similar construction, but broader beamed and more seaworthy, was the dominant cargo vessel. While these vessels remained viable in their home waters, developments to the south were steadily eroding their importance. The most significant of these was the appearance in around 1200 of the cog, a deep-hulled, double-ended vessel with a sternpost rudder, driven by a single square sail. Seaworthy and an efficient bulk-carrier, the cog dominated merchant shipping from the North Sea and the Baltic to Iberia's Atlantic coast until about 1400, when it gave way first to the hulk and then to the carrack. Cogs were easily converted into warships by erecting temporary fighting castles at bow and stern, and impressed cogs formed the core of northern war fleets throughout the fifteenth century, although Mediterranean-style war galleys were used in the English Channel and the Bay of Biscay from the 1200s. Fleets of cogs met in battle on occasion, as we have already seen, but cogs were used in war mainly to haul troops and interdict trade. Galleys and barges, their northern equivalents, were used for coastal raids and attacks on shipping.

Warfare at sea in northern waters was marked by a remarkable degree of strategic and operational continuity. Coastal raids and naval support of land campaigns aside, trade was the main objective. In contrast to eastern and Mediterranean waters, most trade was in bulk commodities, such as grain, timber, fish, salt, wool and wine. Until reduced to third-tier status in the 1530s, the Hanseatic League, led by the port of Lübeck, was able to enforce commercial hegemony with a mixture of interdiction, blockade and embargo. Piracy was endemic – indeed, during the early 1400s, northern pirates, the *Likendeeler* ('equal sharers'), challenged the Hanse hegemony – and, as the scale of trade increased, merchant ships commonly sailed in convoys for mutual protection.

Combat between cogs was a form of mobile siege warfare in which archery and crossbow fire from the fighting castles, supplemented by firearms from the 1370s, cleared the way for grappling and boarding. The replacement of cog by hulk and carrack did little to change this, and neither did the use of increasingly larger guns in the 1400s. Even when, as we shall see, the development of the watertight gunport permitted shipwrights to mount heavy guns low

in the hulls of carracks, sea fights continued to revolve around attempts to grapple and board. Only with the introduction of truly effective heavy ordnance from the 1510s, ironically aboard Mediterranean galleys, did fundamental change begin.

From the Crusades until the mid 1400s warfare at sea in the Mediterranean, as in northern waters, revolved around trade. The only exception of note was the War of the Sicilian Vespers (1282–7), a dynastic struggle between the Aragonese and Angevin empires for control of Sicily, which, to be sure, was commercially important. Even the Crusades had an important commercial dimension, as Venice demonstrated in 1204 by orchestrating the seizure of Constantinople (Istanbul) by Latin crusaders to undercut her rival Genoa. But the similarities between Atlantic and Mediterranean theatres mask fundamental differences, for at the dawn of the gunpowder era the technology of warfare at sea was far more advanced in the Mediterranean, and tactics and strategies more refined. Although partly a product of greater population densities and economic maturity, this was primarily attributable to the Mediterranean's benign environment. In sharp contrast with the Atlantic, the Mediterranean has no perceptible tides, and during the trading and campaigning season, from late March through to early October, the skies are generally clear and storms rare. From antiquity, favourable wind and current patterns channelled trade along trunk routes hugging the Mediterranean's northern coast, a coast flush with harbours and beaches where mariners might pull up for the night or seek refuge from storms. The water is generally clear and the bottom drops off sharply, making it possible for the mariner to approach land safely to establish his position, a process facilitated by the presence of high mountain ranges near the coast that provide convenient landmarks. These factors acted in combination to encourage the early development of maritime trade and specialized warships.

For as far back as there is reliable evidence the design of European seagoing ships tended towards two extremes: round ships for trade and long ships for war. In post-classical times, this tendency found its ultimate expression in the Mediterranean war galley, a highly refined design that evolved as an integral component of a system of warfare and trade peculiarly adapted to the Mediterranean. That system was based on fortified port cities, major centres of trade supported by hinterlands sufficiently rich to provide the wherewithal to build, man and operate fleets of war galleys. The war galley developed in

The storm of Constantinople by Venetian and Latin Crusaders in 1204, painted by Tintoretto three and a half centuries after the event. Though the artist has expunged gunpowder weapons, the galleys, arms, and equipment more closely resemble those of his day, or perhaps a century earlier, than the historical reality. Fleets, particularly Mediterranean galley fleets, were often used in sieges. Note the powerful cranequin-wound steel crossbow in the right foreground.

symbiosis with the port city, defending it from attack and harassing the commerce and coasts of its enemies in a uniquely Mediterranean system of amphibious warfare. The control of outlying ports and seaside fortresses was crucial to this system of warfare, and galley squadrons were a basic means of investing and defending such places. Since galleys, and their smaller derivatives, were designed first and foremost for maximum speed under oars in calm conditions, warfare at sea had a strong seasonal character, a character reinforced by the annual cycles of agriculture, recruiting and trade.

Operationally, galley squadrons sortied in the spring and summer to raid, conduct sieges and, occasionally, to confront one another in battle. Campaigning in autumn and winter was exceptional, generally involving shorter distances and

smaller numbers. The basic ship-to-ship tactic was boarding, preferably after thinning out enemy ranks with crossbow bolts, arrows and, later, firearms. Well-armed war galleys were devastatingly effective against small merchant vessels and coastal villages. They were, however, impotent against competently armed sailing ships of high freeboard, and by the early 1400s well-armed carracks were essentially immune to attack by galleys. The appearance of bombards on the bows of galleys and castles on carracks made surprisingly little difference, amphibious trench warfare in the Venetian lagoons during the siege of Chioggia being the exception.

Few port cities were capable of maintaining and operating major galley fleets, and not all of those that could have did so. The identities and relative strengths of

Genoa in the late fifteenth or early sixteenth century. Possessing one of the best harbours in the western Mediterranean, Genoa was strategically handicapped by the city's accessibility by land. To be sure, the approaches along the narrow coastal plain and through the Ligurian Alps were not easy, but they were passable. Genoa was thus more susceptible to outside pressure than her rival Venice, particularly after the advent of mobile siege artillery from 1494, and fell first under the sway of France and then Habsburg Spain.

those that did changed with time, partly for economic reasons, partly because of changes in the scale of warfare and partly due to changes in the availability of strategic resources. By 1300, the list included Barcelona, Genoa and Venice, all benefiting from their proximity to the northern trunk routes and northern European markets. Naples and Messina possessed the wherewithal to support galley fleets, but Naples dropped from contention after the Angevin defeat in the War of the Sicilian Vespers, while Sicily, and therefore Messina, fell into Aragon's orbit. Alexandria commanded the vast resources of the Nile valley, but the Mameluke sultans, ruling from inland Cairo, were content to enrich themselves by taxing the wealth of the eastern trade in spices, medicinal herbs, porcelain and fine fabrics, bound for northern markets in Italian and Catalan bottoms. Moreover, Egypt lacked timber suitable for ships and barrels. Constantinople had lost her hinterland to the Seljuk Turks following defeat at Manzikert in 1071, and her independence to the Fourth Crusade in 1204. Although restored to Greek rule in 1261, the city dwindled to insignificance save as a trans-shipment point and guardian of the Dardanelles.

It would be an overstatement to assert that Barcelona, Genoa and Venice dominated warfare at sea in the Mediterranean between the Angevin defeat at the

Naples, one of the finest harbours in the western Mediterranean, was never the base of an independent naval power in the early modern era. The object of conflicting imperial ambitions, it fell definitively under Aragon's control in 1442, the date of the event depicted below, the entry of the Aragonese fleet into the harbour.

hands of Aragon in 1287 and the fall of Constantinople to the Ottoman sultan Mehmed II in 1453, but not by much. Lesser powers fielded galley squadrons, some to considerable local effect. Galleys of the Knights of St John for example, operating from Rhodes, were a constant threat to Muslim coasts and commerce in the eastern Mediterranean. In the west, Muslim corsairs operating from Algiers, Tunis and a host of lesser African ports posed a constant threat to Christian coasts and commerce. The Mediterranean was a den of pirates, and the 'little war' of raid and counter-raid, seizure and extortion was constant, cutting across regional and religious lines. By increasing shipping costs the Mediterranean 'little war' worked to the benefit of the maritime nations of the Atlantic over the long term. Over the short term it was background noise in the greater scheme of things.

The big issues in European waters were contested in two overlapping arenas: the fight for commercial dominance of the northern trunk routes and the struggle between Christendom and Islam. The former was settled for a time by the War of Chioggia; the latter gradually assumed major importance, which Venice, victorious in the former struggle, was slow to recognize. The turning point was the fall of Constantinople in 1453. Until then no Muslim power had commanded a resource base of consequence along the Mediterranean's northern rim, and the Christians, fragmented though they were, held the geographic trump cards. Afterwards the Turks, from a commanding position along the trunk routes, could stock the shipyards and arsenals of Constantinople with the vast resources of Anatolia and the Black Sea. The Ottomans were soon gnawing at Venetian positions in eastern Greece and in the war of 1463–79 expelled Venice from Negroponte. The stage was set for a major showdown.

A fine contemporary depiction of mid sixteenth-century war galleys and carracks engaged in combat. In emphasizing the drama of close action, the artist has failed to acknowledge the galley's advantages in stand-off gunnery.

43

The siege of Chioggia, 1379–80

This new plague of artillery, developed many years before in Germany, had been brought to Italy for the first time by the Venetians during their war against the Genoese in the year of Salvation 1380, when the Venetians were defeated at sea and so afflicted over the loss of Chioggia that they would have accepted whatever conditions the victors imposed.

Francesco Guicciardini

The early history of gunpowder's transformation in Europe from a pyrotechnic curiosity into a propellant with serious destructive potential is obscure. Our earliest secure knowledge relates to developments in powder manufacture, gun-founding and tactics that combined with synergistic effect from about 1420 to produce a revolution in positional warfare. Fortifications, hitherto secure against all but disease, starvation and treachery, fell with disconcerting frequency to cannonballs fired in battery against the face of the wall. High walls, hitherto a source of security, became a weakness, serving only to provide additional rubble to fill the ditch. We associate this revolution with France and the reforms of the Bureau brothers, whose guns drove the English from their strongholds in Normandy to end the Hundred Years War, but its essential elements had taken hold in Iberia, Morocco, Germany and the Ottoman domains by the mid fifteenth century. Indeed, our revolution's most dramatic manifestation was the fall of Constantinople to Ottoman bombards in 1453.

This is all reasonably clear, but raises questions, for the Bureaus' guns and the bombards that breached Constantine's wall were a mature technology. That technology must have demonstrated serious potential in adolescence to justify the considerable cost of forcing it to maturity. The question is, when and where? Writing in the 1530s, the historian Guicciardini believed that the siege of Chioggia represented the first effective use of cannon on a large scale in Italy. The evidence supports him, revealing no earlier use of artillery on a similar scale, or with comparable strategic consequences, not only in Italy, but in Europe.

The War of Chioggia, from 1378 to 1381, was the fourth in a series of wars between Genoa and Venice that began in 1253. It marked the end of a multi-sided struggle among the Italian maritime republics for control of the trade routes that hugged the Mediterranean's northern shores. At stake was a rich trade in luxury goods – slaves, wax, honey, sugar, fine textiles and, above all, spices – plus, when justified by price or needed for ballast, high-value bulk commodities, such as timber, wheat, copper and tin, wine, salt, alum and wool. The struggle began in earnest with the increase in trade spurred by the Crusades and was intensified from the mid 1200s by the Italian commercial revolution. As allies of convenience, as wary rivals and in open war, Venice, Amalfi, Naples, Pisa and Genoa fought to control the flow of wealth. The increasing scale of conflict knocked tiny Amalfi from contention in the eleventh century; Naples became the capital of a terrestrial kingdom under Hohenstaufen rule in the thirteenth; Pisa suffered crippling defeat at Genoese hands at Meloria in 1284 and then dropped out as her harbour silted up. That left Venice and Genoa locked in bitter rivalry.

The Venetian–Genoese wars took place across a period of momentous change within Europe and the Mediterranean world. They spanned the first half of the Hundred Years War, the onslaught of the Black Death, the consolidation of the secular power of the Papacy and its eighty-year captivity at the hands of the kings of France, the rise of the Aragonese empire in the western Mediterranean, the growth of the Hanseatic League and the consolidation of the Ottoman sultanate in Anatolia and the Balkans. The Venetian–Genoese wars are of considerable interest, for they spanned not only the economic, demographic and political changes noted, but changes in warfare and seafaring that were of at least equal importance. On land, the armoured man-at-arms who owed his political power to his skills of equestrian combat; who served under feudal obligation; who fought to capture his peers for ransom; and who fought as a shock combatant with lance, mace and sword, gave way as the arbiter of battle to low-born warriors who fought on foot; who fought for pay; who fought to kill; and who increasingly killed from a distance with missile weapons.

The Italians participated in these developments indirectly by hiring English and Swiss mercenaries – longbowmen, halberdiers and pikemen – for their *condottieri* wars, wars in which the mounted man-at-arms retained his traditional importance. But in a broader sense, the Italian maritime republics anticipated developments on land by turning early to the crossbow as an effective means of defending their ships and trading factories. European chivalric élites resisted the crossbow as a challenge to their monopoly of armed violence – Emperor Conrad III of Germany (ruled 1138–52) forbade its use on pain of death – but feudalism had shallow roots in Italy, and by the time of the Crusades Pisan, Genoese and Venetian crossbowmen were renowned for their effectiveness. In Italy, too, there was a curious dichotomy in attitudes towards warfare on land and at sea. City states that were quite content to contract their land wars out to mercenaries were at the forefront of developments in war afloat. Indeed, the upsurge in Mediterranean commerce from the mid 1200s was rooted in changes in weaponry, notably the widespread adoption of the crossbow, as well as in advances in navigation and ship design.

The Venetian–Genoese wars show remarkable strategic and operational continuity, broken only at the end. Each city sent galley squadrons to raid enemy coasts and commerce; both responded by concentrating their shipping in convoys. War fleets were dispatched to attack or protect particularly rich convoys, rarely with decisive effect. The first three conflicts were protracted wars of economic attrition. The fourth began in the same way. It ended very differently.

The Fourth Venetian–Genoese War arose out of efforts to influence the Byzantine succession and control Cyprus. Matters came to a head in 1377 when Venetian forces frustrated a Genoese attempt to seize Tenedos, key to the Dardanelles, and the following spring found both cities on a war footing. Genoa had used the intervening months to good effect by forging alliances with King Louis of Hungary and Francesco Carrera, lord of Padua, an inveterate enemy of Venice. At first Venice held the initiative at sea, and the Venetian fleet, ten galleys under the popular and charismatic admiral Vettor Pisani – the scale of operations was small in the aftermath of the Black Death – defeated a Genoese force of similar size off Anzio on 30 May 1378. Genoese losses were serious, and the doge was deposed in the ensuing turmoil.

Despite his objections, Pisani was ordered to winter at Pola, on the Dalmatian coast. The following spring a reconstituted Genoese fleet of twenty-two galleys under Luciano Doria found him there. Although the odds were even in numbers of galleys, Pisani's ships and men were in poor condition. On 6 May 1379 Doria drew the Venetians into battle, holding a reserve out of sight until the Venetians were committed. Pisani led his best galleys in a furious assault on the Genoese centre, killing Doria, but the Genoese reserves turned the tide. Venice lost fifteen galleys and

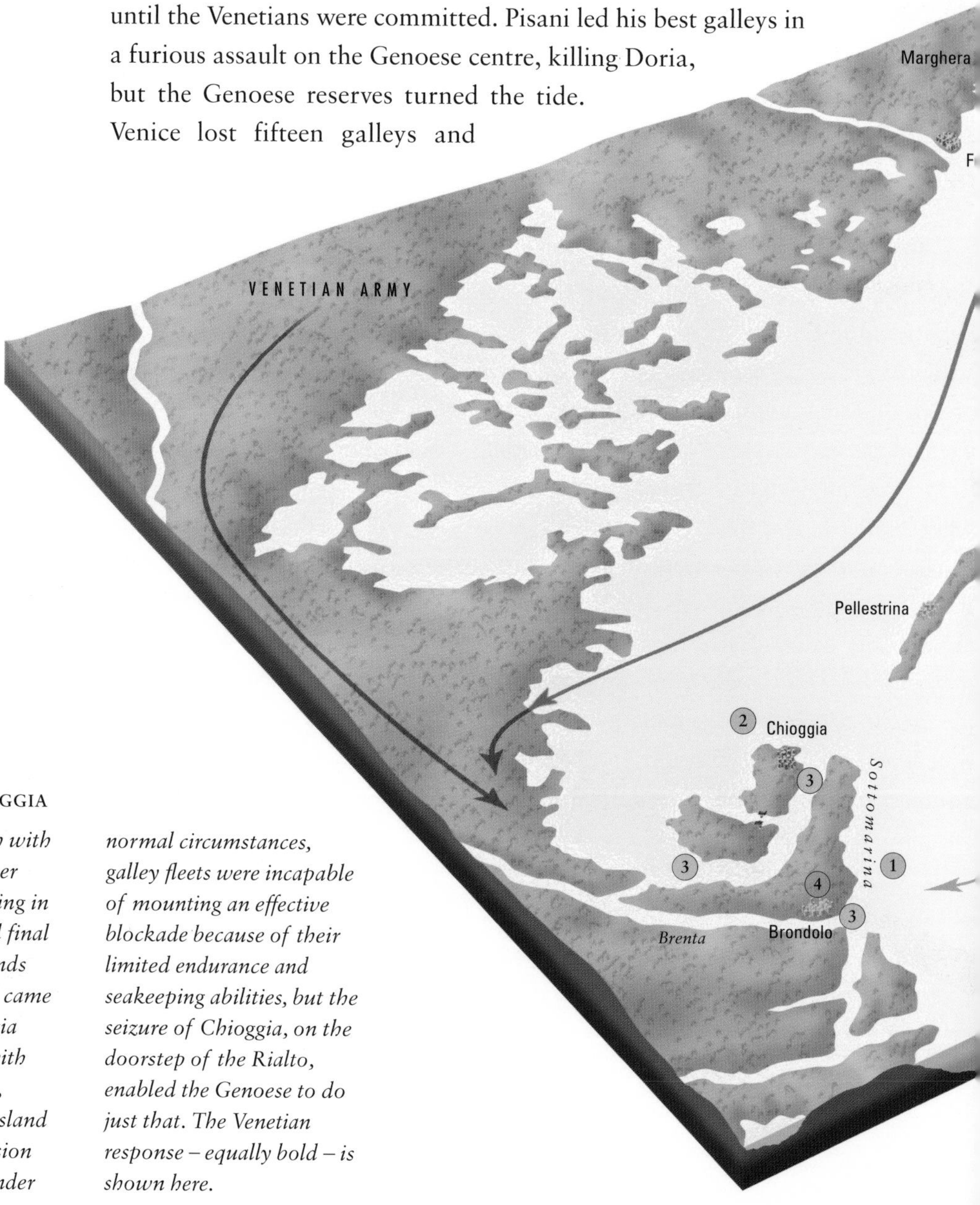

VENETIAN ARMY

Marghera

F

Pellestrina

Sottomarina

2 Chioggia

3

3

1

3

4

Brenta

Brondolo

3

The siege of Chioggia

Venice's closest brush with extinction between her semi-mythical founding in the sixth century and final dissolution at the hands of Napoleon in 1797 came in the War of Chioggia when the Genoese, with uncommon boldness, sought to starve the island republic into submission by close blockade. Under normal circumstances, galley fleets were incapable of mounting an effective blockade because of their limited endurance and seakeeping abilities, but the seizure of Chioggia, on the doorstep of the Rialto, enabled the Genoese to do just that. The Venetian response – equally bold – is shown here.

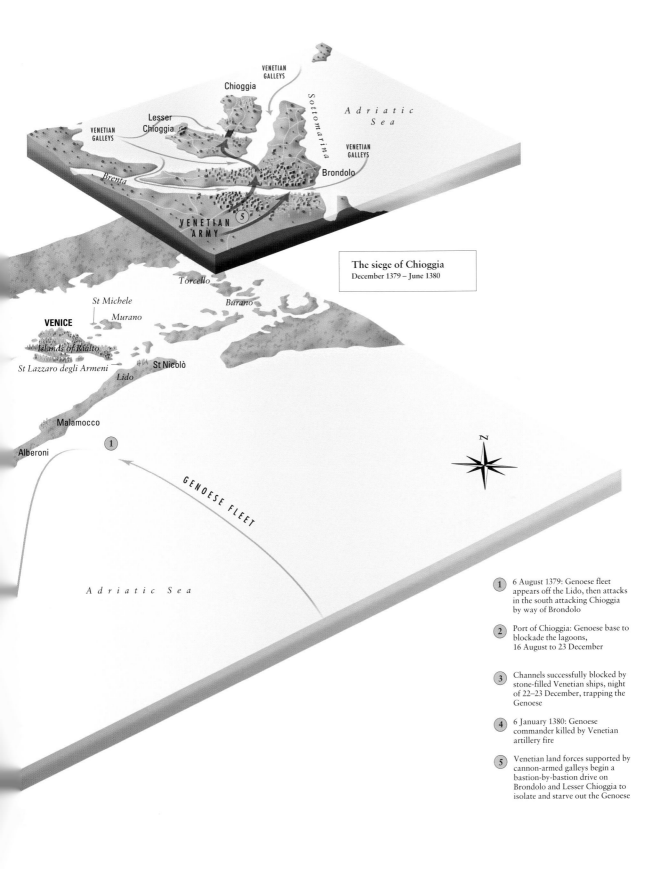

VENETIAN GALLEYS

Chioggia

Sottomarina

Adriatic Sea

Lesser Chioggia

VENETIAN GALLEYS

VENETIAN GALLEYS

Brenta

Brondolo

⑤

VENETIAN ARMY

The siege of Chioggia
December 1379 – June 1380

Torcello

St Michele

Burano

Murano

VENICE

Islands of Rialto

St Nicolò

St Lazzaro degli Armeni

Lido

Malamocco

①

Alberoni

GENOESE FLEET

A d r i a t i c   S e a

N

① 6 August 1379: Genoese fleet appears off the Lido, then attacks in the south attacking Chioggia by way of Brondolo

② Port of Chioggia: Genoese base to blockade the lagoons, 16 August to 23 December

③ Channels successfully blocked by stone-filled Venetian ships, night of 22–23 December, trapping the Genoese

④ 6 January 1380: Genoese commander killed by Venetian artillery fire

⑤ Venetian land forces supported by cannon-armed galleys begin a bastion-by-bastion drive on Brondolo and Lesser Chioggia to isolate and starve out the Genoese

A sixteenth-century painting of the Venetian reduction of the Genoese position on Chioggia. Though painted long after the event the details are credible. Note the close quarters. The siege and counter-siege of Chioggia involved bitterly fought amphibious engagements.

2,400 prisoners, a crippling blow. Salvaging what he could, Pisani fought his way clear with six galleys. Ordered home by the Senate, he was tried and convicted under a law that specified death for commanders who fled a lost battle. It was apparent, however, that once faced with defeat, Pisani had made the best of a bad situation and the vote was close. No doubt partly because of his popularity, Pisani was imprisoned rather than executed. On 10 June Venice dispatched a squadron of five well-equipped galleys under Carlo Zeno to raid the Genoese Riviera.

The Venetian reaction to defeat was conventional. The Genoese response to victory was anything but. Piero Doria, the new Genoese commander, spent the summer in the Adriatic refitting and incorporating the captured Venetian galleys into his force. On 6 August he appeared off the Lido with forty-eight galleys and four galiots, 'all well armed', in the words of the Venetian chronicler Daniele di Chinazzo. Venice responded in panic, fortifying the Lido, removing channel markers and blocking canals with chained beams. Orders went out for Zeno's recall. Then, striking at the heart of Venetian power, Doria launched his force

against the port of Chioggia, at the southern tip of the lagoons, intending to seize a blockading base from which to strangle Venice.

Linking up with Paduan and Hungarian forces investing the lagoons by land, the Genoese fought their way into Brondolo and Lesser Chioggia in turn, storming Chioggia on the morning of 16 August. By evening, the flags of Hungary, Padua and Genoa flew above the plaza and Genoese bombards and trebuchets defended Chioggia's water approaches. Facing ruin, Venice asked for terms. Doria rejected the overtures, boasting that he would first bridle the famous bronze horses atop their columns in St Mark's Square. Moving to mobilize every resource, the Council of Ten met widespread refusal to serve under the designated commander-in-chief, the haughty patrician Thaddeo Giustinian, and popular clamour for Vettor Pisani's release from prison. The council yielded in stages, first releasing Pisani, then appointing him second in command to the aged doge, Andrea Contarini. This took time, and in the meantime the blockade held. By winter, Venice was effectively isolated.

Under Pisani's leadership the Venetians prepared carefully, risking all on a single stroke. As night fell on 22 December – the longest night of the year – they struck, attacking Brondolo as a diversion and using the cover of darkness to extract maximum advantage from their superior knowledge of the waterways. Stone-filled cogs were towed into the mouths of the channels connecting Chioggia with the Adriatic and the lagoons and scuttled. The Genoese repelled the assault on Brondolo, but dawn revealed the extent of their defeat: the channels were blocked and the besiegers were now the besieged. Capping the Venetian victory, Carlo Zeno returned in triumph on 1 January 1380 with fourteen well-armed galleys, having wrought havoc on Genoese commerce.

But it was not yet over. The Genoese fought back with skill and determination, assaulting the Venetian bastions guarding the channels, trying to dislodge or break up the stone-filled cogs and dispatching well-heeled agents to induce treason into Venice's mercenary ranks. To make matters worse, the Genoese defeated a squadron of twelve Venetian galleys under Giustinian sent to bring grain from Sicily, capturing six and taking Giustinian prisoner. Venice faced starvation.

The siege of Chioggia resolved itself into two overlapping campaigns: the first a bastion-by-bastion Venetian drive through Brondolo; the second an unceasing amphibious struggle to dominate the surrounding channels and waterways. In the latter struggle the Venetians' smaller, handier boats and local knowledge gave them the upper hand. They also made good use of galley-mounted bombards, as noted by Daniele di Chinazzo. The overland drive was marked by the effective use of guns as well, notably two large bombards, the first firing 147-pound stone balls and the second, named *la Trevisana* after her founding place in Treviso, firing balls weighing no less than 205 pounds. The chronicler's account is reminiscent of First World War trench warfare, with artillery bombardments of bastions alternating with infantry assaults under cover of crossbow fire.

On 6 January, according to di Chinazzo, *la Trevisana*, 'returning to her

origins' – that is, firing north towards Treviso – 'fired several stones, the last of which struck the belltower of Brondolo, dislodging a large piece of masonry that killed miser Piero Doria, Captain General of the Galleys of Genoa and of the army in Brondolo.' Nor was *la Trevisana* finished: on 22 January, she collapsed another section of wall, killing twenty-two Genoese. Gunpowder ordnance had made its debut as a serious actor on the stage of history.

Doria's death was an emotional turning point, but Venice was nearly as exhausted as the Genoese garrison, and if Genoese supplies were running short, their money held good. They fought on, and Venetian mercenaries could still be tempted… and were; some were hanged for their troubles. Not until 19 June did the Genoese, down to the last ditch and last crust of bread, ask for a parley. They surrendered two days later and the Venetians entered Chioggia on 24 June, taking 4,000 Genoese prisoners and nineteen galleys.

Venice had survived; that was important. More so, Venice had learned – and demonstrated – gunpowder's potential. For this, there were precursors ashore, though none so dramatic as *la Trevisana*'s exploits. There were none afloat.

The triumphant return of Doge Andrea Contarini to Venice following the Genoese capitulation at Chioggia. The painting, by Paolo Veronese two centuries after the events depicted, gives a powerful sense of the remembered importance in Venice of the victory.

CHAPTER TWO

THE WEAPONS OF WAR AT SEA 1300–1650

AN ILLUSTRATION FROM A 1460 TREATISE on warfare, De Re Militari, *by Roberto Valturio. The ship is naïvely drawn, but the arms and equipment are credibly rendered and represent a realistic cross section of the arms and equipment of the fighting complements of contemporary European warships. Crossbows were only just being challenged by firearms and the hand culverineers are firing their pieces mounted above the shoulder, implying modest recoil and destructive capabilities. In a more abstract sense, the drawing accurately conveys the notion that ship-to-ship fights closely resembled the assaults and escalades of siege warfare on land where superior height conveyed important tactical advantages.*

THE WEAPONS OF WAR AT SEA

THE PRECEDING CHAPTERS addressed the basic parameters of armed conflict at sea at the beginning of the gunpowder era, using case studies to show how tactical means were applied to achieve strategic ends. We assumed throughout that those tactical means were largely technologically determined. Embracing that assumption does not diminish the importance of geographic and economic factors, for geography does much to determine which technologies are best suited to the task at hand – this is particularly evident with regard to ships – and economics establish which technologies can be deployed and in what quantities. Nor can technology be understood divorced from its social and cultural context. The reverse side of the coin is that analysis of the technologies of war at sea can tell us a great deal about how these other factors came into play. Subsequent chapters address ships; here we consider weaponry. The war galley became an effective platform for heavy artillery in the 1510s – Chioggia was an aberration – while the galleon was meant to be one from the outset. These developments reflected a decline in the importance of individual weapons. Gunpowder was the main driving force for change, although not in a simple and straightforward fashion.

Boarding was the only reliable means of achieving victory in a sea fight before the advent of gunpowder and remained the preferred means for a long time thereafter. That meant close combat with edged weapons, and the weapons of preference were remarkably uniform across geographic and cultural boundaries: swords and polearms of various kinds, most commonly half-pikes, glaives and halberds. Armour conferred substantial advantages, and armoured men-at-arms comprised an important part of warships' complements. Edged weapons were generally shorter and handier than those used ashore, and armour was lighter, but the differences were not great and warships frequently transported troops with all their impedimenta. The medieval Mediterranean war galley was intended first and foremost to serve as a boarding platform, and by the fourteenth century seasoned mariners had settled on a mix of individual weapons that remained remarkably stable for the next three centuries. The same degree of specialization in warship design does not seem to have prevailed in Asian waters after the Ming emperors allowed their fleet to wither away – the Korean turtle ships were very much the exception – but the same tactical considerations applied.

Turning to individual missile weapons, apart from thrown spears and javelins, the continuity and relative uniformity noted above disappears in the face of sharp regional differences and constant change. At the turn of the fourteenth century, the crossbow was the most important missile weapon in European waters, and probably in Asian waters as well (it was, after all, a Chinese invention). This was not only because it was lethal at both short and medium range, but because it could be quickly mastered and, unlike serious military

bows, did not require great physical strength. The crossbow's liabilities, inaccuracy and a slow rate of fire were mitigated by the conditions of naval combat. While crossbowmen were horribly vulnerable to charging cavalry on land, ships' bulwarks and pavisades gave them protection and time to span their bows, await opportunity and then let fly. European crossbows steadily increased in power in response to improvements in personal armour, and from about 1370 composite bows of wood and horn gave way to steel. The increased range and killing power came with a price: greater complexity and cost.

Hand-portable firearms appeared in the mid 1300s, but only began seriously to challenge the crossbow a century later with the development of efficient lock mechanisms in Germany. The next major technical advance came during the wars of Italy (1494–1559), when the Spanish developed powerful shoulder arms in response to the crossbow's inability to stop charging French men-at-arms and Swiss pikemen with any reliability. Spanish crossbows and *escopetas*, ancestors of the matchlock arquebus, co-existed at rough parity until 1500. Thereafter, the arquebus quickly displaced the crossbow in Spanish service in Europe, and was in turn partially supplanted by the musket, a heavier and more powerful firearm

By Hans Holbein the Younger, c. 1532, the above rendering reflects the enormous changes in warfare at sea since the date of the previous illustration. Though the artist has exaggerated the size of the men, the vessel – a small ship – is realistically portrayed. The fighting tops do not dominate the composition and halberds are not numerous, suggesting the growing importance of powerful deck-mounted ordnance, represented by the lidded gunport on the stern quarter. The unfortunate fellow vomiting over the rail illustrates another constant of warfare at sea.

As long as boarding and entering remained a viable tactic at sea, individual weapons were essentially indistinguishable from those on land. Those on the right are representative of European armies of the late fifteenth and early sixteenth centuries.

This illumination, from a 1483 Swiss chronicle, conveys the uses and capabilities of contemporary weaponry. Individual firearms are growing in importance, but still have limited power.

with considerably greater effective range, some 300 to 500 yards against massed troops as opposed to 100 to 150 yards for the arquebus and crossbow.

Demanding European tactical scenarios drove the Spanish development of individual firearms. Conquistadors used light crossbows against Amerindians to good effect long after Spanish infantry had abandoned them in Europe, and crossbows were required aboard Spanish merchant ships on the Atlantic run for

another half-century. Moreover, social and cultural factors were at work. The French were slow to adopt individual firearms, clinging to the crossbow into the 1600s. Conversely, the Ottoman Turks eagerly embraced individual firearms, overthrowing the Egyptian Mamelukes who resisted them, and the Japanese swiftly adopted the arquebus after its introduction into Japan by European traders in the 1540s.

Firearms were not, however, the premier individual missile weapon during the period of our concern. That distinction fell to the fully developed military bow, meaning, in practical terms, one drawn to the ear with a force of 100–175 pounds and capable of penetrating plate armour. Of these bows, only three survived into medieval times: the Turco-Mongol composite recurved bow, the English longbow and the Japanese samurai's bow. In skilled hands, all were far more accurate than the crossbow, arquebus or musket and all had much higher rates of fire and substantially longer effective ranges. The qualifier was 'in skilled hands', for mastery of these weapons required immense strength and a lifetime of practice. All were products of their users' lifestyles and the social fabric of their communities. The longbow disappeared during the sixteenth century not because of its shortcomings as a weapon, but because of the disappearance of the yeoman archer's way of life. Only the Ottomans, and, on a smaller scale, the Venetians,

The siege of Mortagne, 1378, from a near-contemporary illuminated manuscript. Although longbows and crossbows are the dominant individual missile weapons, cannon have supplanted trebuchets, no doubt in part because of the immense amount of high-grade timber needed to construct a large counterpoise trebuchet. The fortifications are clearly designed primarily to frustrate escalade.

were successful in promoting mastery of the composite recurved bow beyond the nomadic horse archer's tribal lifestyle.

The longbow could be devastatingly effective at sea – it wrought havoc at Sluys – but its importance declined as the pool of yeoman archers dwindled. Turkish horse archers reached the shores of the Mediterranean in the wake of the Byzantine defeat at Manzikert in 1071 and soon learned to raid by sea, but the composite bow in Muslim hands became a significant naval factor only with the consolidation of Ottoman power after the fall of Constantinople in 1453. Archers excelled at delivering a high volume of aimed fire and were effective at ranges that neither crossbow nor arquebus could match, but they needed clear space in which to stand upright, draw and release. By contrast, the arquebus and musket were handy for shooting over bulwarks and through apertures, and at short ranges arquebus balls smashed through pavisades and light planking better than arrows. Although the musket's heavy recoil and weight restricted its use to picked men, its raw stopping power was unequalled. The characteristics of archery and small arms were complementary: the Venetians used archers to cover arquebusiers while they were reloading, and fighting men aboard North African galiots carried both composite bows and muskets on occasion.

With the sole exception of Greek fire, the fabled incendiary that saved Constantinople from the Arabs in the eighth century, crew-served naval weapons were of secondary importance in Europe before the advent of gunpowder, while the secret of Greek fire was lost in the Middle Ages. It was not so in Asia, where the Sung navy used catapults to hurl incendiary munitions and bombs in the 1160s. By 1393, Ming warships were mounting four cannon with 'muzzles the size of rice bowls', that is, firing stone shot weighing about 10 pounds – large for contemporary European naval ordnance – and twenty smaller guns. At that time, the most important crew-served weapons in European waters were war galleys' projecting bows and sailing warships' grappling hooks, both weapons of shock combat. In this context, the Venetian use of shipborne ordnance during the siege of Chioggia was a remarkable divergence. That it was not immediately repeated was probably due to the powder's composition.

Gunpowder was first compounded in Europe with saltpetre consisting mainly of calcium nitrate and made according to the original Chinese recipe. Calcium nitrate is deliquescent, that is, it readily absorbs atmospheric moisture, with obvious implications for use afloat (Chinese and Venetian naval gunners must have taken extraordinary care to keep their power dry; significantly, the Venetians do not seem to have taken bombard-armed galleys outside the lagoons). In around 1400, European manufacturers of saltpetre learned to treat aqueous saltpetre with wood ash to precipitate the removal of nitrate and calcium salts, leaving non-deliquescent potassium nitrate. Guns appear routinely on ships from the 1410s, and while correlation is not causation, the timing is suggestive. These early naval guns were breech-loading bombards of wrought-iron, hoop and stave construction, designed to fire stone balls from barrels 5 to 6 calibres long, that is with bores five to six times as long as their internal diameters, and with powder chambers a half to a third as large around as the bore. They were quite small: if the Warwick Roll artist (see caption p. 89) drew guns and men to the same scale, the guns that he depicted fired projectiles of only 2 to 3 pounds.

Such pieces were not terribly effective, and co-existed with crossbows for a considerable time. The 1445 arms inventory of a Burgundian galley lists large, pedestal-mounted steel crossbows ahead of *veuglaires*, guns about 4 feet long firing a 3-pound stone ball, suggesting that the crossbows were considered more effective. Under these circumstances, ships' bulwarks provided effective protection from missile weaponry and maximized the effectiveness of archers, crossbowmen and gunners firing downwards into a lower-lying enemy. The castles and fighting tops of cogs and carracks were important as dominant points from which to rain projectiles. Prominent among these were stones lifted to the tops with special hoists,

and gads, iron javelins with stabilizing fins. That such weapons played an important role in ship-to-ship combat at the end of the fifteenth century provides eloquent testimony to the initially modest advantages of gunpowder over muscle.

After Chioggia, the first significant use of guns in warfare at sea was not aboard ships, but in shore batteries, notably the Turks' use of huge bombards to close the Dardanelles to Venetian ships in 1453. By then, land ordnance was undergoing rapid development, marked by the appearance of massive siege bombards in Flanders, France, Germany and the Ottoman domains. At the same time, gun-founders were developing pieces of more modest size, with long barrels intended to maximize projectile velocity rather than size. Some of these, ancestors of culverins, were strong enough to shoot balls of cast iron. It was also during this period that guns cast from bronze, copper alloyed with tin in proportions of nine to one, began to establish their superiority over their wrought-iron counterparts.

The optimal materials, size, proportions and projectiles for a given task were anything but clear, and it took time to work things out. Wrought-iron ordnance required little capital investment, but demanded immense amounts of highly skilled labour, particularly for large guns. Bronze guns required considerable capital investment – copper and tin cost far more than iron, and the large refractory furnaces were expensive – but could be made larger without disproportionate increases in cost. Moreover, once the process was mastered, successful designs could be reliably replicated. Finally, bronze was corrosion-

The muzzle of a wrought iron bombard in the collection of the Museu Militar, Lisbon, showing hoop and stave construction. Forged in Goa in 1518, it fired a 200-pound stone ball. The staves were hammer-welded together around a wooden mandrel; the reinforcing hoops were then heated white hot, slid over the staves and hammer-welded into place as they contracted. Corrosion has accentuated the welding joints; they would have been barely visible when new.

ARCHAEOLOGIST'S SITE PLAN

The galleon Santíssimo Sacramento, *flagship of the Portuguese Brazil Company, the Companhia Geral do Comércio do Brasil, went down off Salvador, Brazil, in 1668. She remained undisturbed until 1973 when sport divers found her and began looting the site. The Brazilian navy intervened, and in 1978 mounted an archaeological rescue operation. Forty-two of her sixty guns were accounted for, twenty-six of them bronze and all but two of the twenty-six 11-pounders or larger. These comprise a high proportion of our physical evidence of the armament of transoceanic warships in the final days of the age of the galleon.*

resistant, conferring a durability that had important long-term consequences. Not only did individual guns last longer, but bronze was effectively indestructible, and damaged and worn-out guns were routinely melted down and cast into new ones. Finally, as mining added to the store of copper and tin, the amount of bronze ordnance in circulation steadily increased.

Since stone projectiles were less dense than cast iron, the same velocity could be imparted with less pressure within the gun, and lower pressures meant a greater margin of safety. The same logic relegated projectiles of lead, which were far denser than iron, to small arms. Perriers – stone-throwing guns – could be made thinner and lighter than iron-throwers for the same safety margin, offering considerable cost benefits, particularly with bronze ordnance. Finally, although stone projectiles offered significant advantages – in addition to those already noted, they made a bigger hole – their manufacture required highly skilled labour.

Logic suggested that longer barrels imparted more velocity to the ball, and while this was true only to a degree, bombards were too short to fully exploit gunpowder's propulsive properties. By the early 1500s, gun-founders and gunners had discovered the penetrative effect of long guns firing iron balls in a flat trajectory against stone walls, both challenging and complementing the smashing power of large bombards. To further complicate matters, gunners were learning the superior propulsive powers of fast-burning corned powder ... and the lethal danger of using it in older guns, particularly those of wrought iron. More

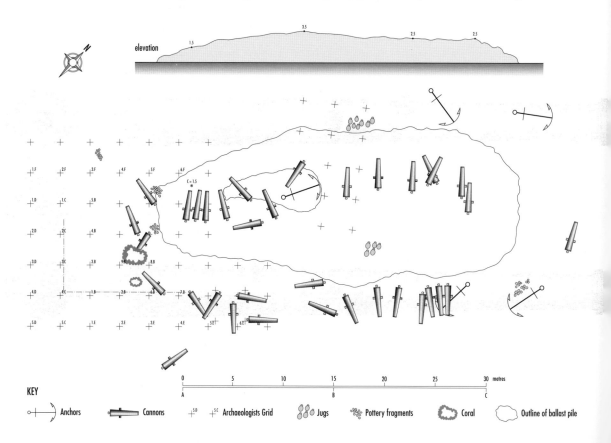

KEY

Anchors　　Cannons　　Archaeologists Grid　　Jugs　　Pottery fragments　　Coral　　Outline of ballast pile

powerful guns demanded better carriages; handier and more mobile carriages multiplied the guns' effectiveness and so on, with synergistic effect.

Unsurprisingly, these developments first took place on land, for guns and powder were expensive, and with few exceptions, those who held the purse strings were landsmen, more concerned with the defence and acquisition of territory than with nautical affairs. The benchmark is the havoc wrought in Italy in 1494 by the siege train of King Charles VIII of France. The agents of destruction were bronze cannon (cannon in the technical sense, as described below), with efficient carriages drawn by horses, rather than oxen as hitherto, using corned powder to fire cast-iron balls of 30 to 50 pounds. Quoting Guicciardini, the guns

…were led right up to the walls and set in position there with incredible speed; and so little time elapsed between one shot and another and the shots were so frequent and so violent was their battering that in a few hours they could accomplish what previously in Italy used to require many days.

Daunting technical challenges had to be overcome before such guns could be used at sea.

By 1500, European artillery was emerging from a period of accelerated development and was being made in increasingly uniform categories. Wrought iron was giving way to cast bronze, and the bombard relinquished its place as the

BRONZE GUNS

Two archaic English bronze guns recovered from Santíssimo Sacramento, an 11-pounder, top, and an 8-pounder. While they are unsigned and undated, their proportions and archaic features, notably their great length and lifting lugs and rings, suggest that they were cast in the early 1500s; the author's best estimate is c. 1535. The weight markings are in pounds avoirdupois; the crest of the Companhia Geral do Comércio do Brasil is inscribed on the breeches. Investigation with magnets revealed iron structures embedded in the gunmetal at the breeches, trunnions and lifting rings, a previously unknown design feature.

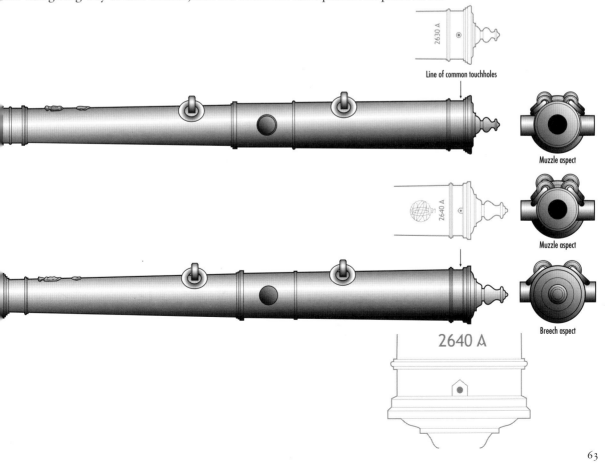

Line of common touchholes

Muzzle aspect

Muzzle aspect

Breech aspect

2640 A

A stand of basilisks in the collection of the Museu Militar, Lisbon. At the rear is a massive 20-foot long Muslim 40-pounder; second from front is a Portuguese 42-pounder cast in 1537, probably in India. The lesser size of the Portuguese piece speaks volumes for the skill of its founders. Cast atop its barrel, on the right, is a baby basilisk, a graphic representation of the fierce mythical beast, half bird of prey and half serpent, sneering eternally at Portugal's enemies.

sine qua non of heavy ordnance, first to the basilisk – named after the mythical beast, half serpent and half bird of prey – and then to cannons and culverins. Basilisks could either be of cast bronze or, rarely, wrought iron; the common denominator was that they were big, long and powerful. Cannons and culverins were of cast bronze. In the early 1500s, cannons had barrels of 26 to 28 calibres in length and culverins, successors to the basilisks for a time as the apotheosis of destructive power, had barrels of 30 to, exceptionally, 40 calibres. The advantage of these long barrels was not, as one might suppose, greater range, but greater safety. Cannons and culverins were cast muzzle up, and the molten metal at the breech solidified under pressure. The longer the gun, the greater the pressure; the greater

Line of common touchholes

Two 20-pounders by John and Richard Philips
cast in 1590 (above), and 1596 (below)

Two 11-pounders by George Elkine
both cast in 1597

1	2	3	4	5	6 feet

1	2 metres

ENGLISH DEMI-CANNONS

Four English demi-cannons recovered from Santíssimo Sacramento. *Cast by known English founders, they were from seventy to seventy-eight years old when* Sacramento *went down, indicating a previously unsuspected longevity for naval ordnance. Their harmonious proportions and lack of elaborate raised ornamentation are characteristic of English – and Venetian – ordnance. Volume calculations reveal that their bronze was denser, and thus stronger, than that of* Sacramento's *other guns. Their weights in pounds avoirdupois, shown below, and in Portuguese* arreteis *(pounds) are stamped on the breeches. All of* Sacramento's *English guns bear such double markings and calculations reveal that the guns were weighed by their new owners with impressive precision.*

the pressure, the denser the metal; the denser the metal, the stronger and safer the gun. At the same time, foundry practice steadily improved, and the great cost of bronze provided a powerful incentive to make guns as light as possible. Barrel walls gradually became thinner and guns progressively lighter, but the biggest changes were in length; by the mid 1600s, the best cannon in naval service were substantially shorter, with bores of 20 calibres or less, and culverins were obsolete.

A class of efficient stone-throwers, the perriers, emerged, which weighed a third to a half less than iron-throwers for the same weight of ball. These came in all sizes, ranging from 6,000-pound full-cannon equivalents down to naval swivel guns, called *medios cañones* in Spanish, weighing perhaps 600 to 900 pounds.

SACRAMENTO'S GUNS

The superimposed outlines of a 28-pounder and 11-pounder from Sacramento *by the same Portuguese founder, Antonio Gomes Feio, illustrates the artistic individuality and technical consistency of the best gun founders. It also illustrates the inherent inefficiency of smaller guns.*

Perriers were considered particularly effective in naval service – the Portuguese *camelo* combined the best characteristics of cannon and perrier – but were progressively put out of business by stonecutters' rising wages. They had almost entirely disappeared from English gundecks by 1588, but hung on in the Ottoman domains and Portuguese India into the eighteenth century.

Our primary concern is guns with hull-smashing – and wall-smashing – capabilities, and the weight and recoil of such guns were not easily contained

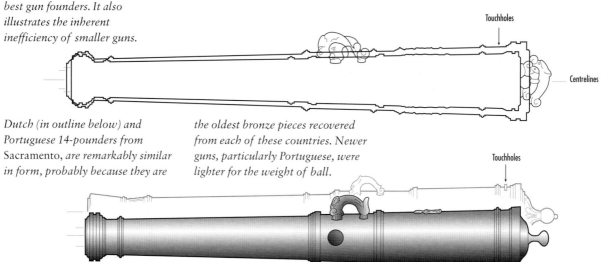

Dutch (in outline below) and Portuguese 14-pounders from Sacramento, *are remarkably similar in form, probably because they are*

the oldest bronze pieces recovered from each of these countries. Newer guns, particularly Portuguese, were lighter for the weight of ball.

Sixteenth-century bronze Ottoman guns in the collection of the Askeri Musesi, Istanbul. The piece in the centre, a 50-pound pedrero (stone-thrower), might well have served as the main centre-line bow gun on a Turkish galley at Prevesa or Lepanto.

(large bombards were tried at sea, but with indifferent results, as we shall see in our discussion of the battle of Zonchio). The French had solved the problem on land by 1494. It was solved at sea by about 1510, almost certainly in Venice, as discussed in Chapter 4. The solution was to suspend a galley's main centre-line bow gun from its trunnions in a stout wooden box that was mounted on a track and allowed to slide backwards on recoil. These mounts for the first time combined the operational advantages of water transport with the tactical power of first-rate, French-style, heavy ordnance. Expensive in terms of manpower – a

MOULDS USED TO CAST SACRAMENTO'S CANNON

The author's reconstruction of moulds used to cast Sacramento's Portuguese 26-pounders, left, and her Dutch 15-pounder. The moulds were made of pottery clay mixed with finely sifted horse manure and wool fragments, built up around a wax-coated positive of the gun that was removed when the mould was dry. The moulds were then fired to melt out the wax and burn away the wool and manure fragments, leaving a sintered surface to absorb the water vapour released when the molten bronze reacted with silicates in the clay. The moulds were sunk in pits surrounded by rammed earth for casting. The wrought iron chaplets centring the cores remained embedded in the bronze. The Dutch mould reconstruction is conjectural, based on chaplet placement.

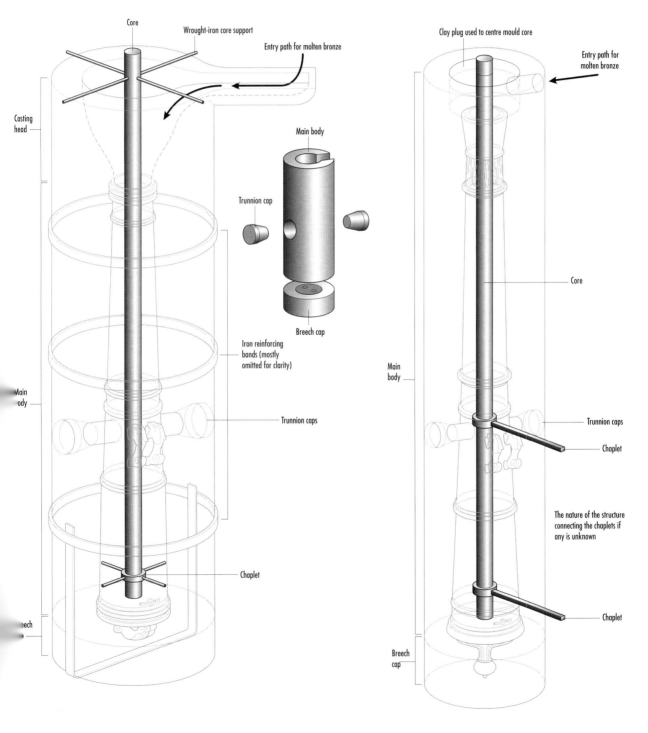

BRONZE ORDNANCE

Sacramento's best heavy bronze ordnance, six 26-pounders by the founder Matias Escartim cast in Lisbon in 1649–53, and an undated, but probably earlier, 28-pounder by the founder Antonio Gomes Feio (AGF). The Matias Escartim pieces weighed an average of 3,729 pounds and the AGF piece weighed 4,047 pounds. Sacramento also carried some sixteen cast-iron pieces, probably half of them 24-pounders and half 11-pounders based on the gross external dimensions of the eight recovered. They would have been substantially larger and heavier than bronze pieces firing the same weight of ball.

galley's entire complement of oarsmen was needed to train the gun – these were the most efficient artillery carriages of their day and Mediterranean seamen quickly grasped their advantages.

The problems of mounting heavy ordnance on sailing ships were less readily solved. The earliest carriages were wooden sledges. These effectively mated the large breech-loaders' powder chambers and barrels; adding wheels at the front made training easier and the rear could be raised and lowered to control elevation. Even so, they were still heavy and unwieldy. Such cumbersome mounts were common well into the sixteenth century – they predominated on the *Mary Rose*, sunk in 1545 – as were land carriages, with their large wheels and long trails. The slow development of gun carriages for sailing ships is partly attributable to the need to develop supporting technologies, notably securing tackle and the watertight gun port. The solution, although it was neither quickly nor universally adopted, was the truck carriage, a stout wooden box on four small wheels in which the gun was suspended from its trunnions, a compact arrangement well suited for use in the confined space of a gundeck. As an added benefit, the small wheels allowed the barrel to protrude well beyond the gun port, permitting wider angles of traverse and keeping the muzzle blast clear of the hull. In its final form, perfected by 1700, the truck carriage was restrained by an elaborate tackle and trained in azimuth by handspikes; elevation was adjusted with a wedge beneath the breech and the gun's recoil was used to bring it

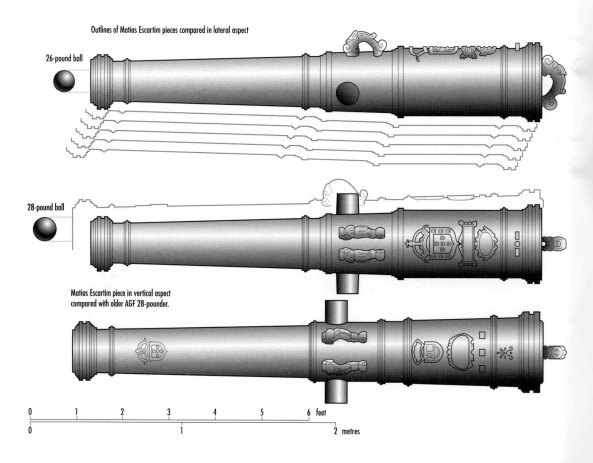

Outlines of Matias Escartim pieces compared in lateral aspect

26-pound ball

28-pound ball

Matias Escartim piece in vertical aspect compared with older AGF 28-pounder.

```
0      1      2      3      4      5      6  feet
0                      1                      2  metres
```

inboard for loading. When and where all these elements came together is unclear.

The earliest evidence of truck carriages is found in the 1513 survey of Henry VIII's navy, which lists four large guns aboard *Trinity*, mounted on carriages with 'trotill wheeles' and four carriages for large guns on *Henry Grace à Dieu*, with 'trotills, 'wheles' or – the clincher – 'on four wheels'. These were not the equals of their eighteenth-century successors: a truck carriage raised from the *Mary Rose*, although similar in appearance, was less solidly constructed. Still, they were vastly superior to sledges and land carriages. For all its seemingly obvious advantages, the truck carriage was slow to take hold, however, except in England. In 1588 the bulk of the Spanish Armada's guns, if not all, were mounted on sledges and land carriages.

We now turn to ballistic performance, leaving a more complete treatment of mounting arrangements to our discussions of caravel, carrack and galleon. Culverin, cannon and perrier alike were smooth-bore guns firing spherical projectiles, and as such they shared common limitations. First, the projectiles were inert (mortars firing exploding shells played a minor role on land and none at all at sea until the 1680s). Because of aerodynamic drag, destructive energy fell off sharply with range, and the angle of impact steepened, limiting penetration. Next, the ballistic properties of black powder placed an absolute limit on muzzle velocities of about 1,200 to 1,500 feet per second. Finally, cannonballs had to be appreciably smaller than the bore to preclude their getting stuck, a serious

DUTCH BRONZE GUNS

Five of the bronze guns recovered from Sacramento *were captured Dutch pieces, indicative of a shortage of good ordnance in 1649–50 when she was commissioned. The three larger pieces were cast in 1622, 1634, and 1649, respectively (top to bottom). The shorter and less massive barrels of the newer pieces as a function of projectile weight is suggestive of improving foundry practice. The Dutch pieces were more elaborately decorated than their Portuguese or English equivalents.*

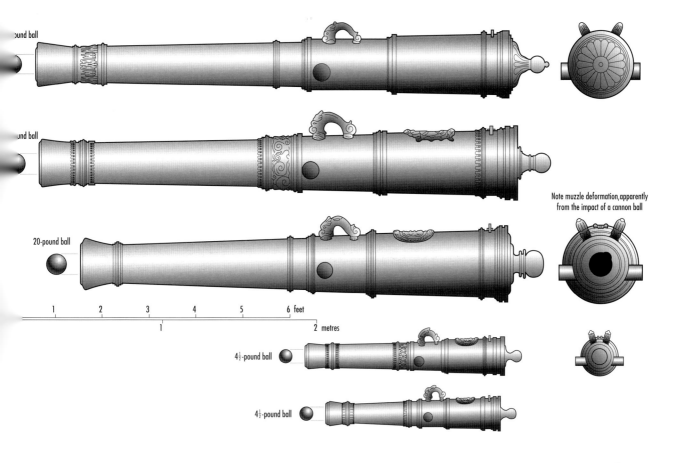

Note muzzle deformation, apparently from the impact of a cannon ball

ound ball

und ball

20-pound ball

4½-pound ball

4½-pound ball

1 2 3 4 5 6 feet

1 2 metres

problem as powder residue accumulated rapidly when firing. In consequence, the cannonball bounced, or balloted, from side to side as it went down the bore, departing at an unpredictable angle. Whatever spin it acquired en route was at right angles to the line of flight, resulting in a 'hook' or 'slice' like a golf ball. Not only was the spin unpredictable, but there was very little of it and the aerodynamic forces on a slowly spinning sphere are also unpredictable, causing the projectile to 'wobble' like an American baseball pitcher's knuckle ball, with obvious implications for accuracy. Although a galley's main centre-line gun could do better under ideal conditions, these factors generally limited the effective range of naval artillery to 200 to 300 yards, a figure that dropped when the gun was fired from a rolling deck. To be sure, any piece larger than a swivel gun could throw its projectile thousands of yards, but with few exceptions – 'long shots' that brought down a fleeing enemy's rigging or disabled a pursuing foe – that was irrelevant. Carriages and mounting arrangements improved steadily, though incrementally. The range, striking power and accuracy of good naval ordnance in the hands of first-rate gunners would not increase materially until the advent of rifled artillery in the 1850s.

There were nevertheless significant national differences in the quality of bronze ordnance. Writing after the battle of Lepanto (1571), Spanish gunner Luis

A sketch of gunners loading and swabbing guns from outboard by the Dutch artist Willem van de Velde, probably the Elder (1611–93). The extent to which outboard loading was used and how long the practice endured is a matter of debate among naval historians. What is clear is that using the recoil of truck-carriage mounted broadside guns to bring them inboard for loading was uncommon until well into the seventeenth century, even on English vessels.

Collado considered German and Flemish guns best, with Venetian ordnance close behind, although Venetian guns were lighter for the weight of ball. Collado acknowledged the excellence of French ordnance; conversely, he considered Genoese guns cast for export 'the worst in Europe'. He had a high opinion of Spanish guns, particularly those cast in Malaga, though they were heavier and longer than their Venetian, French and German equivalents. He considered Ottoman guns cumbersome, though sound. Modern scholarship confirms Collado's judgements, but his experience was Mediterranean and he said nothing about Dutch or English guns. Dutch ordnance was sound, although, based on surviving examples, heavier than equivalent English or Portuguese pieces. The English came late to gun-founding, and Henry VIII imported Flemish founders early in his reign, but English founders learned quickly, and by the 1540s were casting some of the finest bronze ordnance in the world.

By the 1520s bronze muzzle-loaders were solidly established as the European naval ordnance of choice, although wrought iron continued in use, particularly aboard merchant ships. The production and use of cast-iron guns grew steadily from the 1550s, but their use aboard warships was exceptional and of necessity rather than choice. This began to change in the 1620s, when economic reality began to force the adoption of iron guns on state warships. That in turn forced

An English 9½ pound demi-cannon cast in 1571 by Robert and John Owen, in the collection of the Museu Militar, Lisbon. This was a compact and efficient piece and underlines the high quality of the best contemporary English bronze ordnance. It is also noteworthy for its uncommon beauty and harmonious proportions; the spiralled breech has eleven facets and the muzzle has ten.

changes in warship design that culminated in the eighteenth-century ship-of-the-line, a development beyond the scope of our analysis. Meanwhile, economic factors were paramount: in 1570, bronze cost £40–£60 per ton in England, 3⅓ to 6 times more than iron; by 1670, bronze cost £150 per ton and the ratio had increased to 8⅓ to one. Cast-iron naval ordnance was important over the short term because its cheapness made it widely available. It was important over the long term because its greater weight forced the changes in warship design mentioned above. The net result was to place global hegemony within the grasp of those nations that were capable of building and arming fleets of ships-of-the-line and arming them with heavy, cast-iron ordnance.

ZONCHIO, 1499

> … a forest on the sea, when described incredible but when seen stupefying.
>
> A Venetian galley captain's description of the Turkish fleet, 1470

The fall of Constantinople to Sultan Mehmed II's bombards in 1453 shifted the strategic balance in the Mediterranean, not least by compromising Venice's hold on the Aegean and the Levant trade. More importantly over the long term, Constantinople's dockyards and arsenals, as well as the resources of Anatolia and the Balkans, gave the Ottomans a solid basis for sea power. That, however, was not immediately apparent, and Mehmed initially contented himself with absorbing the Byzantine domains and consolidating his hold over the Balkans. Venice and the Turks had a strong mutual interest in peaceful commercial relations, but inveterate Ottoman expansionism against the backdrop of Pope Pius II's calls for a general European crusade pushed them towards war. The spark was provided by Albanian border disputes and Ottoman expansion in the Morea (the Peloponnese).

Unchallenged at sea, and at the height of her naval prestige, Venice struck in June 1463 by occupying the Morea. But numbers counted on land: the Morea was lost that autumn and the Turks undertook a massive naval build-up. Worse still for Venice, Pius died the following year, and, his crusading impulse having died with him, Venice was left without allies in the Mediterranean. The war's defining moment came in 1470, when an enormous Ottoman fleet, variously reported as numbering 300 to 450 vessels, carrying seventy thousand soldiers and the imperial siege train, sortied from Constantinople to rendezvous with an army led overland by Mehmed himself. The target was the island fortress of Negroponte, key to the Aegean. Facing overwhelming odds, the Venetian covering squadron of fifty-five galleys failed to engage and withdrew to Crete. By the time it returned with reinforcements, the Turks were solidly ensconced ashore and had mounted two general assaults. Fearful of Turkish shore batteries the Venetian fleet failed to relieve the city. Ten days and two assaults later, it fell.

The war dragged on, in part because of Ottoman distractions in Persia and

Albania. Having taken Negroponte, the Ottomans abandoned the sea while Venetian squadrons raided at will and took Cyprus. Still, the loss of Negroponte was a major blow, and the disruption of trade was intolerable over the long haul. Venice sued for peace in 1479, surrendering Negroponte and several other Aegean islands and agreeing to pay a sizeable annual indemnity in return for restored trading privileges.

In 1480, with Venice sidelined, Mehmed attacked Rhodes, the home of the Knights of St John and a perpetual thorn in the side of Muslim commerce. The attack failed, but the next year an Ottoman army seized Otranto, at the heel of the Italian boot. Mehmed's fleet had shown that it could transport his army to Italy, and that army had no Christian equal. Until the Spanish infantry learned to combine arquebus and musket fire with pike drill during the wars of Italy, something not evident before the battle of Pavia in 1525, no Western army could handle horse archers in the open field, and armoured *sipahi* horse archers were the core of Mehmed's host. The threat to Italy – and even to Rome, Mehmed's stated objective in legend, and probably in fact – was palpable.

It evaporated when Mehmed died in 1481 and his empire descended into the throes of a hard-fought succession struggle between princes Bayezid and Cem. Otranto's garrison withdrew to support Bayezid's ultimately successful bid, but Cem – uncharacteristically for an Ottoman prince – sought refuge in enemy lands, first Mameluke Egypt and then, after a renewed bid for the throne, in Rhodes. Under Ottoman succession law, either prince's claim was equally valid, and Cem enjoyed considerable support. Bayezid was thus strategically hamstrung as long as Cem remained at large and in the hands of Bayezid's enemies, at first the Knights of St John, then the Pope and ultimately Charles VIII of France.

When Cem died in 1499 Bayezid immediately attacked Venice, going for her coastal enclaves in Greece. The climactic engagement took place on 12 August 1499 off Zonchio, on the south-western coast of the Morea. In strategic outline it mirrored the engagement off Negroponte in 1470: a Venetian attempt to prevent an Ottoman fleet from delivering a siege train and reinforcements to an imperial army besieging a fortified port. That the target was Lepanto, on Greece's western coast, is clear evidence of the Turks' growing might at sea. The ensuing clash was both instructive and decisive. On the day of battle, the Ottoman fleet under Daud Pasha numbered 277 vessels, including 60 ordinary galleys, 30 galiots and *fustas*, 3 heavy galleys, 2 large carracks and 18 large sailing ships. Uncertain of their ability to confront the Venetians, the Turks advanced cautiously, keeping close to the shore.

The Venetian fleet, under Antonio Grimani, numbered 110, including 4 carracks of 1,800 tons, 24 armed roundships of lesser size, 44 ordinary galleys and 12 heavy galleys. In an apparent breakdown of discipline, the only Venetian ships fully to engage were carracks under Andrea Loredan and Albano d'Armer, who attacked the largest Turkish carrack commanded by Burak Re'is, a noted corsair. Larger than its Venetian opponents, Burak's carrack was stuffed with

OVERLEAF: *A Venetian woodcut of the battle of Zonchio, showing the climactic struggle between two Venetian carracks and a Turkish carrack under Burak Re'is (Chmali). They are depicted with an accuracy that dates the woodcut close to the event. All three carracks have guns in abundance – mostly small bombards firing over the bulwarks, though Burak's mounted a pair of huge stone-throwers – but individual missile weapons dominate the fight with a veritable rain of stones, arrows and gads cascading down from the fighting tops. Composite bows are much in evidence, particularly among the Turks. The flames that ended the fight are shown licking at all three carracks.*

NAVE·TVRCESCHA·

NAVE·DE·LARMER·

janissaries and armed with two broadside bombards, firing 150 to 200-pound stone balls. Based on a near-contemporary woodcut of the battle, all three carracks were plentifully supplied with light wrought-iron bombards firing over the wales. Significantly, the waists of all three carracks are shown covered with anti-boarding netting.

The big Ottoman bombards sunk a 600-ton Venetian ship and a smaller vessel outright, no doubt helping to explain the Venetian reluctance to engage. Indeed, to justify his caution, Alvise Marcello, the commander of the Venetian round ships, later emphasized the physical and moral impact of 150-pound stone cannonballs striking his ship. The big guns, however, played no further role in the fight, probably because they were mounted in rigid beds and loaded from outboard. This was an awkward procedure, and to make things worse, bombards used dry-compounded serpentine powder that had to be tightly confined by driving a wooden plug into the chamber, a suicidal task when undertaken outboard with an enemy ship alongside. Although the Turkish galleys intervened to no effect – bow-mounted swivel guns were their largest ordnance – the struggle lasted for four hours. The Venetians must have pressed Burak Re'is hard, for he turned in desperation to burning pitch and the flames spread to all three carracks, destroying them. Deterred by the horrible results, the Venetians held off thereafter, and on 25 August the Turks entered the Gulf of Corinth. Learning that the approaching fleet was Turkish and that it carried the siege train, Lepanto's garrison surrendered without a fight.

The lessons of the engagement bear consideration. Although the Turkish bombards get partial credit for having deterred the bulk of the Venetian fleet, the battle was dominated by anti-personnel missile weapons fired from the carracks' bulwarks, castles and fighting tops. Based on the woodcut, the composite recurved bow was more common among the Turks than the Venetians. Individual firearms were rare on both sides, though more common among the Venetians. Over a fifth of the individuals depicted are brandishing weapons of shock combat, and several Venetians are wearing armour, clear evidence of the perceived importance of boarding. Finally, there is an impressive rain of projectiles from the fighting tops, including gads, rocks and barrels, perhaps containing quicklime or incendiaries. Clearly, gunpowder was not dominant.

Strategically, Ottoman numbers on land, and their ability to transport heavy siege guns by sea, had neutralized Venetian skill afloat. The Turks exploited the combination the following year. Venetian attempts to impede the progress of the Ottoman fleet were again ineffective, and Modon and Coron, the main Venetian bases in the Morea, fell. Having achieved their land objectives, the Turks abandoned the sea while Venetian squadrons raided at will and consolidated their hold on the Ionian islands. France, Spain and Portugal, concerned by the spectre of an expansive Osmanli state, sent assistance, Hungary going to war with the Turks. In early 1502 the Ottomans and Venice concluded a peace treaty that restored Venice's commercial privileges, but the seeming reversion to the status quo was illusory. Venice was still in many respects the premier Mediterranean naval power – this was certainly true in terms of warship design – but henceforth it would fight the Turks out of necessity, not choice.

THE MALABAR COAST, 1503

How it came to pass that Portugal carved out a maritime empire halfway around the world a full century before any other power attempted anything remotely similar remains one of the puzzles of history. In natural and human resources, Portugal would have seemed an unlikely candidate for a world hegemon as Europe recovered from the Viking and Arab invasions and the Black Death. Indeed, in 1385 Portugal had preserved its independence under the house of Avis by a thread, defeating, with English assistance, an attempt by King John of Castile at Aljubarrota to seize the Portuguese throne. But, having expelled the Muslims a full two centuries before the Spanish, the Portuguese turned early to overseas exploration, combining crusading impulses with the Avis kings' commercial interests. The initial draw was gold and slaves from south of the Sahara, and by the mid 1300s Portuguese mariners were exploring the African coast with royal encouragement, seeking a way to intercept the trade at its source. The Portuguese discovered the Madeiras, and probably the Azores, before 1400, and in 1415 they seized the Muslim port of Ceuta on the Moroccan coast opposite Gibraltar.

Efforts to extract wealth from the Atlantic were not uniquely Portuguese: the Spanish conquered the Canaries and Italian entrepreneurs, particularly Genoese, searched for new lands and profit. But the Avis kings sponsored development of the technologies needed for the task: ships, navigational methods and, at an early stage, guns. Moreover, they had ambitious objectives: to tap into the Mediterranean spice trade at its source by finding a direct sea route to India, and to locate and render aid to the lost Christian kingdom of Prester John.

The Avis research and development programme – for that is what it was – was systematic and effective. By the last quarter of the fifteenth century, the Portuguese had developed a coherent system of deep-sea navigation aimed at commercial profit and underwritten by armed violence. It was based on experimentally derived knowledge of solar and stellar navigation; superior nautical charts; ships that could reliably traverse the broad reaches of the Atlantic and serve as effective gun platforms; and steadily expanding geographical knowledge, not least the wind patterns and currents of the southern Atlantic.

At the core of the system, from about 1440, was the caravel. Derived from Atlantic fishing boats, caravels were relatively small, typically about 30–100 tons displacement. Exceptionally seaworthy, weatherly and of comparatively shallow draught for their displacement, caravels were ideal for exploration. Finally, the caravel's stability and low freeboard made it possible to mount a limited number of heavy guns on deck. This was important, for the Portuguese had learned the destructive effect on a ship's hull of heavy shot fired *ao lume do agua* – at the

THE BATTLE OF THE MALABAR COAST

In the first phase of the battle, the Portuguese, sailing in line with Vicente Sodre's weatherly caravels in the lead and da Gama following with his squadron of carracks, worked their way to windward of the oncoming Muslims. In the second, Sodre's broadside ordnance wreaked havoc among the relatively flimsy Muslim craft, leaving da Gama to mop up with fire from the castles and waists.

The Malabar Coast
February 1503

---

① February 1503: da Gama moves north towards Calicut in 2 squadrons totalling some 15 ships, meets a force of 80 local vessels of varying sizes

② A local force manoeuvres to close with the first of the 2 Portuguese squadrons

③ The Portuguese manoeuvre into line-ahead formation, bringing their heavy guns to bear on the enemy

④ The local ships, exposed to the overwhelming gunfire of the Portuguese, are unable to close and board the enemy and are eventually driven off with heavy losses, leaving the Portuguese in control of vital trade links

waterline – before they reached Asian waters. The biggest and best of those guns were of a uniquely Portuguese pattern: called *camelos*, they fired stone balls and had proportions quite different from other European ordnance. As we have already seen, the lower density of stone projectiles, as opposed to iron, made thin barrels feasible, and the resultant pieces were remarkably light when compared with their destructive power.

By 1434, the Portuguese had rounded Cape Bojador, on the African mainland opposite the Canaries. Within half a century, they were reaching far out into the Atlantic before turning south-east to catch the prevailing westerlies to make landfall on the African coast. In 1487, the navigator Bartolomeu Diaz turned the Cape of Good Hope and returned to report that he had found the route to India. No record survives of further expeditions prior to Vasco da Gama's departure from Lisbon in July 1497, but it seems unlikely that the Portuguese curtailed their exploration, and Arab sources report strange shipwrecks in the Madagascar

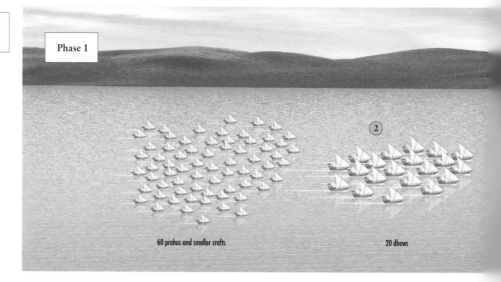

Phase 1

60 prahus and smaller crafts

20 dhows

Phase 2

Channel during the ten-year interval. However that may be, da Gama proceeded without any sign of uncertainty, reaching the Cape of Good Hope after an unprecedented thirteen weeks out of sight of land. His fleet consisted of three naos, full-rigged ships, one of them a supply vessel intended to be emptied and broken up en route, and a caravel, all heavily armed. Proceeding through the Madagascar Channel, da Gama obtained an Arab pilot and, catching the south-west monsoon, arrived at Calicut on the Malabar coast in late May 1498.

Da Gama's reception was unenthusiastic, for the Portuguese, not expecting to find a sophisticated civilization, had brought with them trade goods – cheap textiles, coral beads, hawk's bells and the like – suitable for exchange on the African coast. Calicut's Hindu ruler, the zamorin, scorned da Gama's goods and subjected his party to harassment and humiliation. That notwithstanding, the Portuguese obtained a cargo of pepper, cloves, cinnamon and other spices and set off for home, reaching Lisbon on 28 September 1499.

SÓDRÉ (1)
5 caravels
2 naos

DA GAMA
6 carracks
2 naos

(4)

The second Portuguese expedition, comprising ten ships under Pedro Cabral, departed from Lisbon in March 1500 and reached Calicut in September. As before, the reception was ambiguous: the zamorin was willing to do business with the Portuguese and assigned them facilities ashore, but refused to expel Muslim traders as they insisted. Muslim–Christian enmity spiralled out of control and a massacre of Portuguese ensued. Cabral took his survivors aboard and bombarded

A near-contemporary depiction of the ships of Pedro Cabral's 1500 expedition to India. Note the mix of carracks, caravels and naos. Cabral encountered storms in the Atlantic and, as the picture suggests, several vessels were sunk or turned back. Only six reached India. En route, Cabral made the first recorded landing by Europeans on the Brazilian coast, claiming the land for Portugal. The sources treat this feat with an offhandedness that suggests an earlier discovery.

the port in retaliation, wreaking havoc before sailing to Cochin and Cannanore – nominally the zamorin's vassals but rivals eager to ally with the Portuguese – to top off his cargo. He reached Lisbon in the summer of 1501, with a cargo of spices that had been purchased cheaply so as to ensure enormous profits, all the more so as news of the Portuguese bombardment of the principal Indian spice emporium drove prices sharply upwards.

The third Portuguese expedition sailed in March 1502, under da Gama. Consisting of six carracks, four naos and five caravels, to be followed by an additional five small ships in May, it differed from its predecessors in that it was organized and equipped to establish a permanent presence in Asian waters. Reaching India by autumn, da Gama established a blockade of Calicut, basing his forces on ports hostile to the zamorin, or at least susceptible to Portuguese pressure. Brutally enforced, the blockade extended to the transport of Turks and pepper, striking not only at Calicut, but at the Egyptian Mameluke sultanate's tax base. During the winter, the zamorin and Muslim merchants mustered their forces and prepared to confront da Gama with two squadrons, one of sixty prahus and small craft assembled locally and the other of twenty Red Sea dhows, under a commander seconded by the Mamelukes. They planned to descend on the Portuguese in port while they were loading spices for the return trip, but da Gama was tipped off by local agents and avoided the trap. Still, the odds weighed heavily against the Portuguese. The zamorin boasted of a twenty to one advantage in ships, and spies advised da Gama that he was outnumbered ten to one.

They met off Calicut in February 1503, the Portuguese standing northwards on an offshore breeze in two squadrons, five caravels and two or three of the smaller, and more weatherly, naos under da Gama's principal subordinate, Vicente Sodre, in the lead, followed by the carracks and the remaining naos under da Gama. According to the chronicler Gaspar Correia, da Gama ordered 'the caravels to come one astern of the other in a line … firing their guns as much as they could, and he did the same with the carracks to their rear.' His clear intent was to fight a stand-off artillery action. The caravels, with crews of only thirty, carried 'four heavy guns below, and six falcons above (two of them firing astern), and ten breech-loaders placed on the quarter deck and in the bows'. The carracks carried 'six guns on each side below, with two smaller ones at the poop and the prow and eight falcons and many smaller breech-loaders on deck, with two smaller guns that fired forward'. The guns carried 'below' were probably *camelos* or *cameletes* firing stone shot of 12 to 18 pounds; the falcons were large swivel guns firing stone balls of about 4 pounds or, more likely, scatter shot; the breech-loaders were *berços*, swivel guns with a bore of about 2 inches firing scatter shot.

The Muslims closed from the north, the Red Sea dhows in the lead and local craft behind forming two heterogeneous squadrons, strung out and ill-ordered. Working shorewards to gain the weather gauge, Sodre's squadron engaged the dhows, using his broadside ordnance to good effect: the first volleys left the Egyptian admiral's vessel dismasted and sinking. Handily avoiding Muslim attempts to close and board, Sodre's caravels left shattered hulls in their wake. As da Gama's squadron took care of the surviving dhows, Sodre engaged the local craft, sailing straight through the mass, wreaking havoc with heavy ordnance and swivel guns. Muslim gunfire and archery was intense, but, apart from swivel gunners who sustained the bulk of the casualties, the Portuguese were safe behind their ship's solid bulwarks. In a matter of hours it was over, with the surviving Muslims fleeing for the safety of land.

The Atlantic and Indo-Arab spheres of warfare at sea merged, with enormous consequences. Henceforth, merchants who sailed the Indian Ocean without *cartazes*, licences purchased from the Portuguese, did so at risk to life, limb and property. The cost of spices in Europe escalated, to the benefit of the Portuguese crown and the Flemish port of Antwerp, where the Portuguese marketed their goods. Traditional brokers found ways to circumvent Portuguese authority, however, and the Levant trade largely recovered within a decade. But in the interim the Mameluke sultanate had lost much of its revenue, creating a power vacuum that the Ottoman sultans would fill. Challenges to Portuguese control of the Indian Ocean would henceforth come from without.

The first of these, a Mediterranean galley fleet formed in the Red Sea, was mounted under the aegis of the Mameluke sultanate, bankrolled in part by Italian commercial interests and commanded, and largely manned, by expert artillerists and mariners seconded by the Ottomans. With the sultan of Gujarat's aid, it defeated a Portuguese squadron at Chaul, on India's western coast, in 1508 and at heavy cost, only to be annihilated by a Portuguese counterstroke at Diu the next year. It was the furthest eastward penetration of a Mediterranean empire. The Portuguese in their turn consolidated under Affonso d'Albuquerque, governor general of the Estado da India, Portugal's Indian possessions (1509–15) and the architect of Portugal's empire, seizing Goa, on India's western coast, as a permanent base in 1510, and in 1511 taking Malacca, the principal emporium linking the Indo-Arab and Chinese commercial spheres. Probing eastwards, the Portuguese unsuccessfully tested Ming China during the 1520s – that they would even try, given the staggering disparity in resources, is breathtaking – and in 1535 established a factory (and bridgehead for Jesuit missionaries) in Vietnam. They found the kingdom of Prester John – in fact, Ethiopia – and in the late 1540s saved it from defeat at the hands of an expanding Ottoman-surrogate Somali Muslim kingdom. By the late 1550s, exploiting Ming China's corrupt administrative underbelly, the Portuguese had secured the approval of local officials to establish a trading station at Macao in order to tap into the Japanese trade with China, otherwise forbidden by Ming decree.

The Portuguese were not universally successful. Their attempt to take the port of Aden, at the head of the Red Sea, failed in 1513, although by way of compensation Albuquerque took by coup the island of Ormuz, at the head of the Persian Gulf, in 1515. In 1517 an audacious attempt to capture Jiddah, gateway to the holy city of Mecca, was repulsed by a Mameluke force under a seconded Ottoman commander. The sultans of Aceh, with Ottoman technical assistance, established themselves as a local sea power and, in combination with Gujarati merchants sailing stout junks, largely restored the traditional spice trade. Nevertheless, by the 1520s the Portuguese were solidly ensconced in the Indian Ocean as a transoceanic empire, the first of its kind.

CHAPTER THREE

CARAVELS
AND CARRACKS

WOODCUT OF A CARRACK *by Willem A. Cruce, drawn in preparation for the 1468 wedding celebrations of Charles the Bold of Burgundy and Mary of York. At one of the wedding banquets large models of carracks, symbolizing the Duke's power, graced the serving platters of roast meat and the woodcut was used to guide the model-builders. Accurate and informative, it is the earliest depiction of a carrack – kraeck in Flemish – explicitly identified as such. Gunpowder was clearly expected to play a subsidiary role in combat. The vessel's offensive punch was the overhanging forecastle, a point underlined by the grappling hook beneath the bowsprit. The circular holes in the fore and stern castle rails were no doubt loopholes for crossbowmen and handgunners.*

CARAVELS AND CARRACKS

Scale model of the so-called Bremen cog in the Deutsches Shiffahrtsmuseum, Bremerhaven, based on the hull of an early fourteenth-century cog recovered almost intact from the Weser River in 1962. A high proportion of our knowledge of the design and construction of cogs derives from study of the recovered hull. The Bremen cog also formed the basis for a full-sized reconstruction that proved to have surprisingly good sailing qualities, though the vessel was wet in all but the gentlest seas.

THE EVOLUTION OF European sailing vessels capable of projecting power overseas was anything but straightforward, nor is the process completely understood today. The designs ancestral to the ships-of-the-line, frigates and specialized bulk carriers of the eighteenth century established their lineages not because they were necessarily superior to their competitors on the high seas, but because they were well suited for conditions in their home waters, and because those who operated them had incentives and resources to modify their designs and construction progressively in order to operate further from home. This was certainly true of the cog, the most important sailing warship in northern European waters at the dawn of the gunpowder era.

The cog's origins lay in Anglo-Saxon designs that were no more seaworthy or efficient than their contemporary Viking ships. But as trade expanded, the cog's owners and operators modified it, refining the efficiency of its rig, making it larger to increase cargo capacity, replacing the steering oar with a pintle-and-gudgeon rudder, thus making further increases in size feasible, and so on. Throughout all of this, the cog retained its single mast and square sail, keel, flat bottom, with flush-joined planking, straight stem and sternposts and clinker upper planking. So successful was the cog that certain features of its design, particularly the sternpost rudder and square sail, were widely adopted in the Mediterranean for use in conditions quite different from those in which it had evolved. Ultimately, certain design features, notably the single mast and square sail that limited its size and handiness, rendered the cog obsolete and it gave way first to the hulk and then to the full-rigged ship. Similarly, the cog's flat bottom, which was useful for loading and unloading in small ports with extreme tides, became irrelevant for large vessels, as trade swelled in volume and as an increasing proportion passed through major ports with wharves and proper loading facilities. Over the long haul, then, it was not just the inherent qualities of a type of ship that counted, but also who operated it, why, and with what resources. Of this there is no better example than the caravel.

The caravel began as an Atlantic fishing boat, incorporating a mixture of Atlantic and Mediterranean design features. When it becomes identifiable as a distinct type in the fourteenth century, the smallest was an open boat with a single mast. The defining characteristics were a flush-planked hull built skeleton first – that is, carvel-built – a sternpost rudder, lateen rig and, above all, a reputation for seaworthiness and weatherliness. Caravels' hulls had a length-to-breadth ratio of nearly five to one (by comparison, that of cogs was just over two to one). At this point, the caravel was one type of deep-sea ship among many, and it is unlikely that it would have supplanted the ancestors of the nao (about which more below) had not Portugal's kings embarked on an aggressive campaign of exploration along the African coast. The caravel proved ideal for this, and by the 1440s was the preferred vessel. The caravels that found their way to India probably displaced from 80 to 130 tons; most had three masts, the largest had four. Although lateen sails were awkward for frequent tacking – to come about, the sail had to be furled and the foot of the boom brought around the front of the mast – they were more weatherly than contemporary square sails and ideal for the long reaches out into the Atlantic that were needed to reach the Cape of Good Hope. Eventually a mixed rig, with the foremast square-rigged and the rest lateen, proved best. In Columbus' day caravels were superior to naos in terms of their seaworthiness and weatherliness, but could not be made as large without sacrificing their sailing characteristics. In addition, caravels lacked cargo capacity, and for extended voyages the Portuguese routinely supported caravels with supply ships, naos, that were abandoned when their stores were depleted.

The Portuguese also used caravels as warships from the 1450s to defend the Guinea trade from Castilian and French interlopers. The caravel's weatherliness and superior speed in moderate conditions provided an effective defence against boarding – a point of vulnerability because of the caravel's low freeboard – but guns were needed to make the caravel an effective warship. The caravel's stability and low freeboard enabled the Portuguese to mount heavy ordnance on her main deck, firing over the bulwarks or through apertures within them. The caravel's small size dictated that these pieces would be few in number – perhaps only one – mounted amidships to fire broadside; there was no other option. Furthermore, their weight topside posed stability problems, even in moderate seas; the guns were therefore stowed below and hoisted up only when battle was imminent. The four lifting lugs atop Portuguese *camelos* and *cameletes* – and lifting lugs they surely were, although they may also have served other purposes – are clear, if indirect evidence, of this. When the Portuguese began using heavily gunned caravels we cannot say, but the matter-of-fact competence with which they were used in early encounters in the Indian Ocean suggests that it was well before they turned the Cape of Good Hope.

The caravel represented only a partial and specialized solution to the problem of combining heavy ordnance with ocean-going sailing capabilities. Confronted by a carrack or large nao, a caravel could avoid combat because of its superior weatherliness and, under ideal conditions, bombard from afar; but it could not close in for the kill without being overwhelmed from above by anti-personnel

weapons. The problem was exacerbated in the early 1500s when carracks began carrying heavy ordnance low in the hull. Caravels retained their utility throughout the sixteenth century, but were never first-line warships in European waters.

Meanwhile, the design of naos – precursors to the full-rigged ship, more stoutly built than caravels and with beamier and more capacious hulls – progressively improved. They were better cargo-carriers from the outset and, as they became more seaworthy and weatherly, the caravel's advantages dwindled. At the turn of the sixteenth century, caravels still enjoyed significant advantages in terms of their speed and weatherliness – the contrast in performance between Columbus' lubberly *Santa Maria*, a nao, and the caravel *Niña* is an apt illustration – but the caravel had reached an evolutionary dead end. The future lay with the ship, of which, for a considerable time, the carrack was the most important type built for war.

The full-rigged ship emerged from a fusion of Atlantic and Mediterranean technologies that began during the thirteenth century and accelerated rapidly from about 1300. At that time, deep-sea Atlantic vessels had a single mast, a single square sail and, if they were of any significant size, a sternpost pintle-and-gudgeon rudder. With the exception of the cog's flush-planked bottom, they were built shell first of lapstrake construction. Mediterranean sailing vessels were built skeleton first with flush planking nailed to the frames, were lateen-rigged and had

Two carracks from an illustration in the so-called Warwick Roll (c. 1480), detailing the activities of the Earl of Warwick. The exaggerated size of the human figures notwithstanding, the carracks are clearly large, as indicated by their double mizzen masts. Note the bombards protruding over the midship rail of the closer one.

The outbound 1519 Portuguese India fleet, from a book published half a century afterwards. Despite the time lapse, the ship depictions are credible. Most are carracks, though the vessel with the triple lateen mizzen is clearly a caravel.

quarter rudders. Vessels of any significant size had two masts and acquired a third from about 1400. The ensuing process of borrowing and adaptation was complex, and the precise sequence debatable, but the outlines are clear: Mediterranean shipwrights borrowed first sternpost rudder and then square rig; Atlantic shipwrights adopted multiple masts and began setting a lateen sail on the rearmost to aid in trimming the ship.

The next crucial step was the adoption of skeleton-first, carvel construction by Atlantic shipwrights. The reasons for the shift are unclear; skeleton-first construction was less dependent upon traditional skills and probably cheaper, although how important those factors were we cannot say. More importantly over the long term, shell-first hulls were built by eye, whereas skeleton-first construction required systematic planning. Frames had to be lofted and the shape of the hull determined before the planking was applied, rewarding those who planned best and bringing better designs to the fore more rapidly. That began happening in Europe with increasing frequency; it did not elsewhere, however – a

matter of no small importance. Finally, carvel construction was more adaptable to the strengthening needed to accommodate the weight and recoil of heavy guns.

By the 1450s, the process outlined above had produced the nao, a carvel-built vessel with a pintle-and-gudgeon rudder, three masts and a bowsprit. The hull had a length three to five times the breadth, with permanent fighting structures at bow and stern. The fore- and mainmasts were square-rigged and the mizzenmast lateen-rigged, while a square spritsail was hung beneath the bowsprit. By the century's end, topmasts were being fitted to carry square topsails, further increasing the power of the rig. The result was the full-rigged ship, or simply ship. Hulls became progressively more seaworthy and efficient, and by the mid 1500s well-designed ships could perform as well as caravels. They did not, however, dominate in battle; that distinction fell to the carrack.

Carrack has a fairly specific meaning in English and other northern European languages, but this is not true elsewhere, and terminology can be misleading. The idea behind the carrack was nevertheless clear: to gain tactical advantage from

A large Portuguese carrack, almost surely the Santa Catarina do Monte Sinai, *about 1520, shown with a twenty-four-bank ordinary galley* alla sensile, *right foreground, in a painting attributed to Joachim Patinir (1485–1524). All three carracks in the centre appear to be different views of the same ship. Square main- and foresails were not lowered for furling, as shown here, until much later. The mainsail has two laced-on bonnets to extend its area.*

size and height, particularly by means of the high, projecting forecastle and large fighting tops that were the carrack's distinguishing features. Carracks might be clinker-built, carvel-built or a combination of both. Nor was the carrack defined by sail plan and rigging: some early carracks had two masts, or even one. It became an important type only after its hull and fighting superstructures were combined with the ship's sail plan.

The carrack emerged from a dual need: to secure cargoes from piratical attack and to project armed might afloat. Assuming a seaworthy and reasonably

An anonymous 1520 Flemish woodcut showing the provisioning of a carrack. The crew are embarking in disorder, no doubt under the influence of alcohol; the hoisted stein in the hand of the sailor on the quarterdeck is indicative! The artist's depiction of individual weapons is exemplary, making the absence of firearms all the more noteworthy. The absence of lidded gunports is noteworthy as well.

weatherly vessel, which the ship-rigged carrack was, sheer size and height served both purposes, and by the first decades of the fifteenth century it had acquired its characteristic form. This is shown in the engraving of a *kraeck* by the Dutch master WA (Willem Cruce) and the Warwick Roll illustrations. Depicting carracks of about 1476 and 1480 respectively, these sources provide telling details. Forecastles are considerably higher than stern castles, indicating the preferred tactics: to come alongside the enemy vessel bow first, grapple to hold the enemy fast – the grappling hook dangling prominently from the bowsprit of WA's

carrack makes the point – dominate the enemy's waist with missile fire, board
and capture. As we saw in our discussion of Zonchio, gunpowder ordnance did
little to change this tactical prescription at first, and the small bombards that
were initially the carrack's main gunpowder weapons were primarily defensive.
This is clear on WA's carrack: the stern gallery and mizzen crow's-nest are armed
with guns, whereas the waist and forecastle have none. Moreover, the main- and
foremast crow's-nests have hoists for stones and are liberally festooned with gads.

Carracks were the first sailing ships to mount heavy guns low in the hull

behind watertight gunports, although when and where is unclear. A strong, albeit undocumented, tradition attributes the invention of the watertight gunport to a French shipwright in around 1500, and there may be a grain of truth in this: the large French ship *La Cordelière*, built during the 1490s, was armed with sixteen large guns on the lower deck, and it is difficult to see how else they could have been mounted. Be this as it may, the first really effective heavy guns aboard sailing ships were a defensive response to the galley: basilisks firing through ports on either side of the carrack's rudder in what would become known as the gunroom.

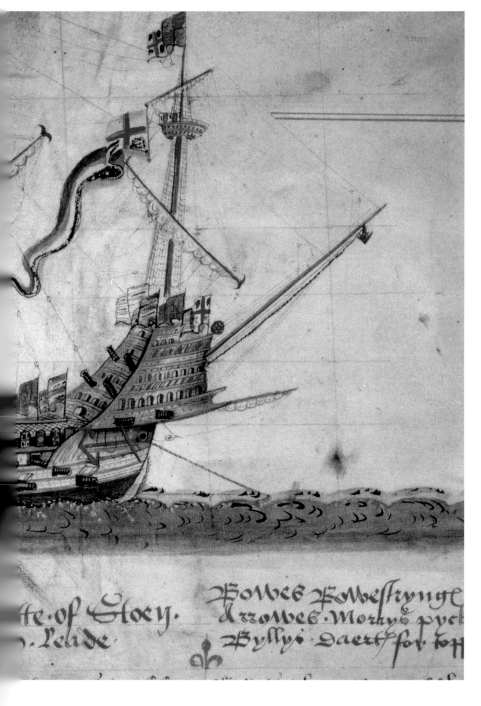

The famous Mary Rose *depicted on the Anthony Anthony Roll of 1545. Built in 1509,* Mary Rose's *original displacement was about 1,050 tons. Here she is shown after rebuilding in 1536. Anthony recorded her armament as including two cannon, two demi-cannon, two culverins, two sakers and one falcon, all bronze, and a considerable number of wrought iron pieces, notably twelve port-pieces, large breech-loaders intended for use afloat. Sunk by misadventure off Portsmouth on 19 July 1545, most of her hull was recovered by nautical archaeology in the 1970s and is now on display in Portsmouth. By the time of her sinking, her forecastle had been considerably reduced in height.*

To modern sensibilities, a rearward-firing mount seems a peculiar location for one's heaviest ordnance, but there were good reasons for the choice. Given the carrack's underwater lines, the stern was the only place to mount really heavy ordnance, and the carrack's flat counter was a logical place to experiment with watertight ports. Finally, when conditions were calm enough for galleys to stalk carracks they were also sufficiently calm for the carrack's crew to put out boats and kedges to slew the ship into position to return fire.

When and where this first happened is unknown, but the first strategically meaningful use of heavy guns on sailing ships was by King James IV of Scotland against land targets. The evidence is by inference, but clear: we know that James's carracks mounted heavy ordnance, and in asserting royal authority over Scotland's Western Isles, his forces reduced by gunfire in 1504 the island fortress of Cairn-na-Burgh, over a mile from the nearest landfall. Atlantic shipwrights soon learned to cut watertight ports in carracks' curving sides and, by the 1520s, heavy broadside ordnance was common. That does not mean that the 'broadside sailing ship' had been discovered, however. To the contrary: ideas about how best to mount and use heavy ordnance aboard sailing ships were in flux, with the apparent goal to maximize the weight of fire directed forwards, no doubt to match the galley's main, centre-line gun. The carrack's hull form put this goal effectively beyond reach, but did not discourage attempts to attain it. When *Mary Rose* went down in 1545, she mounted a bronze, 9-pound demi-culverin on a truck carriage – presumably one of a pair, and one of the best and most modern

A MEDIUM SIZED IBERIAN CARRACK *c.* 1500

This carrack is ship-rigged, that is, it carries square sails set on the fore- and main masts and a lateen sail on the mizzen. Columbus's Santa Maria *was not all that different from the ship depicted here, though some 10 feet shorter at the waterline and only lightly armed. Like* Santa Maria, *the vessel shown was probably called a nao, reflecting a general lack of consistency and precision in terminology.*

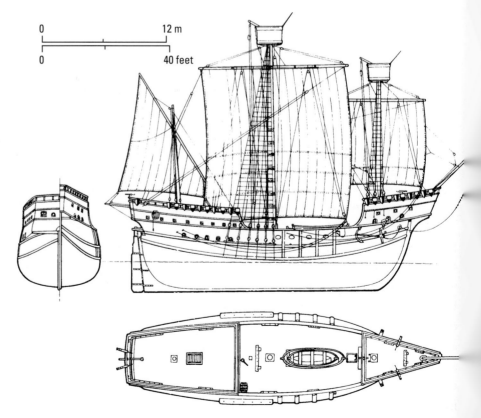

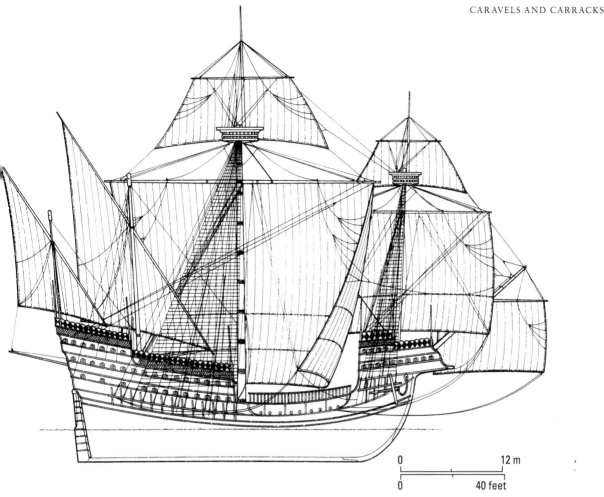

0   12 m

0   40 feet

guns on board – atop the forward end of the stern castle, firing obliquely forwards past the forecastle.

For all the guns aboard the carrack from the 1510s, size and height were still its chief tactical virtues, more so as carracks were efficient bulk carriers. This was particularly true in Eastern waters, where the main threat was boarders from smaller craft. In European waters the cannon-armed war galley was the problem, and galleys rarely ventured on to the high seas beyond the English Channel and the Mediterranean. The Portuguese appreciated these factors, and caravels soon gave way to ever-large carracks on the Carreira das Indias, the annual spice convoy.

To recapitulate, the heavily armed caravel was an expedient that perfectly suited Portugal's initial thrust into the Indian Ocean, but declined in utility once the Portuguese had suppressed local opposition afloat. The caravel did not spawn the long-term solution to the problem of mounting heavy guns on sailing warships, nor did its use by the Portuguese stimulate the further development of broadside tactics. Carracks could carry impressive numbers of heavy guns low in the hull, but those guns were mainly for defence. The carrack's underwater lines, and the bulk and weight of the forecastle, effectively ruled out heavy bowchasers, and its high freeboard and towering castles made it a poor sailor windward. Carracks retained their utility well into the seventeenth century, but the carrack, like the caravel, was doomed to reach an evolutionary dead end.

SANTA CATARINA DO MONTE SINAI

A modern drawing of Santa Catarina do Monte Sinai in about 1520. For all her size – she was one of the largest warships of her day – she carried no heavy ordnance below decks; most of her 140 guns were relatively light railing pieces or swivel guns.

THE RISE OF SWEDISH SEA POWER, 1535–70

Although the details are unclear, heavy shipboard guns appeared in the Baltic towards the beginning of the sixteenth century, paralleling contemporary developments in the Atlantic. Their strategic impact, however, was quite different, reflecting the geographic, economic and political peculiarities of the region.

In the Baltic, as in the Mediterranean, warfare at sea in the Middle Ages was fought primarily over trade and was dominated by mercantile city states. There the similarities end. Unlike their Italian equivalents, the German port cities of the Baltic made a common cause, banding together in a trade cartel called the

Hanseatic League (Hanse). Their foremost city was Lübeck, whose wealth and importance derived from its location at the base of the Jutland peninsula, connecting the Baltic and Atlantic through Hamburg. Most trade was in bulk commodities – grain, fish, timber, salt and naval stores – and the Hanseatic cities lacked the power to control extensive territories. The Hanseatic towns were important centres of seafaring and shipbuilding and possessed the financial wherewithal to turn their trading fleets into war fleets by hiring mercenaries and later by manufacturing and purchasing guns. The Hanse's use of trade as a weapon was effective, but brought it into conflict with the emerging monarchies of the region, notably Denmark–Norway, whose ability to tax shipping in the Sound, the narrow passage connecting the Baltic with the North Sea, gave Danish kings a source of revenue beyond the control of the land-holding aristocracy that could be used to build a navy. By the 1510s, that navy was well provided with guns and included some of the largest warships in the world.

The Swedish nobility had revolted against Danish rule in 1501, and King Christian II (who ruled Denmark from 1513 to 1523) used his fleet to reassert his sovereignty, occupying Stockholm in 1520. Under the leadership of Gustav Vasa, the Swedes responded by building up their naval strength, initially by purchasing armed merchantmen from the Hanse and then with an indigenous building programme. The struggle acquired a new dimension in 1523 when Christian was overthrown by rebellious nobles and fled with his fleet to the Netherlands, from whence he sought to return with Habsburg support. Growing Swedish naval strength, helped by an infusion of assets seized while reforming the church in 1527, enabled Gustav to consolidate his power. Christian's threatened intervention materialized in 1531, in the form of an invasion of Norway, but the Baltic forces – Denmark, Sweden and the Hanse – banded together and defeated it, capturing Christian. Lübeck played the role of spoiler, siding first with the Swedes – a Lübeckian fleet took Stockholm for Gustav in 1522 – and then with one or the other of the contenders for the Danish throne, but consistently striving for commercial advantage and gaining control of Copenhagen and the Sound between 1534 and 1535.

The struggle was effectively resolved when a combined Swedish–Danish force defeated Lübeck's fleet between 1535 and 1536, landing an army that secured Copenhagen

Plan of a mid sixteenth-century Swedish warship. A comparatively small vessel, it has a broadside battery of ten guns a side, no doubt newly cast of Swedish bronze, and a full ship rig. At this point, Scandinavian naval architecture was rapidly approaching par with the best European practice. Not ordinarily required to cruise far from home, Swedish warships could carry heavier offensive ordnance at the expense of provisions.

THE BALTIC, 1563–70

The sixteenth century saw momentous change in power relationships in the Baltic, driven by the increasing importance of gunpowder at sea and the political fallout of the Reformation. Fuelled by taxes levied on shipping in the leads connecting the Baltic and Atlantic, Denmark built up its fleet and by the 1510s possessed a powerful navy. But the Swedes rose against Danish rule in 1501 and – though it took over three decades – established Vasa-ruled Sweden as a major power. Both Sweden and Denmark went Protestant, converting Church property to royal control, and in 1525 the Grand Master of the Teutonic Knights declared himself a Lutheran, and dissolved the order. The Livonian Knights, earlier absorbed by the Teutonic order, briefly asserted their independence only to have their territories carved up by Russia, Poland–Lithuania, and Sweden. Meanwhile, Denmark and the Hanseatic League lost out to the cannon-armed Swedish navy in the struggle for Baltic hegemony.

and the island of Zealand for Christian III, the Protestant claimant to the Danish throne. Nevertheless, Habsburg intervention in favour of Christian II remained a possibility until 1544 when Emperor Charles V abandoned his cause. Meanwhile, the Swedes and Danes eyed one another warily and the Swedes continued their naval programme, building a significant galley fleet from the 1540s.

Apart from the emergence of Sweden as an independent power, the most important consequence of this struggle was the imposition of a *pax Baltica*, whereby Sweden and Denmark purged the Baltic of piracy by implicit agreement. Neither nation had a large merchant marine, and the principal beneficiaries of this policy were the Dutch, whose efficient unarmed ships swelled their profits. The next decades saw a steady rise in Swedish naval power, marked by the mass production of bronze cannon and the construction between 1560 and 1563 of seven major warships of 600–1,800 tons displacement, as well as smaller vessels. Swedish attempts to regulate trade in the eastern and northern Baltic inevitably led to friction with Denmark and Lübeck, and the accession in Sweden and Denmark of Erik XIV (who ruled Sweden from 1560 to 1568) and Frederik II (Denmark's king from 1559 to 1588), both young, ambitious and energetic, led to war.

Danish interference with Erik's plans to marry a Hessian princess provided the *casus belli*. On 30 May 1563 Danish and Swedish squadrons joined in battle off Bornholm in the first of seven major naval engagements in what historian Jan Glete has termed the first modern naval war, modern in the sense that fleets fought not to transport armies to their objectives, but to achieve what naval theorists would later term control of the sea. The battles were hard-fought and chaotic, and the details have been largely lost, but some generalizations can be made. The Danes and Lübeckers preferred traditional tactics of boarding and entering, while the Swedes, with a newly formed navy and lacking in maritime traditions, relied on stand-off gunnery, often using booms to hold enemy ships at bay while the guns took their toll. Both fleets organized their vessels in groups of three, with two smaller ships supporting a larger one, reflecting Edward III's tactical arrangements at Sluys two centuries earlier. With the Danes and Lübeckers, the intent seems to have been to provide reinforcements for the larger ship that played the pivotal role in a boarding fight. The Swedes seem to have relied on the gunfire of the larger ship, using the smaller ones in support where necessary. All three navies possessed large warships, although the Danes and Lübeckers continued to place heavy reliance on armed merchantmen. Purpose-built Swedish warships increasingly asserted their superiority as the war progressed.

The climactic engagement was the second battle of Bornholm, on 7 July 1565, in which a Swedish fleet of 49 ships, under Klas Horn, engaged 22 Danish and 14 Lübeck ships, under the Danish admiral Otto Rud. The allies began the engagement shortly after noon with the advantage of the wind, Rud laying his flagship, *Jegermesther,* alongside Horn's *St Erik*, both vessels of 90 guns although we know nothing of their size. In the chaotic action that followed, the Swedish

The Baltic 1563–70

- 🏛 headquarters of Hanseatic League
- ◆ member city of the Hanseatic League
- → trade routes
- amber trade goods
- Livonian Knights
- ◎ the Sound, source of Danish tax receipts

- Russian territory
- Swedish territory
- Danish territory
- Polish territory c. 1570
- under Polish suzerainty

Barents Sea

Norwegian Sea

LAPP NOMADS

White Sea

Kola Peninsula

RUSSIA

Arctic Circle

Trondheim

NORWAY

SWEDEN

FINLAND

Finland

Gulf of Bothnia

Lake Onega

Lake Ladoga

Bergen
Hansa
priviledges
lost 1559

Oslo

Uppsala

Åland

Helsingfors

Gulf of Finland

Reval
Wessenberg

Narva

Ivangorod

slaves, furs, amber

Novgorod

Tver

Stockholm

Norrköping

Estonia
LIVONIAN
KNIGHTS

Dorpat

Pskov

Helmed

Alvsborg
(Gothenburg)

Gotland

Visby

Wenden

Livonia

Riga
grain, timber, naval stores

Corland

Velikiye Luki

fish

Skagerrak

grain

North
Sea

Varberg

Kalmar

Öland

Dünaburg

Polotsk

Smolensk

Kattegat

DENMARK

Baltic Sea

Memel

Kovno

Chasniki

to Western Europe

Copenhagen

Lund

Funen Zealand

Bornholm

grain, timber, naval stores

wine, salt

Königsberg

Holstein

Stralsund

Rostock

Danzig

Elbing

PRUSSIA

POLAND-
LITHUANIA

Wismar

Stettin

Lübeck

Hamburg

Groningen

Bremen

Lüneburg

BRADENBURG

Berlin

Warsaw

SMALL STATES

Grip was rammed and sunk by a large Lübecker and the battle resolved itself into a series of ship-to-ship duels that emanated outwards from the flagships. The issue was settled after nightfall when the Swedish *Gyllende Lejon* caught fire and exploded, scattering the two fleets and leaving *Jegermesther* surrounded. Rud struck his colours at 21.30 hours.

Jegermesther surrendered, with 1,100 killed or captured; a Danish vessel and a Lübecker were sunk. The Swedes lost *Grip* and *Gyllende Lejon* as well as a third ship captured, losing 362 killed and 523 seriously wounded, in addition to the complements of the vessels lost, significantly fewer casualties than the allies. The Swedes had taken the measure of their more experienced enemies; stand-off gunnery was their chosen instrument. It was a major benchmark in warfare at sea.

By 1566 the Swedish advantage was apparent. After a partial and indecisive engagement off Öland on 26 July 1566, the allies disengaged. Two days later an unseasonable storm struck, and 11 Danish and 3 Lübeckian ships were driven ashore, with the loss of some 6,000 men. The Swedes also suffered damage, particularly among their larger ships, but weathered the storm. The Swedish navy was unchallenged in 1567, but domestic turmoil attending Erik XIV's overthrow the following year prevented the Swedes from pressing home their advantage and the war ended in mutual exhaustion in 1570.

As far as the Scandinavian kingdoms were concerned, the result was a draw in political terms. Denmark was forced to accept Swedish independence while Sweden was unable to bring Denmark to heel. Operationally, the war demonstrated that merchant ships fitted for war by adding men and guns could not stand up to purpose-built warships armed with heavy guns. Lacking the resources to build a specialized war fleet, and undercut commercially by increasingly efficient Dutch shipping, Lübeck was finished as a major power.

The Baltic War of 1563 to 1570 was a milestone, not only in naval strategy but – or so we surmise – in the design and construction of purpose-built, artillery-armed sailing warships. Unfortunately, we know little about them. The Baltic is small, so they did not have to be provisioned for extended voyages. In principle, more and heavier guns could have replaced provisions. In fact the Swedes seem to have done just that, although the details are missing. Our one firm data point is a single ship, the Lübeck-built *Jesus of Lübeck*, a carrack of some 1,050 tons displacement. Purchased by Henry VIII of England in 1544, and documented in the Anthony Anthony Roll, an illustrated naval ordnance inventory of 1545, she ended her career in September 1568 as part of John Hawkins's ill-fated expedition to New Spain, caught with the carrack *Minion* and the small barque *Judith* in the harbour of San Juan de Ulloa (Vera Cruz, Mexico) by the entire Flota de Nueva España, the annual treasure fleet. A blistering artillery duel ensued, and within an hour English gunfire had 'blown up' the *Almirante* [the vice flagship] and so shattered the *Capitana* [the flagship] and another vessel that they settled to the bottom'. *Minion* and *Judith* escaped. *Jesus*

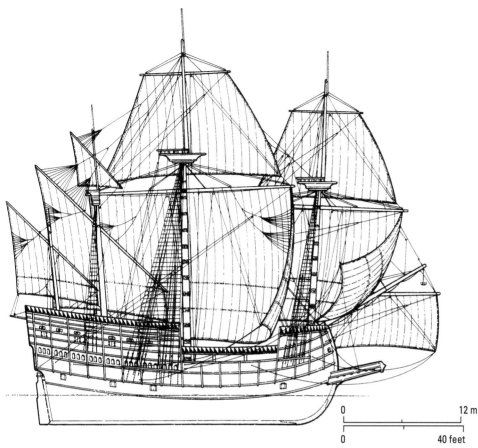

A modern rendering of an armed merchantman, probably Flemish, based on a 1565 drawing by Pieter Brueghel the Elder. The ship's type is indeterminate, but the projecting beakhead suggests an affinity with the galleon. The standing and running rigging and sail plan are fully developed and are representative of those of large European sailing vessels until the advent of the spritsail topmast around 1600. Lateen topsails, shown here on the mizzen mast, must have been terribly awkward to work.

was abandoned, to be meticulously surveyed by Spanish scribes. Due to their labours, and the Anthony Roll, we know a good deal about her armament.

Her biggest guns were 24–25 pounders (I have calculated projectile sizes based on the recorded barrel weights). She had only nine of these: two in the gunroom in chase and seven on the main gundeck; three of the nine were pedreros. Her heaviest pieces were two bronze culverins in the foremost broadside ports; her upper gundeck included two 6–8-pound sakers in the stern chase and two 10–12-pound half-culverins at the bow. We must be careful, for if *Jesus* was Lübeck-built she was armed in England. Nevertheless, she was probably representative of the more heavily armed merchantmen that contended for control of the Baltic between 1563 and 1570. Just over 2 per cent of her displacement tonnage consisted of ordnance, on average only a third as much as the race-built English galleons that defeated the Spanish Armada in 1588. The first race-built galleon was launched in 1573, so the comparison is not inappropriate, although we should remember that *Jesus* was armed and fitted out to cruise – and trade – far from home. That *Jesus* and *Minion* could wreak havoc on what we must presume to have been the most heavily armed and best-manned Spanish galleons of their day speaks volumes for their effectiveness as gun platforms. It also suggests that the Swedish warships that took the measure of the best that Denmark and Lübeck had to offer between 1563 and 1570 must have been extraordinarily well armed for their day.

CHAPTER FOUR

THE GALLEY

Lepanto, the climactic battle in the struggle for control of the Mediterranean between the Ottoman Turks and Christendom, shown here on a Venetian mural with the cartography of the site. Lepanto was the largest galley fight ever and one of the hardest fought. Some 208 Christian galleys and 6 galleasses carrying some 80,000 men engaged 230 Muslim galleys and 70 galiots, many of them large North African craft nearly as large as galleys, carrying 90,000. Here, the two fleets are shown twice, in pre-battle array on the sides and locked in combat in the centre. In fact, neither side came on so neatly arrayed but the artist has accurately depicted the fustas *and* bergantines *backing up the Christian line.*

THE GALLEY

FROM CLASSICAL TIMES, seagoing ships in European waters fell into two principal categories: round ships driven by sails and intended for trade, and long ships driven by oars and meant for war. In fact, it was not quite that simple: the crews of oared warships often carried trade goods and, in the Mediterranean, larger relatives of oared fighting vessels, driven by sails, but using oars to overcome adverse winds and currents, were used to transport precious cargoes from antiquity until the sixteenth century, when rising wages and improvements in sailing-ship design rendered them uncompetitive. Before heavy gunpowder ordnance became common these large galleys had important military advantages. Our main concern here is the evolution of the Mediterranean ordinary galley – a warship propelled by eighteen or more banks of oars worked from fixed benches mounted on a continuous upper deck – and from that perspective the distinction between long ship and round ship is valid. For completeness we should note that the term galley applied loosely to all specialized oared vessels and had the subsidiary meaning of 'warship'.

The reasons for the divergence in design were straightforward. In antiquity, ship-to-ship fights were generally decided in hand-to-hand combat. Numbers counted, and faster, more manoeuvrable vessels could bring more men into action more swiftly. Early sailing ships moved against the wind with difficulty, and the logical solution was a long, low-lying hull driven by oars. A narrow hull with parallel sides maximized the number of oarsmen as a function of displacement, while a low freeboard gave the oarsmen greater mechanical advantage and efficiency. The advantage was multiplied if the oarsmen were free men and combatants, almost invariably the case until the mid 1500s. Finally, rowing is an oscillatory motion. The vessel slows during the recovery portion of the stroke, so the power stroke must not only overcome the resistance of the water, but the mass of the vessel. Since acceleration is proportional to propulsive force divided by mass, lighter vessels are thus faster.

There were, however, drawbacks: long, narrow hulls with low freeboards are inherently unseaworthy, and the high bulwarks of sailing ships of any size offered important defensive advantages. Nevertheless, oared speed, manoeuvrability and greater numbers usually carried the day. Moreover, the economic benefits of warfare afloat extended to raiding ashore, for which light oared vessels were ideal. Wherever specialized warships emerged as a distinct type, these basic relationships held good into the high Middle Ages; the contrast between the Viking longship and the beamier, cargo-carrying *knarr* is a classic example. But the distinction between long ship and round ship appeared earliest, and was pressed furthest, in the Mediterranean, finding its ultimate expression in the cannon-armed war galley.

The lineage of the cannon-armed galley extends to classical times, although

A Raphael drawing of a late fifteenth or early sixteenth-century Venetian galley under sail. Given the realistic depiction of men and vessel and the fact that it is rowed two men to an oar, a scaloccio, *it is probably a small galiot or* fusta. *Such vessels could make good time in light and moderate winds, but their shallow hulls' limited resistance to sideways drift made them mediocre sailers with the wind abeam.*

not in any straightforward fashion. Both classical trireme and sixteenth-century trireme were propelled by oarsmen who worked in clusters of three; both were inherently offensive and attacked straight ahead; both were highly vulnerable to flank attack; both were most effective when used in ordered squadrons – and that was about that. The classical trireme's waterline ram was designed to shatter enemy hulls; the early modern war galley's equivalent was an above-water spur that served as a bridge for boarding and capture. The classical trireme's oarsmen

Olympias, *a full-sized replica of a classical Athenian trireme, built in 1985–87 and operated for several years thereafter. Propelled by 170 oarsmen rowing on three vertically superimposed levels, such vessels were far faster under oars than their early modern successors. Below, a modern artist's reconstruction of a first-century* AD *Roman trireme. Note the waterline ram, designed to spring the seams of opposing vessels.*

rowed in vertically superimposed layers, the lower oarsmen working deep in the hull; their early modern successors worked side by side on the upper deck, exposed to the elements. The formations of classical galley warfare were many and varied, driven by the fast trireme's extreme manoeuvrability and the striking power of its ram. The early modern galley depended in battle on the line abreast, with each galley protecting its neighbours' flanks.

The lesson to be drawn from the comparison is that the Mediterranean environment fostered first the development, and then the dominance, in two periods widely separated in time, of highly specialized oared warships that pressed the propulsive capabilities of human muscle to the limit. Galley design was not static but evolved constantly in response to changing economic, social and political circumstances. Palaeontologists have recorded the evolution of remarkably similar animal species in widely separated geological eras in response to similar conditions. The evolution of large, unrelated, sabre-toothed, cat-like carnivores – like the war galley, highly specialized predators – on several occasions is an apposite example of this phenomenon. Like the sabre-toothed tiger, the war galley evolved to fill an ecological niche, in the galley's case, in what we might term the strategic ecology of the Mediterranean. As with the sabre-toothed tiger, evolutionary forces pushed the war galley towards greater offensive lethality. And like the sabre-toothed tiger, the war galley flourished only so long as its environment provided adequate sustenance. Although we should not push the analogy too far, it underlines the dynamic nature of design evolution and the manner in which the war galley functioned as part of a complex system.

The development of oared warships in the Dark Ages is obscure. Throughout the eleventh century, full-sized Mediterranean galleys were powered by oarsmen working in two vertically superimposed banks, with the lower oarsmen working below deck. By 1200 the oarsmen were all above deck, and the dominant design was the bireme, rowed by two oarsmen to a bench and four to a

A fragment of the outer rail of a seventeenth-century Venetian galley, probably from the stern based on the sharp upward curve and elaborate carving. Renaissance and Baroque shipwrights did not neatly differentiate between form and function and warships were often elaborately decorated.

bank, each with his own oar. The outer oars were pulled against thole pins set in longitudinal beams, mounted outboard of the hull on an outrigger to give the oarsmen a better mechanical advantage, while the inner oars were pulled through holes in the hull. For long passages galleys were powered by lateen sails set on one to three masts; spars and sails were lowered for combat. By mid century galleys had hinged rudders that could be removed for beaching stern first, although traditional quarter rudders were retained. Christian galleys of the western Mediterranean almost certainly had fighting superstructures at the bow, and perhaps at the stern as well, although we know little about these vessels. During the thirteenth century, the holes in the hull for the inner oars were replaced by thole pins on a second outboard longitudinal beam just below the first, and commanders began squeezing a third oarsman on to the benches to provide additional fighting manpower. The experiment proved beneficial in terms of propulsion, and the third oarsman became permanent.

By 1290, galley design had evolved to exploit the third oarsman fully. The result was the trireme *alla sensile*, 'in the simple fashion' in Italian, although the forest of closely spaced oars hardly seems simple to us. Though we cannot explain why in detail, the rowing system was optimal, for it quickly became standardized and remained dominant on ordinary galleys for two-and-a-half centuries. When the *alla sensile* system was finally abandoned it was not due to the appearance of a superior design, but because of a scarcity of the skilled

Roman relief carving of two oared warships, so identified by the waterline rams. The oarsmen of the vessel at the top appear to have worked on more than one level, though it is difficult to be sure.

A VENETIAN GALLEY
ALLA SENSILE

A 23-bank Venetian ordinary galley alla sensile, *c. 1400. Note the raised prow, handy as a boarding bridge and firing platform when engaging ordinary galleys and smaller vessels. Such vessels were significantly faster under oars than heavy galleys, but engaged them at a significant disadvantage because of their smaller crews and lower height. Later, one bank of oars was left vacant on each side for the skiff (starboard) and the cook's galley (port).*

oarsmen that it demanded – or, more precisely, because of a lack of money with which to pay them.

Ordinary triremes *alla sensile* might have had as few as eighteen banks of oars or, exceptionally, sixteen. From about 1500 until the mid 1530s the most common number was twenty-five banks and twenty-four thereafter, with a bench missing on the starboard side to accommodate the skiff and another on the port side for the cook's galley. Such galleys were described as 'armed with 144 oarsmen

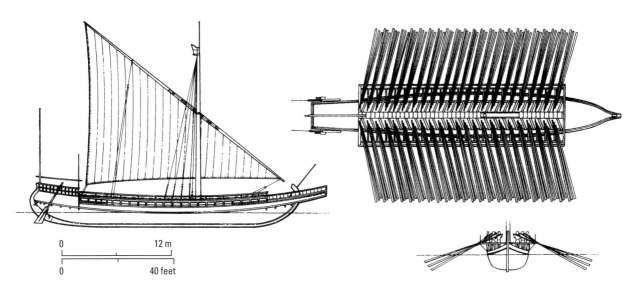

0   12 m

0   40 feet

to row 3 by 3 from poop to prow'. The oarsmen's benches were separated by a narrow raised gangway, the corsia, and were angled forward twenty degrees, forming a series of 'V's pointing towards the stern so that the oarsmen could complete their strokes without fouling one another's oars. The oars were pulled against thole pins mounted on a longitudinal outrigger, the apostis, that was supported by transverse beams, one forward and one aft, to form the rowing frame. The oars varied slightly in length, inboard oarsmen pulling the longest

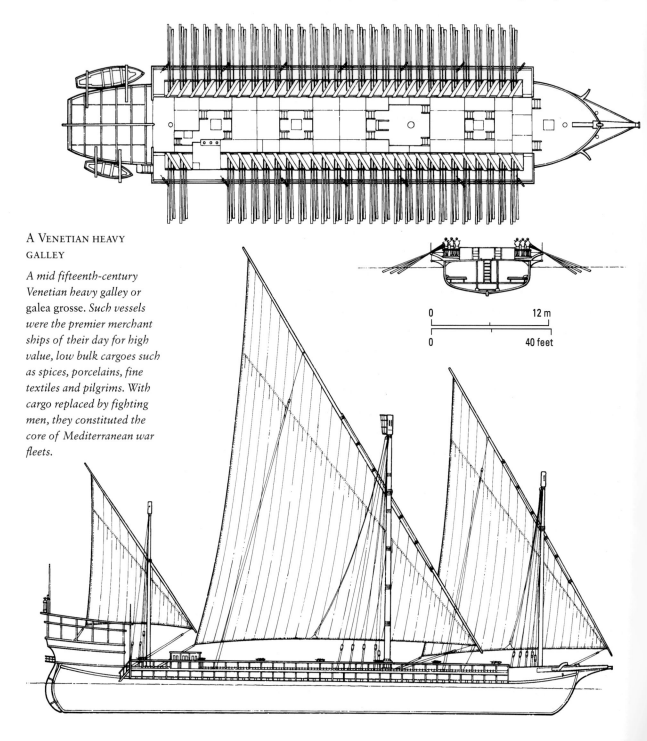

A VENETIAN HEAVY GALLEY

A mid fifteenth-century Venetian heavy galley or galea grosse. Such vessels were the premier merchant ships of their day for high value, low bulk cargoes such as spices, porcelains, fine textiles and pilgrims. With cargo replaced by fighting men, they constituted the core of Mediterranean war fleets.

0   12 m

0   40 feet

and outboard oarsmen the shortest. The poop deck was level with the top of the corsia and tilted upwards at the rear for visibility; this was the galley's 'brain', occupied by captain, pilot, helmsman and reserve fighting men. The bow forward of the rowing frame was the heart of the galley's offensive power, where fighting men would muster to board enemy vessels by means of the spur. The spur was tipped with iron and was sufficiently stout to lodge in an enemy vessel's planking or to ride over an enemy's apostis, breaking it down in a flank attack. In either case, the spur served as a combination grappling hook and boarding bridge. Western galleys often had an elevated fighting platform above the bow, the *arrumbada* in Spanish, from which crossbowmen, archers and later arquebusiers could rain fire. Triremes typically carried two lateen sails on as many masts; sails, spars and even masts could be lowered and stowed inside the corsia before combat.

Ordinary galleys were not the only oared fighting vessels. Great galleys, *galee grosse* in Italian (converted merchant galleys, although some were purpose-built as military transports), formed the tactical backbone of fifteenth-century galley fleets. Slower under oars than ordinary galleys, their high freeboards and stout bulwarks gave crossbowmen, archers and handgunners the advantages of height and protection when engaging lower-lying vessels and made them a difficult proposition for ordinary galleys to handle. As we saw in our discussion of Zonchio, how they were handled could spell the difference between defeat and victory. Mediterranean commanders did not consider tactical homogeneity inherently good and employed larger than normal, or exceptionally heavily armed, ordinary galleys as tactical focal points for victory. The former were called *bastardas*; the latter were called lantern galleys for their ornate triple stern lanterns, vital for signalling and station-keeping at night and the ultimate symbols of authority. Confusingly, not all *bastardas* were lantern galleys, nor were all lantern galleys *bastardas*. The key distinction was how heavily the vessel was armed, and in Mediterranean terms that meant the number and quality of fighting men, artillery entering into the equation later. Perhaps because they were comparatively wasteful in terms of manpower, *bastardas* were not numerous during the era of the trireme *alla sensile*, although quadriremes *alla sensile* rowed four by four were used as lantern galleys. Emperor Charles V's *Real* (royal galley) for the 1535 Tunis expedition was such a vessel, of twenty-six banks (thus requiring 208 oarsmen), as was Andrea Doria's *Capitana* in 1539.

Next, although not necessarily in strategic importance – for galley fleets rarely engaged one another in battle – came smaller oared fighting craft: in descending order of size, galiots, *fustas* and *bergantines*. Galiots were scaled-down galleys, rowed two by two rather than three by three. They were typically of eighteen to twenty banks, but large galiots could have as many banks as an ordinary galley and, although lower, were as long. Although at a serious disadvantage to ordinary galleys in a head-on clash in line abreast, galiots were handier and more manoeuvrable and could – and not infrequently did –

overwhelm galleys from flank and rear in a mêlée. Economical in their manpower demands, galiots were raiding craft *par excellence*. *Fustas* were smaller still, rowed two by two like a galiot, but with fewer banks, ten to fifteen being typical. Like galiots, *fustas* were effective raiding vessels; less demanding of their oarsmen, they were useful in battle for passing messages and transferring reinforcements. *Bergantines* were the smallest of all, with ten to fifteen banks and a single oar and oarsman to the bench. Armed with one or two swivel guns, they were useful raiding and dispatch vessels. Perhaps their most celebrated use was in Mexico in 1521, when prefabricated *bergantines* were constructed at Spanish conquistador Hernán Cortés' orders and were carried overland to Lake Texcoco to blockade the Aztec capital of Tenochtitlán, sealing the doom of Montezuma's empire.

So far we have said little about the relationship of galleys – using the word to encompass all oared fighting craft – to sailing ships, and a few words are in order. Small sailing ships and coastal villages were the war galley's natural prey. By contrast, before the advent of gunpowder, large and well-armed merchant vessels posed a virtually insoluble problem. The fate of the Venetian Levant convoy of 1264, caught without escort by a squadron of eighteen Genoese galleys off Valona, south-west Albania, makes the point. The convoy consisted of twelve *tarettes*, single-decked sailing vessels displacing about 150 tons, half a dozen smaller craft and a single large, round ship, the *Roccaforte,* of 750 tons. After defending the smaller craft for some hours, the outmanned Venetians retreated aboard the *Roccaforte,* where they effectively defied the Genoese. Two points are worth noting: the slowness with which the Genoese, despite their overwhelming numerical superiority, overcame Venetian resistance, and the *Roccaforte*'s unassailability. The lessons are clear: before the advent of heavy gunpowder ordnance, galleys engaged sailing vessels of moderate size at a tactical disadvantage and were effectively impotent against competently defended large ones; improvements in sailing-ship design and construction made the problem worse. By the 1420s the Genoese were building carracks of 600 to 900 tons displacement, and they were not alone. Such vessels, prestige state warships *par excellence*, were essentially immune to attack by galleys.

The above relationships changed fundamentally with the appearance during the 1510s of ordinary galleys armed with main, centre-line bow guns firing balls of 30 to 50 pounds or more, with hull-smashing velocity. The resultant tactical revolution depended on an awareness of the potential of heavy naval ordnance, upon a willingness to expend money to develop that potential and on the realization that centre-line gun-armed galleys were enormously more effective when employed in squadrons in line abreast. Technically, it required the development of a recoil system that could harness the weight and power of such guns without causing damage to the hull. The solution was a wooden box in which the gun was suspended from its trunnions, mounted in a track along which it slid backwards into the corsia on recoil, hence the name *cannone da corsia* in

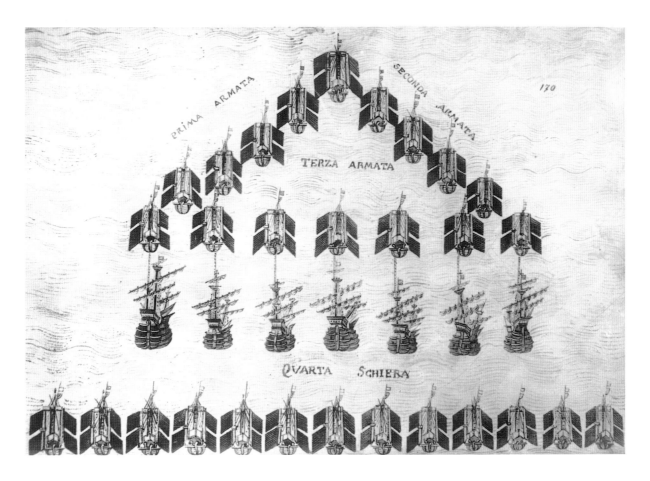

Italian. As an added benefit, the gun could be pulled back nearly to midships to trim the galley for easy rowing and heavy weather; no small matter with a gun weighing 7,000 pounds mounted on the bow of a hull displacing 170 tons, figures representative of mid sixteenth-century Venetian triremes. Shipwrights compensated for the weight by designing hulls that were fuller at the bow and finer at the stern, giving the underwater lines a graceful, fish-like shape.

This elegant solution to a difficult problem was almost certainly a product of the Venetian Arsenal. The first report of a really powerful gun mounted on a galley's bow involves a basilisk – a generic term for a long gun of exceptional power, firing a ball of 50 pounds or more – on a Venetian *galea grosse* in 1501. (Venice's disastrous defeats of 1499 and 1500 were no doubt a powerful spur to innovation!) Although there is no evidence that the Venetians learned to combine an ordinary galley's speed and mobility with the power of a basilisk in time to influence the outcome of the war with the Ottoman Turks from 1499 to 1503, they must have done so shortly thereafter.

Whatever their origins, war galleys with hull-smashing centre-line bow guns left their first imprint on the historical record in April 1513 in a series of combats in Brest Roads, when a squadron of six French galleys shattered an English fleet that included some of the largest and most heavily armed carracks of the day, the famous *Mary Rose* among them. The galleys were surely the cream of twelve

Diagram from the Venetian Admiral Cristoforo da Canal's treatise, Della Militzia Maritima, *written about 1550, showing a battle formation integrating galleys and sailing warships. In fact, the disparate capabilities and limitations of the two rendered tactical co-operation all but impossible and it was seldom achieved.*

ordinary galleys built in 1511 for Louis XII of France in Genoa and Savona and of two *bastardas* built in Venice.

The combat sheds light on capabilities at a pivotal time, and illustrates in microcosm our revolution in firepower. The French commander, Prégent de Bidoux, had brought his galleys north from the Mediterranean the previous autumn and had based them in northern Brittany, poised to descend on the English coast as had Genoese galley squadrons during the Hundred Years War. Frustrated by the winter weather, he found himself outflanked when Henry VIII's fleet, under Sir Edward Howard, arrived off Brest in April 1513, threatening to take the city and cutting de Bidoux off from the main French fleet. Prégent de Bidoux came south, shooting his way through Howard's force and sinking one ship outright in the process. The English were shocked by the power of the French guns, almost certainly bronze basilisks charged with corned powder. Handling his force with a sure confidence that suggests prior experience, de Bidoux withdrew into a narrow bay flanked by shore batteries, his galleys pulled up stern first against the shore, with their guns pointed to sea, a classic and all but unassailable defensive tactic. Howard sought to rally his shaken force with a bold move: a direct assault with all of his oared vessels. It failed in the face of superior French firepower and Howard was killed in the attempt. It was, as Nicholas Rodger has said, an entirely new way of waging war at sea.

By the 1520s Mediterranean war galleys commonly sported main centre-line

An eighteenth-century engraving based on a contemporary painting of the engagement between the French and English fleets off Portsmouth, 19 July 1545. The Mary Rose has just gone down, a victim of overloading, open lower gunports, ill discipline among her crew or some combination thereof. Her topmasts can be seen in the centre of the channel. The action – perhaps the largest naval engagement to date – illustrated the difficulty of controlling in battle combined fleets of oared and sailing warships.

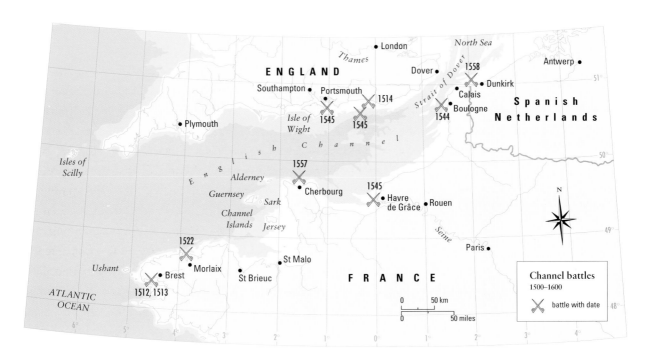

CHANNEL BATTLES, 1500–1600

France and England were at war from 1492 until 1525, again from 1543–46 and yet again in 1549–50. The wars' naval dimensions are suggested by the dates and places of notable engagements, above. Imperial ambitions, notably those of England's Henry VIII, were a rich source of conflict; so was the spillover from England's wars with the Scots, whom the French were perennially ready to assist.

bow guns with hull-smashing – and wall-smashing – power. So armed, the ordinary galley quickly elbowed the great galley from the line of battle and progressively reduced the tactical viability of the carrack until, by the 1570s, none was left in the Mediterranean. The cannon-armed galley established the basis of a system of warfare that dominated the Mediterranean until the 1630s. That system had an enormous thirst for human and fiscal resources that only Habsburg Spain and the Ottoman Empire – and France, when it chose – could meet. As the system matured, second-tier naval powers – Genoa, the Papal States and the North African Muslim emirates – were reduced to subsidiary status. Venice hung on – barely – by dint of shrewd diplomacy, superior technology and operational competence. But as powerful as they were, the galley fleets that formed the operational bedrock of the Mediterranean system of warfare at sea carried within them the seeds of strategic decay. To understand why that was we must examine the war galley in some detail, focusing on the period from 1530 to 1570 when the galley fleet's tactical power and strategic potential reached their apogee.

Tactically, the war galley with a heavy main, centre-line bow gun was

A woodcut of a 1561 battle between galleys and carracks ... or so we presume; the low projecting spur on the bow of the large sailing vessel, centre, is a feature known only from Flemish artists' depictions. It is unlikely that the galleys would have closed to within small arms range of their loftier opponents, as shown, before bombarding them into submission.

inherently offensive. Engagements between individual galleys and small squadrons tended to be all-or-nothing affairs, with the losers suffering heavily and the winners getting off scot-free, or nearly so. Conversely, large, full-blown engagements, in which both sides were able to form in line abreast, tended to be inconclusive. Galleys could row astern and, covered by fire from their bow ordnance, retreat to a beach or anchorage and pull up stern first. A key limiting factor was the number of galleys that could effectively manoeuvre in line abreast. As any aircraft pilot with formation experience can attest, line abreast is the most difficult of formations: errors in station-keeping propagate outwards from the lead ship, multiplying their effect in crack-the-whip fashion. In practical terms, this imposed an inflexible limit of fifty-three to fifty-four galleys on a squadron required to manoeuvre, and perhaps ten more for a squadron that only had to move straight ahead. The galley's lean and speedy look notwithstanding, large formations would have been hard-pressed to maintain more than two knots, with the outboard galleys' oarsmen working themselves to exhaustion.

Beyond inherent physical limits, the Mediterranean powers used galleys that were effectively indistinguishable in very different ways. The Spanish galley was a

The 1583 Spanish assault on Terciera, from murals in the palace of Don Álvaro de Bazán at Viso del Marques in La Mancha. From contemporary accounts of the action we know that the galleys supported the boats filled with assault troops with cannon fire. In tactical sophistication the action was well in advance of the 1915 Gallipoli landings.

tactical assault vessel, designed to bring the maximum load of ordnance and fighting men to the battle line without compromising dash speed; the French galley was also a tactical assault vessel, but with more emphasis on artillery; the Venetian galley was a strategic assault craft, designed for maximum speed under oars to reinforce seaside fortresses and port cities under threat, without being embroiled in a boarding fight; the Turkish galley was a strategic transport, designed to carry men, ordnance and supplies to the site of a siege and to support them once there. These differences were consistent, significant and accurate reflections of differences in strategic goals, resource availability, organization and social structure. Differences in design and construction were marginal, mainly involving fighting superstructures that could be quickly added or removed. More important were the socially based differences: Venetian oarsmen were predominantly free men until after the battle of Lepanto in 1571, while Spanish oarsmen were almost entirely convicts and slaves by 1550. Unsurprisingly, the Venetians placed greater emphasis on accurate gunnery and so on.

Returning to performance, a 24-bank trireme *alla sensile* armed three-by-three and with a 30–50-pound main centre-line gun, fully manned and with a freshly cleaned, well-greased bottom, free of barnacles and weeds, could manage a dash speed under oars of some $7^1/_2$ knots (nautical miles per hour) for about 20 minutes and a cruise speed of $3^1/_2$ to 4 knots for 8 hours or so. These things were done at a cost, for the *ciurma*, the rowing gang, required immense amounts of biscuit – hard tack, a daily ration of 26 ounces per man, supplemented by fresh bread when hard rowing was anticipated – plus perhaps three-quarters of a cup of beans or garbanzos (chickpeas), an occasional fish or meat ration, small amounts of olive oil, wine and vinegar and, above all, water. Water was critical, tactically because the oarsmen would collapse in the Mediterranean summer if their intake fell below an absolute minimum of half a gallon a day, and strategically because the galley's slender hull left little room for stowage. Galleys had to land frequently – two weeks at most – to recharge their water barrels and more frequently as, for reasons explained below, crews grew larger. The water requirement placed stringent limits on individual galleys and squadrons and restricted fleets even more severely, tying them closely to shore.

To compound matters, the inexorable tactical logic of galley warfare dictated a constant increase in the amount of forward-firing ordnance, and galleys began sporting flanking pieces alongside the main centre-line gun, ideally 12-pound demi-culverins or perriers of equivalent weight, throwing a somewhat heavier stone ball. By the mid 1530s, the most heavily armed ordinary galleys had a second, smaller pair of forward-firing guns at the bow: *sacres* (sakers) or *medios sacres* (half-sakers), firing balls of 6–9 pounds. Most western galleys mounted swivel guns on the *arrumbada*.

The weight of ordnance could be impressive. In 1536, the *Capitana* (flagship) of Don Álvaro de Bazán the Elder, Captain General of the Galleys of Spain, carried a *cañon grueso* (large cannon), two half-culverins, three *sacres*, a *pedrero* (stone-thrower) and an array of swivel guns on the *arrumbada*. Assuming representative weights for the guns and a hull 140 feet long, 16½ feet wide, and drawing 4⅓ feet, Bazán's *Capitana* displaced about 186 tons and carried 9¾ tons of ordnance. Some 5.2 per cent of the galley's displacement tonnage thus consisted of ordnance, a figure not matched by sailing warships until the English navy's first race-built galleons were commissioned half a century later. Moreover, in contrast to galleons, the majority of a war galley's ordnance – all but about half a ton in this case – was purely offensive. Bazán's *Capitana* was exceptional: of the twenty-three galleys under his command, only nine approached it in weight of metal. It was not, however, unique. The weight of ordnance aboard Mediterranean galleys grew steadily, displacement increasing accordingly, reaching 200 tons for an ordinary galley by mid century and 300 tons a century later. That growth had important long-term consequences.

The difficulty was the tactical importance of dash speed under oars, for increased weight entailed disproportionate numbers of additional oarsmen if speed was not to be compromised. Venetian experiments in the 1520s with a quinquireme *alla sensile*, five men and five oars to the bench, showed that a 50 per cent increase in displacement required a 100 per cent increase in power – oarsmen – if dash speed was not to be compromised. That was indicative, and the problem went beyond the technical and tactical to encompass socio-economic factors. The trireme *alla sensile* was an optimal design, but it was strictly limited in size and depended on highly skilled, salaried oarsmen. By the 1550s inflation had put oarsmen's salaries beyond the reach of western Mediterranean powers and they instead turned to slaves and convicts, by definition less skilled and motivated. Individual oars gave way to a single large oar for each bench, pulled by grips attached to the oar's rear with ladder-like attachments, from whence is derived the Italian name *a scaloccio*, 'like a ladder'. With this system, three men to an oar proved inadequate, for a single oar was less efficient than individual oars pulled by skilled oarsmen. Four men to an oar were needed to equal the trireme *alla sensile*'s dash speed, and the additional oarsmen entailed an increase in displacement. That was the bad news; the good news was the *a scaloccio* system's flexibility. Only one skilled oarsman per oar was needed, and oarsmen could easily be added or removed according to the tactical situation.

Commanders *in extremis* might promise slaves their freedom in exchange for victory – as did both commanders-in-chief at Lepanto – and arm them if they were co-religionists, but servile oarsmen were not combatants, and additional soldiers were required to guard them. That further increased displacement, requiring still more oarsmen to maintain tactical dash speed. The result was a self-regenerative feedback loop that called for more and more oarsmen and larger hulls, progressively eroding tactical flexibility and strategic radius of action. A Spanish ordinary galley of the 1520s with 144 free oarsmen carried 40 to 90 *compañeros sobresalientes*, sailors doubling as marine infantry, and 20 to 25 *oficiales*, an untranslatable term that requires explanation. *Oficiales* were the war

An allegory of Lepanto by Giorgio Vasari, showing the opposing fleets about to clash against the backdrop of the Greek coast. The spectre of death hanging over the battle is real enough, but the geometric regularity of the arrayed fleets is anything but, and Vasari's Muslim order of battle inaccurately mirrors that of the Christians.

A seventeenth-century engraving of a Venetian squadron approaching the island of Tinos, a key position in the Central Aegean. It accurately suggests the symbiotic relationships among ports, seaside fortifications and galley fleets.

galley's technical experts: sailing master, pilot, boatswains, gunners, caulker, carpenter, cooper, rowing master, master-at-arms (significantly, in charge of water distribution), barber-surgeon, chaplain and able seamen; but they were more than that, for they were primary combatants as well. Such men were never numerous, for the Mediterranean, unlike northern European waters, lacked the fisheries that were their natural breeding ground. They were *the* critical manpower requirement of galley warfare.

By 1560, Spanish ordinary galleys were ideally rowed four-by-four by 160 oarsmen and carried 30 to 40 *oficiales* and 50 soldiers, with additional oarsmen added for important undertakings. The numbers are hard to track because of the *a scaloccio* system's flexibility and because the demand for fighting men varied enormously according to circumstances, but they grew steadily. The figures for the galleys of Spain and of Gian Andrea Doria, wintering at Messina after Lepanto, are indicative. Ordinary Spanish galleys mustered 50 *oficiales*, 27 sailors, 35 soldiers and 200 oarsmen while Doria's ordinary galleys had 50 *oficiales*, 35 soldiers and 164 oarsmen. An entrepreneur close to home, Doria cut

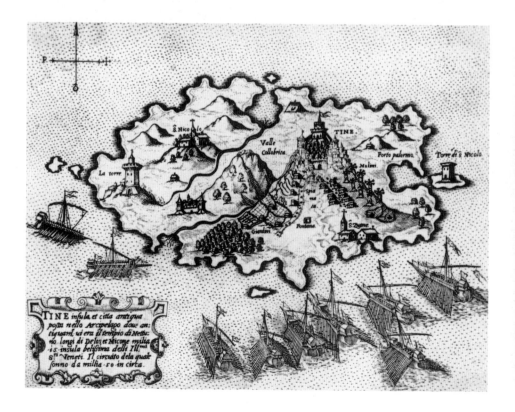

A galley laid up in port, attributed to the school of Pierre Puget (1620–94), showing the increase in the size of ordinary galleys during their waning days. Venetian galleys much like the one depicted here fought in the final sea battles in which Mediterranean galleys played a significant role, during the 1645–69 War of Crete. Though still effective firing platforms for their heavy main centre-line guns, such vessels were costly to operate.

his manpower rolls to save money, confident that he could obtain oarsmen and hire seamen in the spring. By contrast, the Spanish were far from their sources of manpower and carefully conserved their oarsmen, laying in special stores of wine, rice, olive oil and 'medicine' – in fact, high-protein food – for those who fell sick. While I have confined myself to Spain and its Italian clients since better documentation survives, and while these data reflect peculiar circumstances, the problems they illustrate were universal.

The trireme *alla sensile* endured in the eastern Mediterranean – most Venetian and many Muslim galleys that fought at Lepanto were triremes *alla sensile* – but lantern galleys grew inexorably larger. Don Juan of Austria's *Real* at Lepanto had 30 banks and 6 men to an oar – no less than 360 oarsmen – and a fighting complement based on 300 Sardinian arquebusiers as well as over 100 gentlemen volunteers. The lantern galley of his Muslim opposite, Ali Pasha, was even bigger, with a fighting complement centred on 300 janissaries and 100 archers. Those of Sebastian Venier, Venice's Capitano Generale da Mar (Captain

General of the Sea), and Marc Antonio Colonna, the Pope's captain general, must have been nearly as large.

The increase in manning density had two causes: first, the increased weight of ordnance and, second, the reduced efficiency of the *a scaloccio* rowing system. The effects were straightforward: a sharp decrease in strategic radius of action, combined with a geometric increase in costs exacerbated by rising inflation, particularly in the West. Like the sabre-toothed tiger, the galley continued to dominate its environment and to grow larger and more powerful – in the seventeenth century ordinary galleys normally had twenty-six banks – but at the same time the numbers of galleys in commission steadily declined. Lepanto thus marked the galley fleet's apogee, technically as well as strategically.

LEPANTO, 1571

They sail in badly made vessels poorly furnished with artillery, but they fight with desperation.

Venetian characterization of the Turks, MATTHEO CIGOGNA,
Il Primo Libro del Trattato Militare, 1567

The struggle for control of the Mediterranean that peaked at Lepanto is traditionally dismissed by historians as peripheral. It produced, after all, only minor transfers of territory: a few coastal presidios, the islands of Rhodes, Chios and Cyprus, and border adjustments in coastal Dalmatia. Moreover, the principal actors in the drama, the Ottoman Empire, Spain and the Venetian Republic, were in decline by the time of the battle of Lepanto, or so it seems in retrospect. Contemporary declamations that Lepanto delivered Christendom from the Turk are dismissed as rhetorical flourish. A closer look suggests otherwise.

Lepanto was a product of the fusion of two naval struggles: the first between the Ottomans and Venice for control of the north-eastern Mediterranean and the second Spain's extension of the *Reconquista* (reconquest) into North Africa, a strategic impulse that found its counterpart in the Ottoman commitment to the expansion of the *Darülislam*, the abode of those who submit to the will of Allah. The overall contest interacted with, and was shaped by, three regional conflicts: the wars of Italy, the intermittent struggle between Spain and France for Italian hegemony between 1494 and 1559; that between the Ottomans and the Egyptian Mamelukes; and Ottoman expansion into the Balkans.

The wars of Italy ended in 1559 when the Treaty of Câteau-Cambrésis confirmed Spain's claim to Italian hegemony. Their main effect on the Mediterranean struggle was the diversion of Spanish resources; indeed, from the 1520s, French kings and Ottoman sultans co-ordinated their efforts with precisely that in mind. The same point applies to Ottoman expansion in the Balkans, though the diversion of resources cut both ways from 1519 when Charles I of Spain was elected Holy Roman Emperor, ruling the Habsburg domains in Germany, the Netherlands, Spain and the Americas as Emperor Charles V. The Ottoman thrust into the Balkans ended in stalemate, with Süleyman I's repulse from Vienna in 1529, although that was not apparent until long afterwards. The Ottoman–Mameluke conflict ended very differently, with Ottoman victory in 1517 placing Egypt's immense agricultural wealth at the Turks' disposal and giving the Ottomans control of the eastern termini of the Mediterranean spice trade.

The Mediterranean was not the only arena in which Spain, the Ottomans and Venice engaged. In the first decades of the sixteenth century, Spain carved out a rich empire in the New World, unleashing first a trickle, and then a torrent, of gold and, above all, silver, that loomed large in the strategic balance by multiplying Spain's military might – and unleashing the ravages of inflation. The Ottomans opposed the Portuguese in the Indian Ocean and Persian Gulf, with

Khaireddin Barbarossa in a 1540 portrait. Born on Mitylene, Barbarossa and his elder brother Uruj fled west to escape the turmoil of the Ottoman succession struggle that put Sultan Bayezid II on the throne. He inherited the mantle of leadership when Uruj was killed in 1518 and became a champion of North African Muslims resisting Spanish expansion. Perhaps the finest naval commander of his day, he is shown here in old age, the red beard from which he got his name having turned white.

tacit Venetian backing. They also kept a wary eye on the Persian Safavids, mounting imperial campaigns to the east in 1514, 1534–5 and 1554–5.

For Spain, however, as long as the Turkish threat was real, the Mediterranean was the strategic linchpin, the axis around which all else pivoted. When Charles V received the Inca emperor Atahualpa's ransom of gold, he spent it not on the Danube to defend Austria, but to finance the conquest of Tunis. Even after the Netherlands erupted in open revolt, the Mediterranean retained its priority. The absence of mutinies in the Mediterranean provides strong, if indirect, evidence. As important as Flanders was to Philip II of Spain, his soldiers there were habitually unpaid, which inevitably led to mutiny. That did not occur in the Mediterranean, however, and not because of economic surplus as Spanish bankruptcies in 1557, 1560 and 1575 attest.

The first tentative step towards generalizing the Mediterranean struggle came in 1495, when Sultan Bayezid II dispatched the corsair Kemal Re'is to western North Africa, where he made contact with sea ghazis, raiders for the faith, who had made common cause with expelled Iberian Muslims thirsting for revenge and were inclined to take seriously the Ottoman sultans' legitimacy as protectors of the faith. In the following decades, these ghazis struggled to establish themselves in the face of repeated Spanish offensives aimed at stopping their raids by controlling their ports, either by occupation or through fortifications erected at their mouths. By 1520 the most successful among them, Khaireddin Barbarossa, had seized Algiers – although the Peñon, the fortress controlling the harbour, remained in Spanish hands – and had formally accepted Ottoman overlordship. In 1529, using

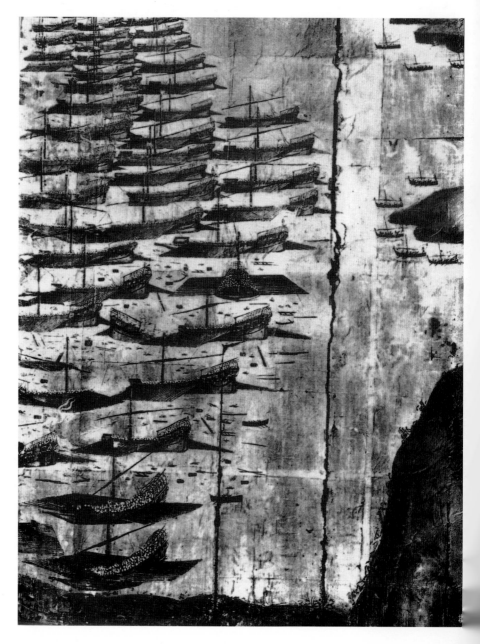

A contemporary engraving of a late sixteenth-century galley fight. It conveys an accurate impression of the slow pace of galley warfare, of the incredible human congestion, and of the carnage. Unusually, the artist has recorded the debris of battle and the small fustas *and* bergantines *that transferred reinforcements from ship to ship and carried dispatches and orders.*

a siege train provided by Francis I of France, Barbarossa took the Peñon, a counterpoint to his imperial master's repulse before Vienna in the same year. Meanwhile, in 1528 the great Genoese naval condottiero Andrea Doria transferred his allegiance from France to Spain, becoming Charles V's Captain General at Sea. Doria's switch secured Habsburg communications in the western Mediterranean and helped force France to seek peace with Spain in the following year.

Charles launched Doria on a series of raids against the North African coasts and in 1530 installed the Knights of St John, homeless since their expulsion from Rhodes, in Malta and Tripoli. In 1532, Doria took Coron. Süleyman responded by summoning Barbarossa to Constantinople in 1533 and appointing him Kapudan Pasha, naval commander-in-chief. Barbarossa recaptured Coron the

Sultan Süleyman I interviewing Kapudan Pasha Barbarossa in an Ottoman miniature done just over a decade after the great admiral's death.

next year, but Charles led a massive expedition to Tunis in 1535, taking the city in a brilliant campaign. The Ottoman response was not long in coming. Having secured his eastern flank by taking Baghdad in 1534, Süleyman entered into a secret agreement with Francis I of France to mount a co-ordinated invasion of Italy in 1537.

The Turks deemed control of Corfu essential to an invasion of Italy, for a powerful squadron there could control the Straits of Otranto. That meant war with Venice. Spain and the Pope came to the republic's aid, forming a loose alliance. By May 1537, Süleyman and the imperial army were in Avlona, opposite Corfu. Although eight thousand cavalry were taken across to raid Apulia in anticipation of a major invasion, Süleyman's plans came up against hard reality: Italian engineers had learned well at the hands of French and Ottoman siege guns

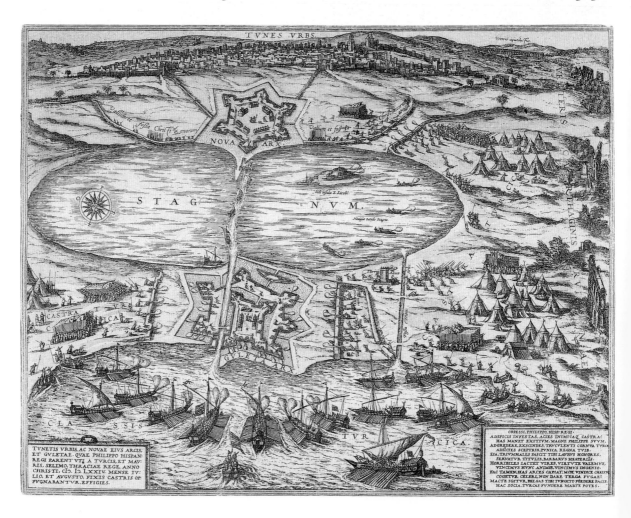

Tunis, shown here under siege in 1574. Taken for Christendom by Charles V in 1535, Tunis was captured by Uluj Ali's forces in 1569, then taken for Spain by Don Juan of Austria in 1573. Uluj Ali's reconquest in 1574 placed the city permanently in Muslim hands.

in the preceding decades, and Corfu was defended by up-to-date *trace italienne* fortifications. From 18 August to 6 September the Turks hurled themselves against them to no effect and, threatened with being cut off from their bases by converging allied squadrons, withdrew.

The economic logic of Ottoman mobilization, based on an elaborate system of decentralized taxes in kind, militated against campaigns by the imperial army in successive years since the *sipahi* horse archers, who constituted its core, needed time to attend to the land holdings that supported them. Süleyman's army thus stayed at home in 1538, leaving hostilities to the fleets. The Venetians were first out, threatening Ottoman bases along the Dalmatian coast. Knowing that he would be outnumbered, Barbarossa came west, taking shelter in the Gulf of Prevesa. Doria, the alliance's captain general, did not reach the Adriatic until

Portrait of Andrea Doria by Sebastiano del Piombo. Wealthy merchant, naval condottiero, Genoese patriot and shrewd politician, Doria was Genoa's de facto leader for much of his life. His defeat by Barbarossa at Prevesa in 1538 notwithstanding, he was one of the most skilled naval commanders of his age.

September 1538 and stopped at Corfu, where the allied fleet lay plagued by internal dissension, with the Venetians clamouring for aggressive action. The Pope's captain general, Marco Grimani, took the initiative, landing troops and guns in an attempt to seize the Ottoman batteries guarding the narrow entrance to the gulf and to bottle Barbarossa up inside. That brought Doria south.

The odds favoured the Christians, with 130 galleys and a fleet of supporting sailing ships to Barbarossa's 90 galleys and 50 galiots, but the appearance of Ottoman land forces in strength forced Grimani to withdraw. That left the Christian galleys off a hostile shore, expending energy, provisions and water.

It was late in the season, and the threat of storms was real; on 27 September Doria ordered withdrawal under cover of darkness. The wind failed during the night and dawn found the Christian fleet scattered, much of it within reach of

Barbarossa's galleys, which promptly sallied forth. Tactically, the battle of Prevesa was little more than a skirmish. The Christians lost a handful of galleys and round ships. The most notable episode was the successful resistance of a Venetian galleon.

Strategically, however, Prevesa was decisive. Furious at what they considered to be Doria's indecision – even treason, for he was believed to have been negotiating with Barbarossa – and with their commercial lifeline cut, the Venetians concluded a separate peace in 1540, leaving the Turks supreme in the Levant and free to campaign westwards. This notwithstanding, Charles struck next, attacking Algiers in 1541. He achieved strategic surprise by sailing late in the campaigning season, but his boldness was rewarded with disaster when his fleet was smashed by a great storm on 24–26 October. Half a world away, an equally bold Portuguese attack on Suez miscarried in the same year.

France re-entered the Italian wars the next year, and Barbarossa raided Calabria in 1543, wintering in Toulon. It was the high point of Ottoman–French naval co-operation. Then, after helping the French to take Nice, Barbarossa declined to assist in a proposed siege of Genoa. France left the war in 1544 and Süleyman focused his attention on Persia and Hungary. The crisis had passed.

Nevertheless, the Turks had the upper hand. During the 1550s Turkish

An idealized representation of the battle of Prevesa by Bernardino Poccetti (c. 1542–1612). At Prevesa, Barbarossa's shrewd tactics gained him a signal victory that split the Christian alliance and gave Turkish galley fleets access to the western Mediterranean for a generation.

squadrons raided the Balearics and Malta and expelled the Knights of St John from Tripoli. French–Ottoman naval co-operation from 1552–54 and from 1557–58 added to Spain's woes. Worn out by the struggle, Charles abdicated in favour of his son, Philip in 1556. Then, with the French threat lifted by the Treaty of Câteau-Cambrésis, Spain took the offensive. Doria's great-nephew and heir, Gian Andrea Doria, then aged only 20, was at sea early in 1560, with 54 galleys, 5 galiots, 29 sailing ships and 35 miscellaneous small craft carrying an army of five thousand. Aiming for Tripoli, Doria vacillated and attacked the corsair island base of Djerba, off the Tunisian coast. News of his expedition reached Constantinople, and Piali Pasha, Kapudan Pasha following Barbarossa's death in 1546, sortied in early March. His force swelled to 86 galleys by North African reinforcements, Piali Pasha caught Doria in disarray on 11 May and inflicted a crushing defeat, capturing or sinking 28 to 30 galleys, half of the sailing ships and nearly all of the smaller craft. That represented a large proportion of Habsburg naval power – the galleys of Sicily were nearly wiped out and the Papal fleet crippled for years to come – but the real loss was in skilled manpower: some 600 *oficiales* were lost, along with 2,400 sailor-arquebusiers. Few in number, and the products of a lifetime of experience, the *oficiales* were irreplaceable in the short term and the latter could not be replaced at all.

Forced to embark regular infantry to replace the sailor-arquebusiers, and with inexperienced *oficiales*, Spanish galleys suffered a series of disasters in subsequent years, and when the Ottomans concluded a truce with the Austrian Habsburgs in 1563 they found Spain vulnerable in the Mediterranean. Spanish officials, notably Don Garcia de Toledo, Philip II's Viceroy of Sicily and Captain General at Sea, accurately predicted that the Turks would strike in force in 1565. Don Garcia also anticipated the target: Malta, with an excellent harbour well placed to support Turkish operations against Italy or even Spain itself. The Knights of St John were well fortified and could be relied upon to mount a stout defence, but thick walls and determination alone could not offset Turkish superiority at sea. That superiority was manifested in early May when a fleet of 130 galleys, 54 galiots, 8 *maonas* (great galleys used as transports) and 11 large sailing vessels under Piali Pasha arrived off Malta, transporting a powerful siege train and an army of 30,000 men, for which the galleys' oarsmen and fighting complements were reserves. Against this, the Knights of St John could muster only 2,500 professional fighting men including 500 Knights plus 1,000 armed Maltese.

Unable to confront the Muslims at sea, Don Garcia reinforced the island's garrison and, after a particularly dangerous assault in early July, sent in four picked galleys with a relief force of 700 infantry and 40 Knights. The siege lasted into September and was resolved when enormous casualties among the janissaries, *sipahis* and oarsmen left Piali Pasha's fleet wasted, enabling Don Garcia to throw in a relief of 11,000 infantry and 200 Knights carried in 28 galleys. The Knights vilified him for excessive caution, but Don Garcia's skill in playing a weak hand had saved Malta. Of equal importance, Spain's galley

A contemporary depiction of the 1565 siege of Malta. One of the hardest-fought and most closely contested sieges in history, it was a vital defensive victory for Christendom.

squadrons were allowed to complete their post-Djerba recovery, rebuilding their corps of *oficiales*.

Large galley fleets were mobilized in the ensuing years, but to little effect, for both sides understood the strategic and tactical calculation. A galley fleet's strategic potential lay in its ability to seize forward bases, yet that was becoming increasingly expensive, all the more so as a numerically inferior but well-handled galley force could effectively support the place under attack. For the Turks the effectiveness of the Habsburg armies, with their hard core of Spanish infantry,

ruled out objectives in Sicily or Italy. Finally, as galley fleets grew larger, their strategic radius of action diminished. The Spanish refused to chance a fleet encounter with inferior numbers, and the result was a stand-off. The Ottoman seizure of Chios, Genoa's last possession in the eastern Mediterranean, in 1566 was unopposed.

After Süleyman's death on campaign in Hungary in 1566, offensive action in the Balkans ceased and his successor, Selim II, 'The Sot', turned to the sea, perhaps as part of a grander design, for the sultans of Aceh, aided and abetted by

Selim II, 'The Sot,' in a sixteenth-century painting from the Top Kapi Museum. In their youth, Ottoman princes were trained in a craft as part of their imperial education. Selim's was that of a bow-maker, hence the bow in his hand.

the Ottomans, were becoming a serious threat to the Portuguese in the east, attacking Malacca both in 1568 and in 1571–5. Frustrated at Malta, the Turks chose a target closer to hand: the rich Venetian island of Cyprus, hard up against the coast of Asia Minor, no doubt reasoning that its proximity to their bases would offset Venetian strength at sea. Rejecting an ultimatum to cede Cyprus, Venice approached Spain and the Pope for help, and swiftly commissioned between 120 and 130 galleys, the majority laid up in the Arsenal, a remarkable

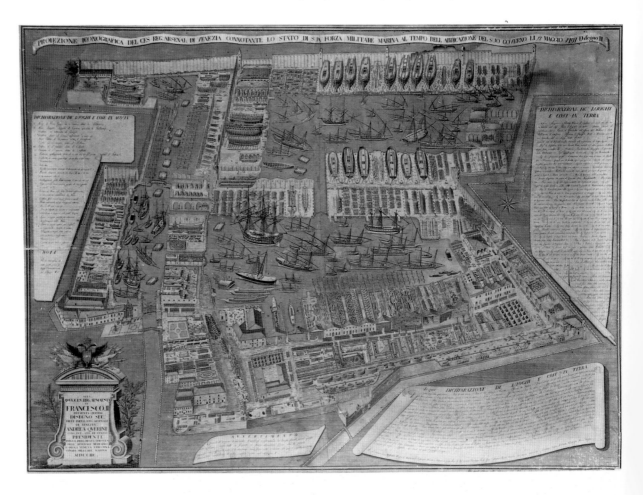

Depicting the Venetian Arsenal near the end of its long existence, this engraving gives an idea of the scale and scope of activities carried on within its precincts. In addition to being a major shipyard and cannon foundry, the Arsenal stored the Republic's reserve galleys in time of peace.

achievement. Also in the Arsenal were ten merchant galleys – *galee grosse* – that had been laid up when rising salaries rendered them unprofitable. Chronically short of manpower, Venice possessed a surfeit of first-rate ordnance and these merchant galleys were converted into galleasses, with batteries of heavy guns.

The ensuing campaign was a fiasco for Christendom. Supported by 150 to 160 galleys under Piali Pasha, the Turks invaded Cyprus in July and quickly overran the island. Sickness among his crews forestalled an early counterstroke by Girolamo Zane, the Venetian Capitano Generale da Mar, and the Spanish and Papal contingents, under Doria and Marc Antonio Colonna, reached the Levant only in late August. The allies now had 180 to 190 galleys, but internecine squabbling reduced the force to impotence. The capital of Cyprus, Nicosia, fell in

September, leaving the port of Famagusta the only remaining Venetian position. The only bright spot was a brilliant Venetian relief of Famagusta in January which resulted in Piali Pasha's dismissal as Kapudan Pasha.

Thoroughly alarmed, in May 1571 Spain, Venice and the Pope consummated the Holy League, a much tighter alliance than that of 1538. They agreed to maintain 200 galleys, 100 sailing vessels, 50,000 infantry and 4,500 cavalry for three years, the costs being borne by Spain, Venice and the Pope in a ratio

An allegorical depiction of the formal ratification in May 1571 of the Holy League of Spain, the Papal States, and Venice, showing Philip II of Spain, Doge Alvise Mocenigo of Venice, and Pope Pius V. In fact, the provisions of the alliance were hammered out in Rome by diplomats representing their respective powers and the three never met face to face.

*The struggle for control of
the Mediterranean began in
earnest around 1500 and
expanded in scale and
geographic extent as the
main centre-line bow
gun-armed war galley
matured as an effective
weapons system. The
concurrent consolidation
of the Habsburg and
Ottoman resource bases
gave the principal
contenders the means to
pursue their ambitions.*

of 3:2:1. The allied fleet would have a single commander-in-chief, and since
Spain paid the most, the appointment was Philip II's, who named his 24-year-old
bastard half-brother, Don Juan of Austria.

In 1571 both sides mobilized on an unprecedented scale, a lengthy process.
Complicating matters for the allies, Don Juan was engaged until July in
suppressing a major Morisco revolt in southern Spain. Colonna with 12 Papal
galleys arrived at the agreed rendezvous of Messina on 20 July, shortly followed
by 58 Venetian galleys and 6 galleasses under Sebastian Venier, the new Venetian
Capitano Generale da Mar, Zane having been imprisoned after the previous
year's débâcle. Don Juan reached Messina with 24 galleys on 23 August, followed
a week later by 60 Venetian galleys from Crete. That gave Don Juan about 190
galleys and 6 galleasses, not counting galiots, *fustas* and sailing vessels carrying
soldiers and supplies. Christian strength grew as additional galleys trickled in.

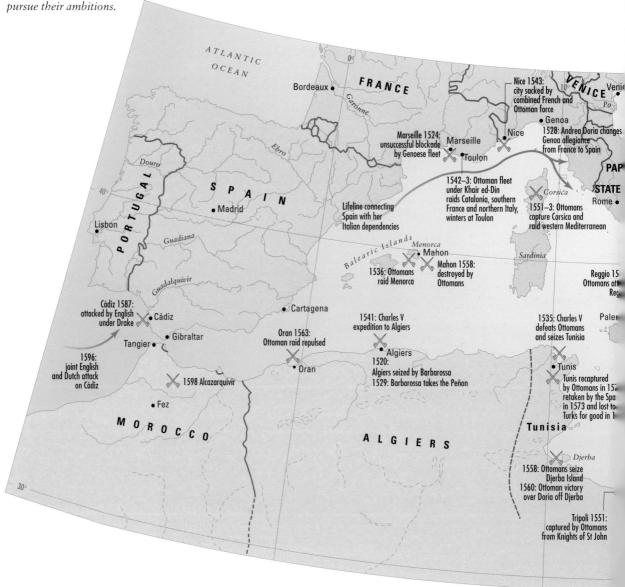

Meanwhile the Ottoman fleet under its new Kapudan Pasha, Müezzenzade Ali Pasha, had worked its way around the Morea (Peloponnese), penetrating as far north as Prevesa. Forty North African galleys and galiots under Uluj Ali Pasha, heir to Barbarossa and one of the most skilled galley commanders of the age, brought the Muslim fleet up to a final strength of some 230 galleys and 70 galiots.

In the meantime, Don Juan confronted daunting challenges. Deep-seated enmities existed between his various contingents, exacerbated by imbalances in their respective capabilities. Venetian–Genoese distrust, particularly Venetian distrust of Doria, ran deep, and the matter was complicated by the Venetian manpower shortage. Colonna, Don Juan's second-in-command, proved effective in smoothing over the differences, but the problems went beyond simple distrust. The Venetians arrived at Messina with only thirty *scapoli*, fighting men, per galley, far below the minimum of one hundred that western commanders

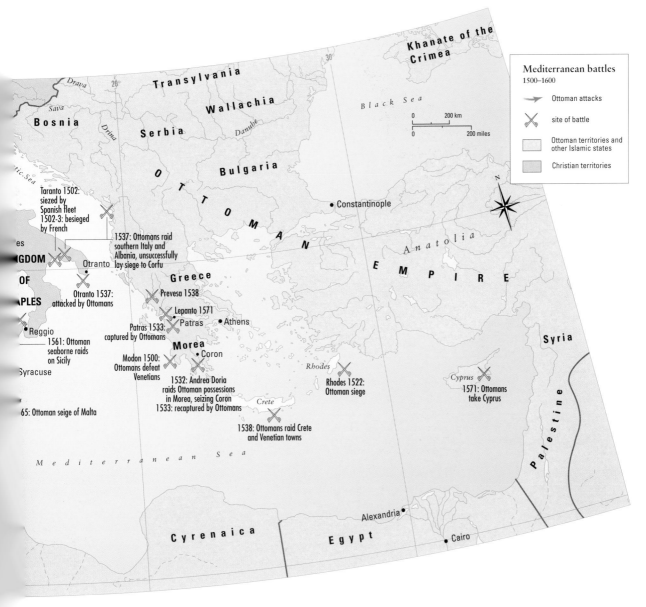

Mediterranean battles
1500–1600

→ Ottoman attacks

✕ site of battle

Ottoman territories and other Islamic states

Christian territories

0   200 km
0   200 miles

Khanate of the Crimea

Black Sea

Drava
Sava
Drina
Danube

Transylvania
Wallachia
Serbia
Bosnia
Bulgaria

OTTOMAN EMPIRE

Constantinople

Anatolia

Syria

Palestine

Taranto 1502: siezed by Spanish fleet 1502-3: besieged by French

1537: Ottomans raid southern Italy and Albania, unsuccessfully lay siege to Corfu

Otranto

Otranto 1537: attacked by Ottomans

Greece

Prevesa 1538

Lepanto 1571

Patras 1533: captured by Ottomans

Patras

Athens

Reggio

1561: Ottoman seaborne raids on Sicily

Syracuse

65: Ottoman seige of Malta

Modon 1500: Ottomans defeat Venetians

Morea

Coron

1532: Andrea Doria raids Ottoman possessions in Morea, seizing Coron 1533: recaptured by Ottomans

1538: Ottomans raid Crete and Venetian towns

Crete

Rhodes

Rhodes 1522: Ottoman siege

Cyprus

1571: Ottomans take Cyprus

Mediterranean Sea

Cyrenaica

Egypt

Alexandria

Cairo

KGDOM OF NAPLES

considered necessary for a stand-up fight. Don Juan therefore proposed that the Venetians embark Italian, Spanish and German infantry to make good the deficiency. Venier rejected the Germans out of hand, but, pressed by Colonna, accepted the Italians and Spaniards. Spanish infantry and Venetian *scapoli* were a combustible mix, and fights escalated into mutinies. Venier had a Spanish captain hanged, and until cooler heads prevailed the alliance was in jeopardy.

One of Don Juan's earliest and most successful decisions was to intermingle the Holy League's galleys, leaving no contingent intact under its own commander. That this unprecedented arrangement was accepted is elegant testimony to the urgency of the situation. Don Juan then divided the fleet into a centre, two wings and a reserve, commanding the centre personally. Doria commanded the right wing; Agostin Barbarigo, the Venetian second-in-command, the left; and Don Álvaro de Bazán the reserve.

The Christians left Messina on 16 September 1571. On 26 September, they

The commanders of the fleet of the Holy League at Lepanto in a near-contemporary painting: from left, Don Juan of Austria, Captain General of the League; Marc Antonio Colonna, Papal Captain General and second in command; and Sebastian Venier, Venetian Capitano Generale da Mar.

reached Corfu, where they heard of the fall of Famagusta. Meanwhile Ali Pasha had gone south, sheltering at Lepanto. The Christians followed him four days later with an advance guard drawn from the right and reserve, followed by the right, centre and left, pausing between Cephalonia and Ithaca on 5–6 October to replenish and take on water. Both commanders-in-chief had good intelligence, but each underestimated his adversary's strength. Both determined to seek battle; indeed, Ali Pasha was under explicit orders from his sultan to do so.

Thus it was when the Christian advance guard, entering the Gulf of Patras shortly after dawn on 7 October, sighted the Muslim fleet off to the east. The strengths of the opposing forces given in the table below do not reflect late arrivals and are thus low, particularly for the Christians, who gained as many as seventeen galleys. Putting the numbers in perspective, Fernand Braudel, the great French historian of the Mediterranean, has estimated that a total of 500 to 600 galleys were operating in the Mediterranean at the time of Lepanto. If that was the case,

THE ORDERS OF BATTLE OF THE CHRISTIAN AND MUSLIM FLEETS 7 OCTOBER 1571

CHRISTIANS			MUSLIMS		
Squadron	**Commander**	**Strength**	**Squadron**	**Commander**	**Strength**
Left	Barbarigo	53 galleys 2 galleases	Right	Mehmet Suluk	60 galleys 2 galiots
Centre	Don Juan	62 galleys 2 galleases	Centre	Ali Pasha	First line: 62 galleys Second line: 25 galleys 8 galiots
			Reserve		8 galleys 22 galiots 64 *fustas*
Right	Doria	53 galleys 2 galleases	Left	Uluj Ali Pasha	61 galleys 32 galiots
Reserve	Bazán	38 galleys			

and Braudel's estimate is credible, then somewhere between 70 and 90 per cent of all Mediterranean war galleys in existence met at Lepanto, clear evidence that the principal actors believed the stakes to be very high indeed. Reinforcing the point, Venice retained only fourteen galleys and two galleases in the upper Adriatic.

The opposing orders of battle seemingly mirrored one another, but were based on very different premises. The Christian left wing was overwhelmingly Venetian, evidence of Don Juan's concern that the Muslims might turn his inshore flank and precipitate a mêlée, with fatal consequences for his less manoeuvrable galleys. The Venetian galleys' speed under oars was his best counter, and so he put them there, under a Venetian commander, who posted himself on his extreme inshore flank, a decidedly unconventional position. Moreover, Don Juan assigned only three of his twenty-five lantern galleys to the left, where speed would count more than power.

For his part, Ali Pasha knew that the greater height and firepower of the Christian galleys, particularly those of Spain and her Italian clients, would grind him down in a head-on fight. He therefore planned to turn the Christian flanks, by better knowledge of the soundings on his right and – he hoped – by Uluj Ali Pasha's tactical magic on his left. Personally commanding his centre, he would counter Christian superiority head-on by feeding in reinforcements from his second line and reserve, holding on long enough for his wings to bring victory. It nearly worked.

Don Juan staked all on the ability of his squadrons to maintain line abreast, reinforced by *fustas* and *bergantines* shuttling men to threatened segments of the line. Leading from the centre, and correctly anticipating that Ali Pasha would do the same, he posted the galley of Don Luis de Requesens, Comendador Major of Castile, at his stern to provide reinforcements and Venier's and Colonna's lantern galleys on his flanks. Finally, he ordered the galleasses to be towed in front of

A contemporary artist's view of Lepanto from the State Archives of Siena. The artist has done a commendable job of showing the confusion of battle.

their respective squadrons. Those on the left and centre made it before the initial clash; those on the right, with a greater distance to travel, did not. As the fleets closed, Don Juan ordered the spurs of the Christian galleys to be cut off, so that their main centre-line guns could be depressed to bear at the shortest possible range for maximum effect. In giving the order he confirmed implicitly that – at least in the centre – he had precipitated the head-on clash in line abreast that he wanted. Unlike Ali Pasha, he did not need to pre-commit his reserve. Employed independently, it would be his final safeguard against the mêlée that the Muslims desperately needed.

The inshore squadrons engaged at around noon, the Muslim galleys parting ranks to bypass the galleasses, which punished them with their heavy guns as they passed. Mehmet Suluk broke for the shallows to slip between Barbarigo's left and the shore to precipitate a mêlée. He made it with four or five galleys and the battle hung by a thread. Eight Venetian galleys were sunk, and Barbarigo was

THE BATTLE OF LEPANTO

The maps on the following pages can only hint at the chaos with which the opposing commanders had to deal. Their eye level was only 12–15 feet above the water, and although masthead lookouts could see farther, little would have been visible through the gunpowder smoke once battle was joined. The fustas *and* bergantines, *used to pass orders and information, transfer reinforcements, and protect galleys against attack from the rear, were omitted for clarity. A large number of these vessels were present, particularly on the Christian side.*

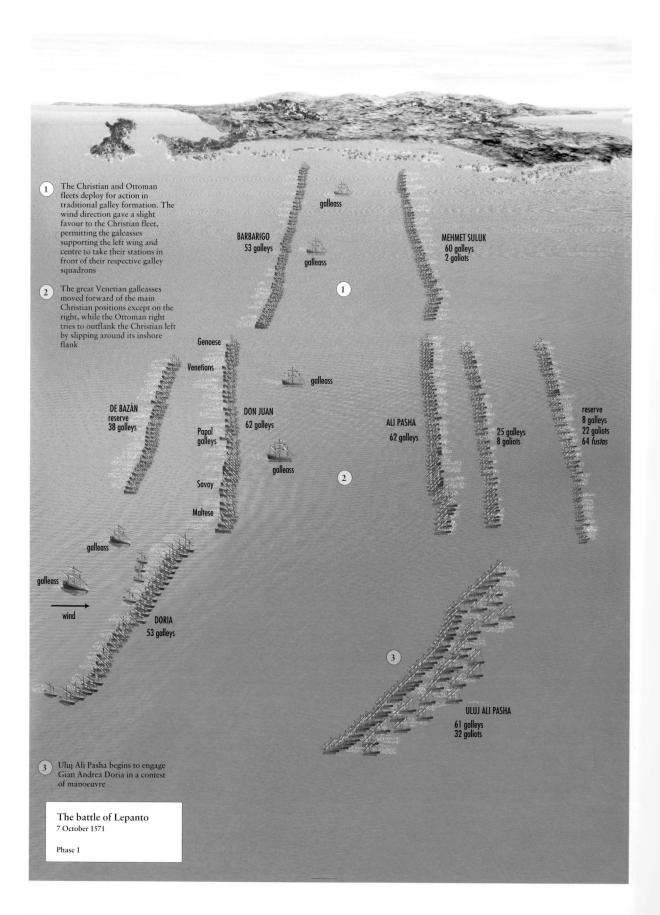

1 The Christian and Ottoman fleets deploy for action in traditional galley formation. The wind direction gave a slight favour to the Christian fleet, permitting the galeasses supporting the left wing and centre to take their stations in front of their respective galley squadrons

2 The great Venetian galeasses moved forward of the main Christian positions except on the right, while the Ottoman right tries to outflank the Christian left by slipping around its inshore flank

galleass

BARBARIGO
53 galleys

galleass

MEHMET SULUK
60 galleys
2 galiots

1

Genoese

Venetians

galleass

DE BAZÁN
reserve
38 galleys

DON JUAN
62 galleys

Papal
galleys

galleass

ALI PASHA
62 galleys

25 galleys
8 galiots

reserve
8 galleys
22 galiots
64 *fustas*

Savoy

Maltese

2

galleass

galleass

wind

DORIA
53 galleys

3

ULUJ ALI PASHA
61 galleys
32 galiots

3 Uluj Ali Pasha begins to engage Gian Andrea Doria in a contest of manoeuvre

The battle of Lepanto
7 October 1571

Phase 1

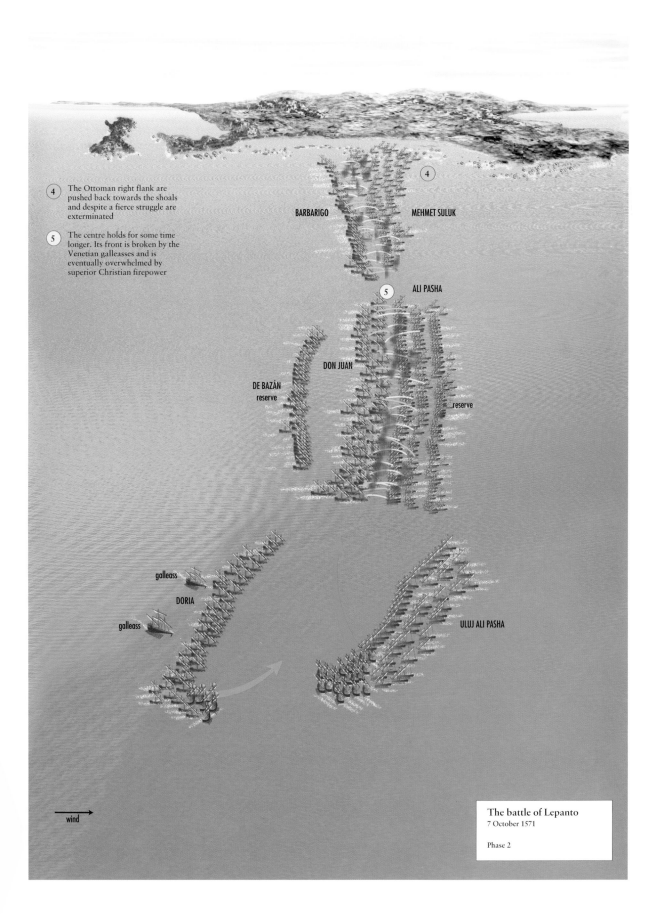

④ The Ottoman right flank are pushed back towards the shoals and despite a fierce struggle are exterminated

⑤ The centre holds for some time longer. Its front is broken by the Venetian galleasses and is eventually overwhelmed by superior Christian firepower

④

BARBARIGO

MEHMET SULUK

⑤ ALI PASHA

DON JUAN

DE BAZÁN
reserve

reserve

galleass

DORIA

galleass

ULUJ ALI PASHA

wind

The battle of Lepanto
7 October 1571

Phase 2

6 Meanwhile on the left, Uluj Ali
Pasha holds the Christians back
until news comes of the collapse
of the rest of the Ottoman fleet.
He then withdraws with 47 of his
original 95 ships plus one
Venetian vessel captured

BARBARIGO

MEHMET SULUK

DON JUAN

ALI PASHA
with reserve

DE BAZÁN

ULUJ ALI PASHA

6

DORIA

wind

The battle of Lepanto
7 October 1571

Phase 3

felled by an arrow to the eye, but first he pivoted his squadron 'like a door', bringing his right forward on line to confront the Turks. His galleasses worked their way back into the fray to deliver the *coup de grâce*. Christian losses were heavy, but the Muslim right was driven against the shore and eliminated.

The centres met at about 12.30 p.m. The Muslims took their quota of punishment passing the galleasses, reformed and then came on. By all accounts, the initial clash was awe-inspiring, firepower pitted against speed and raw muscle, with Muslim galleys penetrating the Christian ranks by as much as a ship's length. The fight was particularly fierce in the centre, where Ali Pasha's *Sultana* forced itself between Don Juan's *Real* and Venier's lantern galley, and smaller Muslim craft sought to force gaps in the Christian line. Twice, boarding parties from the *Real* drove the *Sultana*'s defenders back as far as the mainmast; twice they were repelled by reinforcements from the reserve. Finally, on the third attempt, supported by fire from Venier's galley and bolstered by reinforcements, Don Juan's men succeeded. Ali Pasha was felled by a musket ball, and, as the news of his death spread, Muslim cohesion faltered.

Meanwhile, Uluj Ali Pasha had manoeuvred as if to turn Doria's right, and Doria responded accordingly, moving seawards. Frustrated by the inconclusive

A detail from a contemporary painting of Lepanto by Paolo Veronese (1528–88) accurately conveys the intensely close nature of combat and the dense press of bodies aboard the galleys.

manoeuvring, fifteen of Doria's Venetian galleys, their captains perhaps doubting Doria's intentions, broke formation and headed for the centre. Uluj Ali was closer and shot the gap. He piled into Don Juan's right flank, gobbling up most of the fifteen ill-disciplined galleys en route, engaging Doria's left-hand galleass and the galleys that were towing it into action, and capturing the *Capitanas* (flagship) of Malta and Savoy. It was a close-run thing. Had Bazán not kept the bulk of the Christian reserve uncommitted, Uluj Ali might have pulled victory from the ashes of defeat. As it was, Bazán met the assault head on, while Doria and his second galleass came up belatedly and engaged the rearmost Muslim galleys and galiots in a vicious fight. Seeing the tell-tale signs of defeat in the centre, and no doubt having learned of Ali Pasha's death, Uluj Ali threw in the towel, abandoned his prizes and fought his way clear with thirty galleys, the only sizeable Muslim contingent to escape.

Muslim losses were staggering: 200 galleys, with all of their ordnance, over 30,000 killed and wounded, 15,000 galley slaves freed and 3,000 prisoners as

An engraving of Lepanto from the Museo Correr, Venice, showing the climactic final stages of the battle. The ships are particularly well drawn; note the size difference between the ordinary galleys and galleasses. This depiction is unusual in including significant amounts of smoke.

opposed to Christian losses of 10 galleys, 7,500 killed and 20,000 wounded. Most importantly, at least 4,000 Muslim experts, technical specialists and skilled mariners – *oficiales* – were lost, along with the corps of naval archers. The loss of 600 *oficiales* and 2,400 sailor-arquebusiers at Djerba had hamstrung Spain's galley forces for half a decade, but this was far worse, both proportionately and in absolute terms.

The Ottoman Grand Vizier Sokullu Mehmet Pasha, is said to have reacted to defeat by saying, 'The Christians have singed my beard [meaning the fleet], but I have lopped off an arm. My beard will grow back. The arm [meaning Cyprus], will not'. Either Sokullu Mehmet Pasha was ill-informed on naval matters, which seems unlikely, or he was dissembling, for, as the Spanish learned after Djerba, such beards grew slowly. The Venetian Council of Ten took measures to ensure that it would not grow at all: in June 1572, they polled their prisoners to identify the experts and had them killed. In December the Venetian ambassador to Madrid requested a secret audience with Philip II to inform him of this and to ask

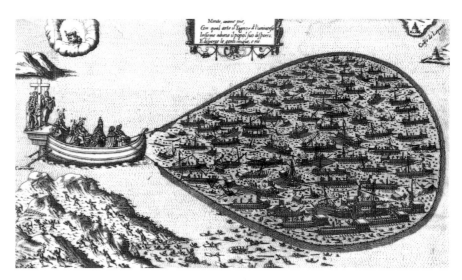

that he do the same. Philip responded that he had already given Don Juan the appropriate orders.

In 1572 Uluj Ali, now Kapudan Pasha, put to sea at the head of a fleet of over 200 galleys, a remarkable achievement although the galleys were hastily built of green wood and their crews were inexperienced. Fearing an outbreak of religious war in France, Philip delayed Don Juan in Spanish waters. By the time he reached the Adriatic in September, Colonna had already sortied, acting in his capacity as second-in-command and encouraged by the new Venetian Capitano Generale da Mar, Giacomo Foscarini (Venier having been

An allegorical engraving celebrating Christian victory at Lepanto. The Pope, with his Spanish and Venetian helpers, is shown pulling in the netted and doomed Muslim fleet.

sidelined to eliminate friction with Don Juan). Catching Uluj Ali off Cerigo on 7 August, Colonna and Foscarini formed line and had their galleasses and armed supply ships towed to the front. Uluj Ali formed line to oppose them. The allies would not engage without the galleasses, while Uluj Ali declined to engage at all.

The two fleets squared off again on 10 August, Uluj Ali again managing to avoid a general engagement. After Don Juan's arrival with 55 galleys, the Christians tried again, finding Uluj Ali at Modon, where he had sought refuge by pulling his galleys ashore stern first, protected by shore batteries. The odds were heavily in the Christians' favour, 194 galleys and 8 galleasses (two of them Tuscan) as opposed to some 200 Muslim galleys, of which 70 or 80 may in fact have been galiots, their crews raw and depleted by sickness. There were signs of panic in the Muslim ranks, and a bold attack might have succeeded, but inter-allied friction had reappeared and Don Juan was reluctant to risk all on a single throw of the dice. The moment of opportunity passed. Distrusting her allies, and with her economic position worsening, Venice came to terms with the Turks the following April.

In 1573 Don Juan led 107 galleys and 30 sailing ships carrying 27,000 troops against Tunis, taking the place without resistance. The success was ephemeral, however. The next year, Uluj Ali, with breathtaking audacity, led 230 galleys and a fleet carrying an army of 40,000 to Tunis. He not only retook the city, but captured the harbour fortress of La Goletta that had been Spanish all along. To the Turks, his triumphal return to Constantinople must have seemed a miracle. The success was never repeated.

With the Turks contained and the situation in Flanders worsening, Philip re-ordered his priorities, scaling down his galley forces and sending Don Juan north in 1576 to take command against the Dutch. The North African *ghazis*, with a hard core of actively campaigning galleys, recovered from Lepanto and remained an active threat to Christian coasts and commerce. The Constantinople-based galley fleet did not. The corps of technical experts and skilled mariners that had been lost at Lepanto was never regenerated, and Western galleys, notably those of the Knights of St John, raided routinely in the Levant, cruising in waters that had hitherto been prohibitively dangerous.

Lepanto yielded seemingly modest strategic dividends, but we must consider the alternatives. As we have seen, victory hung on the narrowest of margins, and the very nature of galley warfare would surely have made any Muslim victory as lopsided as that which obtained. The main loss would have occurred in skilled Christian manpower and, in addition to *oficiales*, would have included the Venetian pool of free oarsmen (only sixteen Venetian galleys at Lepanto were rowed by convicts). With the Mediterranean devoid of expert Christian practitioners of galley warfare, Ali Pasha would have had a degree of operational freedom far greater than that enjoyed by Barbarossa after Prevesa. That the Christian leadership felt constrained to massacre the captured Turkish experts *after* their victory speaks volumes about the threat that these men represented.

Had the Muslims won, it is unlikely that Crete and Malta would have remained in Christian hands for long, and Venice itself would have been at grave risk. Links between North Africa and Constantinople would have been strengthened, the Balearics would have been open to invasion and Ottoman hopes of aiding the Spanish Moriscos would have been real. Perhaps most important though immeasurable, Muslim confidence would have soared, while that of Christendom plummeted.

The evidence thus indicates that Lepanto was indeed decisive, albeit defensively. Süleyman's repulse from Vienna in 1529 is widely regarded as a major turning point, and rightly so, but even had the Turks taken Vienna further advance would have been difficult without major institutional changes – moving the Ottoman capital to Vienna, perhaps – for by 1529 the Habsburg armies were quite capable of taking the Turks' measure in the field. No such constraints would have applied to a victorious Ottoman fleet after Lepanto.

PUNTA DELGADA, 1582

> The most famous naval battles these late years have afforded, were those
> of Lepanto against the Turks ... of the Spaniards against the French at
> the Terceira Islands, and betwixt the Armada of Spain and the English in
> 1588.   SIR WILLIAM MONSON, *c.* 1620

Although it might easily have been otherwise, the Ottoman–Habsburg struggle for Mediterranean dominance now trailed off into stalemate. Uluj Ali Pasha's capture of Tunis and La Goletta in 1574, although operationally brilliant, yielded modest strategic dividends. For its part, Spain commanded inadequate resources for major offensive action, but, in the absence of a significant threat, adopted an aggressive posture. Álvaro de Bazán's galleys ravaged the North African coast with impunity in 1576, showing that war could still cost the Turks. But as the threat diminished in the Mediterranean, Spain's difficulties in the Netherlands grew apace. At the same time, the Ottomans nervously eyed their eastern frontier, where 1577 began a thirteen-year war with the Safavids. That same year, Sultan Murad III concluded an armistice with Philip of Spain that would be periodically renewed until the negotiation of a definitive peace in 1587.

But Spain was not the only Catholic nation with crusading impulses and Mediterranean ambitions, and in 1578 the young Portuguese king, Sebastian, led an army into Morocco to overthrow the sharif, an Ottoman surrogate, and install his own client. The Moroccans were as well supplied with gunpowder weapons as the Portuguese and as skilled in their use, and won a crushing victory on 4 August at Alcazarquivir. Sebastian died in the battle, and his entire army, including the cream of the Portuguese nobility, was killed or captured. The Portuguese throne fell by default to Cardinal Henry, ageing and in ill health, the last legitimate descendant of the Avis line. These developments were noted with alacrity by Philip of Spain, who had a solid claim to the throne through his mother, a

THE STRUGGLE FOR THE AZORES, 1582–3

The map on the right highlights the strategic importance of the Azores as a stopping-over point and provisioning base for returning Spanish treasure fleets and Portuguese spice carracks. In hostile hands, the Azores would not only have deprived the Spanish and Portuguese of a vital place of refuge, but would have been perfect bases for corsairs. The routes of outbound Spanish and Portuguese vessels were further south to take advantage of prevailing winds and current patterns.

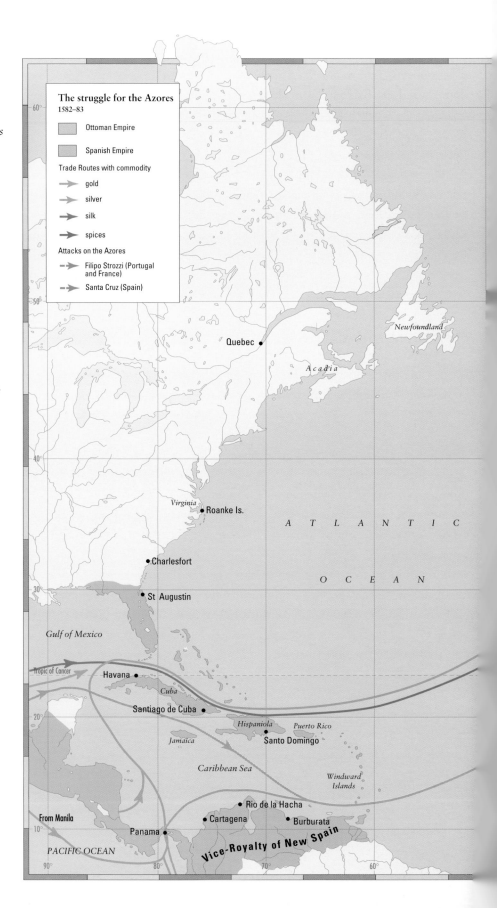

The struggle for the Azores
1582–83

Ottoman Empire

Spanish Empire

Trade Routes with commodity

gold

silver

silk

spices

Attacks on the Azores

Filipo Strozzi (Portugal and France)

Santa Cruz (Spain)

Quebec

Acadia

Newfoundland

Virginia • Roanke Is.

A T L A N T I C

• Charlesfort

O C E A N

• St Augustin

Gulf of Mexico

Tropic of Cancer
Havana •

Cuba

Santiago de Cuba •

Hispaniola   *Puerto Rico*

Jamaica   Santo Domingo •

Caribbean Sea

Windward Islands

• Rio de la Hacha

From Manila
• Cartagena   • Burburata

Panama •   **Vice-Royalty of New Spain**

PACIFIC OCEAN

30°   28°   26°

⚔ 1582 Corvo
      Flores

      Graciosa
São Jorge
Faial   Terceira ⚔ 1583
      Pico

38°

      São Miguel
      1582 ⚔ Punta Delgada
      Ilheus das Formigas

      Santa Maria

NORWAY

SCOTLAND   North Sea

DENMARK

Ireland   ENGLAND   UNITED PROVINCES

London •   Spanish Neth.   SMALL

English Channel   STATES
      • Le Havre
      Paris •
• Brest   SWISS CONFED.

F R A N C E

Bay of Biscay

S P A I N   Mediterranean Sea

Portugal, under Spanish rule 1580–1640   • Madrid

Lisbon •
      • Cádiz
      Oran •   Tunis •

• Sallee   O T T O M A N   E M P I R E

Azores

Madeira

Canary Islands

• Arguin   A f r i c a

Cape Verde Islands

GUINEA

40°   40°   30°   20°   10°   0°

Portuguese princess. Henry died in February 1580, having spent much of Portugal's treasure to ransom *fidalgos,* members of the nobility captured at Alcazarquivir. Philip had used the intervening years to good advantage, discreetly negotiating his terms of succession with Henry, arriving at an arrangement that preserved Portugal's empire and governmental institutions and secured the acquiescence of the nobility and wealthy merchants.

There was, however, considerable anti-Spanish sentiment among the ordinary Portuguese, and Sebastian's illegitimate cousin, Dom Antonio, a wealthy friar, proclaimed himself king with considerable popular support. Philip responded by invading Portugal and dispatching envoys to Portugal's imperial possessions to press his case. The invasion had two arms: an army driving on Lisbon from the east through Estremadura, and a smaller force working its way along the southern coast with naval support. Philip again displayed his skill at selecting subordinates, assigning the main force to the Duke of Alba, ageing but still widely respected; the southern army to the Duke of Medina Sidonia; and naval command to Bazán, getting on in years but thoroughly competent. It was Philip's finest hour as commander-in-chief. Henry's expenditure for ransoms had left little for defence; the Spanish moved swiftly and, in Alba's case, with remarkable restraint. The Spanish forces united and, after a short, stiff fight – Alba's last battle, and perhaps his best – Lisbon surrendered on 18 July 1580. Dom Antonio fled north and on 23 October left the country aboard an English ship.

Philip's lieutenants had left Portuguese governance intact, and internal resistance evaporated. The Indies and Brazil accepted Spanish rule, the latter with some enthusiasm in the light of French designs on its trade. Of the Portuguese empire, only the Azores, excepting the island of São Miguel, held for Dom Antonio, a matter that quickly aroused interest in London and, of greater import, Paris. That interest was heightened when a small Spanish expedition that had been sent in 1581 to reclaim the islands was repulsed. This was a serious matter, for the Azores were vital to the operation of convoys from both the East and West Indies; the Flota de Tierra Firme, Flota de Nueva España and Carriera das Indias, the treasure and spice convoys, used them for watering and provisioning on their way home and as a rendezvous point for their escorts. They were a perfect base from which to prey on Habsburg commerce.

Sensing opportunity, Catherine de Medici, dowager queen of France, resolved to support Dom Antonio's claim and, in the spring of 1582, dispatched an expeditionary force under Philip Strozzi of some 60 ships, half of them large, carrying 6–7,000 soldiers, the largest French maritime expedition until the age of Louis XIV. Sailing with the implicit blessing of Queen Elizabeth, it included several English ships. Alive to the danger, Philip dispatched a fleet under Bazán. Consisting of 2 large Portuguese warships, 19 armed merchantmen and 10 transports carrying 4,500 soldiers, it met Strozzi's force on 24 July 1582. After an indecisive encounter, the two fleets met two days later, some 18 miles south of São Miguel, in a fierce engagement named after the island's capital, Punta Delgada.

The French initially had the advantage of the wind and attacked the Spanish rear with superior forces, but Bazán doubled with his van, precipitating a mêlée. Although the French enjoyed advantages in terms of weatherliness and, initially, in order, the Spanish prevailed by sheer hard fighting. The galleon *San Mateo*, the focal point of the battle, was assailed by no less than seven French ships, including Strozzi's *Capitana* (flagship), in an action that ultimately drew in Bazán's *Capitana*. While the major warships on both sides were amply provided with cannon, it was a battle of boarding and counterboarding that was decided by small arms, edged weapons and valour. The French lost ten ships, including Strozzi's flagship, which was boarded and captured. Strozzi himself took a Spanish arquebus ball and died a captive aboard Bazán's *Capitana*.

Punta Delgada was the first major naval engagement fought far from any continental landmass and would be the last until the battle of Midway in 1942. Although modern historians have largely ignored Punta Delgada, the English sea dog Sir William Monson was quite right to cite its importance. Although French adventurers and Dom Antonio's partisans still held the Azores, save for São Miguel, Punta Delgada was decisive. Bazán returned the next year with a massive armada: 5 galleons, 2 galleasses and 12 galleys, together with 79 sailing ships, 30 large and the rest small, carrying some 15,372 soldiers. Uniting his fleet at São Miguel on 19 July 1582 – the galleys sailed independently, arriving eleven days ahead of the rest – Bazán directed his force at Terceira, the largest of the Azores in French hands. After a careful reconnaissance, he selected the least heavily defended of three feasible beaches and mounted a model amphibious invasion, the galleys providing fire support for infantry carried ashore in small craft. Bazán's account of the action has a strikingly modern tone:

> … receiving many cannonades … the [flag] galley began to batter and dismount the enemy artillery and the rest of the galleys [did likewise] … and the landing boats ran aground and placed the soldiers at the sides of the forts, and along the trenches, although with much difficulty and working under the pressure of the furious artillery, arquebus, and musket fire of the enemy. And the soldiers mounting [the trenches] in several places came under heavy arquebus and musket fire, but finally won the forts and trenches.

With Spanish infantry ashore in superior numbers resistance on Terceira collapsed, the other islands following suit. Dom Antonio got off with his skin and little else. The Azores held for Spain, and the Indies convoys continued unhindered. Flushed with victory, Bazán advised his imperial master that England could be invaded by sea. Thus stimulated, Philip asked his commander in Flanders, Alexander Farnese, Duke of Parma, about the feasibility of such a project. Parma was unenthusiastic, preferring a surprise attack across the Channel to Bazán's proposal to invade from Iberia; Parma did not, however, rule it out.

CHAPTER FIVE

THE GALLEON

ENGLISH VICTORY over the Spanish Armada, detail from a painting by Nicholas Hilliard (1547–1618) in the collection of the Apothecaries Guild, London.

THE GALLEON

THE GALLEON'S ORIGINS are obscure; all we can say about them with certainty is that they are European and included oared warships. The Portuguese used galleons fitted with oars to patrol the Indian Ocean in the 1510s, and early sixteenth-century French sources mention Spanish galleons as feared Mediterranean raiders. Both cases clearly involve warships, and probably ancestors of the fully developed galleon, but we know nothing about them in detail. The galleon's immediate precursors in England were 'galliasses', built from the 1520s to the 1550s, with low, almost flush-decked, hulls. These vessels – which bore no relationship to Mediterranean galleasses – lost their oars by the mid 1540s, yet as late as 1567–8, the Spanish crown built twelve small galleons fitted with oars to defend the Atlantic trade routes.

A Portuguese fleet inventory of 1525 lists twenty-one galleons in the Indian Ocean, and one galleon was built in the Venetian Arsenal between 1526 and 1530. These were oarless and clearly warships – the Venetian galleon fought at Prevesa in 1538 – but our knowledge remains sketchy until around 1540, when galleons became increasingly common in maritime art. Gleaning information from artists' depictions, gear and armament inventories, works of naval architecture and the fruits of nautical archaeology, we can approach the galleon with some confidence from this point. Particularly important in this regard is the Swedish *Vasa*, a ship intermediate between galleon and ship-of-the-line, which was sunk on her maiden voyage in 1628 and was raised intact in the 1960s.

By about 1570 'galleon' was being commonly used to designate the kind of ship that we associate with the word, but the precise meaning varied from country to country. The Portuguese *galeão* was a purpose-built warship, whereas, in Spanish, *galeón* designated warships and armed merchantman alike. The English applied the word more often to foreign vessels than their own, and the Dutch *galjoen* applied only to the vessel's projecting beakhead.

Galleons were ship-rigged with a bowsprit, foremast, mainmast and mizzenmast (or masts: large galleons had a second, bonaventure mizzen). The bowsprit carried a spritsail, the fore- and mainmasts carried square courses and topsails, while mizzens were lateen-rigged. In this respect galleons were no different from naos and carracks. The difference was in the hull which was slimmer than the carrack's, with a length-to-breadth ratio in the order of four to one to the carrack's three to one. Stoutly built to carry heavy ordnance, it had a low forecastle and – the distinguishing feature – a projecting beakhead below the bowsprit. The hull had pronounced tumble-home, that is inward-tapering sides, and the quarterdeck and poop towered above the forecastle, giving the galleon its characteristic crescent shape when viewed from the side. The logic behind these features becomes evident when we consider that the galleon was designed to carry its heaviest ordnance to fire forwards. Like the cannon-armed galley, the galleon's

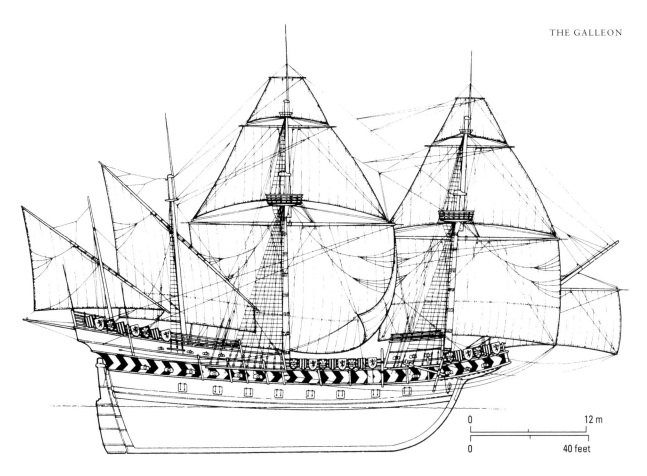

underwater lines provided extra buoyancy at the bow to support ordnance, ideally two heavy bowchasers mounted under the forecastle on either side of the beak and two smaller chasers in the forecastle itself. Like the galley, the galleon's underwater lines were fine at the stern, reducing drag and improving performance. The hull lines of the *Vasa* and surviving contemporary models support this thesis, as do the plans and illustrations of Matthew Baker, Queen Elizabeth's principal master shipwright, preserved in *Fragments of Ancient English Shipwrightry*. From this perspective the beakhead's resemblance to the war galley's spur is obvious, while the forecastle was plainly more akin to the galley's fighting platform than the carrack's towering forecastle.

Galleons were more weatherly and seaworthy than carracks, and the galleon's hull, unlike the caravel's, was sufficiently capacious to carry adequate supplies and provisions for transoceanic voyages and still retain a margin for cargo. They varied widely in size, generally between 450 and 1,500 tons displacement. There were trade-offs – heavier armament and finer lines meant fewer stores and less cargo – but galleons were the first sailing vessels routinely capable of transoceanic navigation that could effectively bring heavy guns to bear offensively. That represented an enormous increase in capability. The stark contrast between the relative ease of Francis Drake's almost offhanded 1577–8 global circumnavigation as the easiest way home with his Spanish loot (with heavy loss of life, to be sure) and the three-year calvary of the 1519–22 Magellan–Del Cano expedition – 4 out of 5 ships and all but 18 of 234 men lost – says it all.

SPANISH GALLEON

Artist's rendering of a Spanish galleon of about 1540, based on a contemporary model in the Museo Naval, Madrid. The rig is fully developed, with topgallants on the fore and main masts and a bonaventure mizzen. Note the laced-on bonnets on the mainsail, foresail and mizzen lateen sail. Characteristically, it has only one continuous gun deck. The guns on the upper deck and castles would have been relatively light.

A contemporary portrait of Sir Francis Drake, one of the most able exponents of the galleon. A dynamic leader and able mariner, he was at heart a corsair, persistent attempts by later historians to see him as a pre-incarnation of Horatio Nelson notwithstanding.

The galleon was valued tactically for combining the full-rigged ship's seaworthiness and manoeuvrability under sail with the war galley's effectiveness as a gun platform. This is best documented for the English, but they were not unique. The heaviest shipboard guns in the 1525 Portuguese inventory mentioned above were four *leões* (lions), bronze pieces nominally firing a 50-pound cast-iron ball; these were mounted 'forward', or 'in the prow' in 4 of the 10 galleons for which ordnance is specified. The next heaviest guns were 18-pound, stone-throwing *camelos*, comprising the bulk of the broadside armament and used as bowchasers in the absence of *leões*. Extremely heavy pieces continued to be mounted as bowchasers on galleons well into the seventeenth century, and there is ample evidence that seamen considered a heavy forward-firing battery the galleon's knockout blow. Broadside guns were considered useful and, to confuse matters, although 'broadside' was used to describe their collective discharge just as we use the word today, their role was defensive. Regarding their galleons' accomplishments, the Elizabethan sea dogs reserved pride of place not for the defeat of the Spanish Armada, but for their successes against galleys in Spanish waters. The Cádiz raids of 1587 and – particularly – 1596 are the benchmarks.

As long as galleons remained a distinct type the design parameters described above remained essentially unchanged, but design was not static. Most importantly, as more and better ordnance became available, armament became progressively heavier and hull design was modified accordingly. This was particularly true in England where the galleon was considered ideal for corsairing and, as it turned out, defence of home waters. To this, add Queen Elizabeth's policy of encouraging her subjects to raid her enemies by sea – as private acts of war, to be sure, to avoid diplomatic embarrassment – while at the same time funding the development of a small but efficient state navy, and the result was the race-built galleon. Developed under the influence of John Hawkins, treasurer of the navy, these galleons were uncommonly sleek, with fine hulls, reduced superstructures to improve weatherliness, and unprecedentedly heavy armament. As Geoffrey Parker has shown, the first of these galleons, *Dreadnought*, launched in 1573, carried ordnance amounting to nearly 4.5 per cent of displacement tonnage – an unprecedented figure; by contrast, galleons commissioned early in Elizabeth's reign carried less than 3 per cent. By the time of the Armada, the figure had increased to 8 per cent, and sometimes even 11 per cent, and, of equal importance, guns with hull-smashing potential accounted for a steadily larger

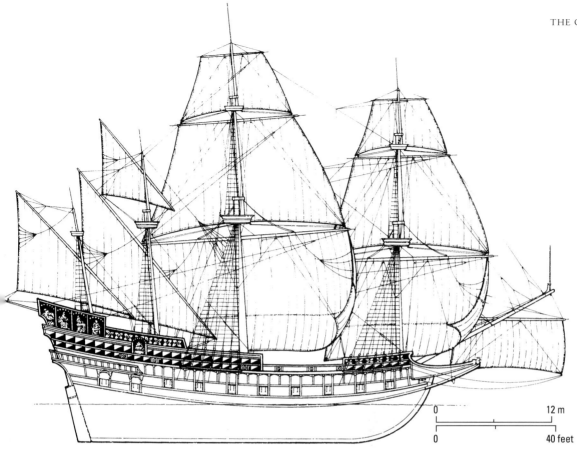

0   12 m

0   40 feet

proportion of the total. Race-built galleons were not true transoceanic warships, however, for their fine lines and heavy ordnance limited stowage, keeping them relatively close to home. Spanish galleons built to escort the annual Indies convoys and to haul silver were substantially less heavily armed: in 1588, these carried only some 3 per cent of their displacement in ordnance, while the Portuguese galleon *San Juan*, reputedly the best-gunned ship in the Spanish Armada, carried only 4 per cent.

There was an important human difference as well, for in contrast to Spanish and Portuguese practice, English crews were not segregated by soldiers having their own commanders and occupying higher rungs on the social ladder than seamen. Instead the ship's company worked as one, and the captain – a mariner – was in undisputed command. This yielded enormous advantages in efficiency, advantages the Dutch would share.

Spanish, Portuguese and Ragusan galleons from Sicily carried less firepower than their English equivalents, particularly in the form of hull-smashing guns, but the biggest technical difference was not in the guns, but in how they were mounted and used. The English used four-wheeled truck carriages, while the others used long-trailed, two-wheeled carriages and land carriages with large wheels. It is clear from analyses of the amount of shot fired and powder consumed that the English guns, particularly their heavy guns, fired more than those of the Armada, and to better effect. The question is how, and why.

There is an understandable tendency to assume that since sixteenth-century English carriages differed little from those of the eighteenth century, the gun drill

ENGLISH GALLEON

A race-built English galleon of the time of the Armada, based on contemporary plans from Matthew Baker's Fragments of Ancient Shipwrightry. *Of about the same size and displacement as the Spanish galleon depicted two pages earlier, it is much more heavily armed. Its largest ordnance would have been mounted in chase and behind the two rearmost ports on the gun deck. Notice that the gundeck is 'stepped' to place the heavy pieces aft lower in the hull for reasons of stability.*

Royal Prince, alternatively Prince Royal, by Willem van de Velde the Elder. Commissioned in 1610, Royal Prince was the precursor of English ships-of-the-line. Repeatedly rebuilt and rearmed, she had a long and distinguished life before being captured by the Dutch in the Four Days Fight, 11–14 June 1666, during the Second Anglo-Dutch War.

was also similar, that is using the gun's recoil to bring it inboard for loading. There is some evidence that recoil was used on English ships of the Elizabethan era to bring guns inboard for loading, but that was certainly not universal practice and may have been confined to the heaviest chase guns. Moreover, neither records of ammunition expenditure nor of the numbers of gunners provided per gun suggest anything like the high rates of fire later obtained. Rather, the Elizabethan sea dogs probably valued the truck carriage mainly for the compactness that permitted greater angles of traverse. The preferred ship-to-ship tactic was to gain the wind; bear down and fire the bowchasers; pull parallel and fire the lee broadside; luff to bring the stern-chasers to bear; then tack to fire the weather broadside before pulling clear to reload. The English had probably adopted recoil-firing on the broadside by the 1630s, but the preferred tactics remained unchanged, for they were perfectly suited to creating advantageous circumstances for boarding and capturing.

Understandably, the Barbary corsairs took to the galleon with alacrity, for it was ideally suited to their work, and in the galleon's heyday, during the 1620s, Algiers possessed Europe's largest war fleet. The Dutch came late to the galleon, and called it by other names, but they used it to good effect: the galleon's swiftness and offensive firepower lent itself well to their interloping expeditions to Africa, the Indies and Brazil, and the first battles of any size between European fleets far from home were fought by squadrons of Dutch and Luso-Spanish galleons. In 1631 the Spanish admiral Don Antonio de Oquendo described his Dutch opponents in the battle of Abrolhos, fought some 150–180 miles off the Brazilian coast, as *galeones gruesos*, 'big galleons'. It is worth noting that Abrolhos was the first naval battle of consequence fought far from land, a mark

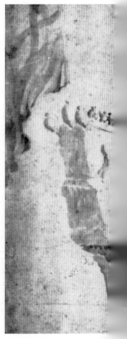

of the galleon's capabilities, and that Oquendo gained victory in a hard-fought boarding fight with the Dutch flagship, despite a manifest inferiority in heavy ordnance.

However firmly ship's masters and captains held to traditional tactics, there was an irreversible logic in the steadily increasing weight of ordnance and the design changes needed to accommodate it. As galleons acquired more and more guns, these were mounted on the broadside, for there was nowhere else to put them. The process ultimately produced the ship-of-the-line, but the ship-of-the-line made little sense without line-ahead tactics, and these were counterintuitive: one does not attack by going sideways. The imperative for royal display weighed in as King James I of England (r. 1603–25) ordered construction of the *Royal Prince*. Commissioned in 1610, *Royal Prince* was a spectacular departure, displacing 1,900 tons and carrying 55 guns mounted on 2 full gundecks – galleons had one only – and a partial third. Interestingly, as Nicholas Rodger has shown, *Royal Prince* was copied from the slightly smaller Danish *Tre Kroner*, designed by a Scottish shipwright who used English lofting methods, circumstances suggesting exchanges of shipbuilding methods in northern European waters. That impression is confirmed by Louis XIII of France's principal minister Cardinal Richelieu's purchase of warships from Dutch yards, one of which, the *St Louis*, delivered in 1626, displaced 1,400 tons and carried 60 guns on 2 gun-decks. *Vasa*'s lines give us a firm anchor on which to base our hypotheses. King Charles I of England (r. 1625–49) commissioned a series of 'great ships', derived from the galleon but larger and with heavier broadside.

In England the *Royal Prince* was followed in 1637 by the even more extravagant *Sovereign of the Seas*, with 100 guns on 3 full gundecks and 2,700

Sovereign of the Seas, the most powerful warship in existence when she was launched in 1637, here in a sketch by Willem van de Velde the Younger (1633–1707). The power of her broadside is evident. Not evident is her richly carved and gilded ornamentation. At first criticized by experienced sea captains as impossibly cumbersome, she served with distinction in the Anglo-Dutch Wars and was known to her enemies as 'The Gilded Devil'.

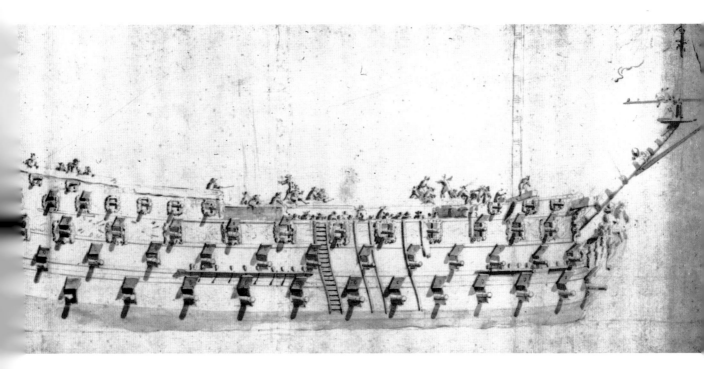

tons displacement. The French *Couronne*, launched in 1638, was even larger, at 2,900 tons, although she carried only 88 guns. *Sovereign*, like *Royal Prince* before her, was criticized by experienced English sea captains, Sir William Monson among them, as being impossibly unwieldy. Such vessels, they argued, could fight only on one side and would be outmanoeuvred and outshot by smaller, nimbler warships that could bring bow, weather broadside, stern chase and lee broadside to bear in turn. Given the tactical precepts of their day, Monson and his colleagues were quite right.

In fact, *Sovereign* survived into the Anglo-Dutch wars and proved herself a thoroughly capable warship, but the tactics with which she would demonstrate her prowess barely existed when her keel was laid. With full hindsight, it is possible to discern the beginnings of the galleon's transformation into the ship-of-the-line by the 1630s, but that transformation would be driven to completion only by the impetus of future wars.

THE 'INVINCIBLE' ARMADA, 1588

> We found that many of the enemy's ships held great advantage over us in combat, both in their design and in their guns, gunners and crews . . . so that they could do with us as they wished. But in spite of all this, the duke [Medina Sidonia] managed to bring his fleet to anchor in Calais roads, just seven leagues from Dunkirk . . . and if, on the day we arrived there, Parma had come out [with his forces] we should have carried out the invasion.
>
> DON FRANCISCO DE BOBADILLA, the Armada's senior military officer,
> 20 August 1588

The defeat of the Spanish Armada marked a major turning point in world history. To be sure, the popular view that the Armada marked the beginning of England's rise and Spain's decline is overstated, but if Philip II's grand design had succeeded we would be living in a very different world. Beyond its immediate consequences – which were considerable – the Armada tells us a great deal about warfare at sea during a pivotal period of change.

The first link in the chain of proximate causation that led to the defeat of the Armada was forged in April 1572, when Queen Elizabeth, bowing to Spanish pressure, ordered Dutch privateers to be expelled from English ports. With good intelligence of Spanish dispositions, and nowhere else to go, they returned home and seized the port of Brill. Welcomed by their fellow Protestants, and finding the Duke of Alba's army overextended, they seized Flushing and Enkhuizen in May, re-igniting the rebellion that the duke thought he had snuffed out in 1567–8.

Unable to stand up to the Spanish in the field, the Dutch proved tenacious in siege warfare and quickly learned the value of their waterways. Alive to the advantages of water transport in a land with more canals than roads, Alba created a navy to support his endeavours, but could not sustain it. Its only success

ELISABETHA
REG: ANGLIÆ.

A portrait of Queen Elizabeth I by an anonymous artist. Painted towards the beginning of her reign, it hints at her shrewdness and keen intelligence. Her judicious naval policies laid the foundations for England's future greatness at sea.

Alexander Farnese, Duke of Parma, in a portrait by Frans Porbus the Younger (c. 1570–1622). Perhaps the finest general of his day, Farnese's strategic vision and dynamic leadership brought the Dutch revolt to the brink of collapse more than once.

was cutting off Haarlem from resupply in the spring of 1573, and from that point Dutch control of inland waters did much to counter the skill and fortitude of the Army of Flanders. The high point of Spanish fortunes came in the summer of 1585, under the captain-generalcy of Alexander Farnese, Duke of Parma. Perhaps the finest general of his day, Parma had confined the rebellion to Holland, Zealand and Utrecht, with a relentless campaign of sieges, taking Antwerp in August. That May the Spanish had embargoed all northern vessels in Spanish ports. All but Dutch ships were eventually released, but the act gave Elizabeth *casus belli*.

Up to that point Elizabeth had condoned a private war against Spain, but stopped short of openly declared hostilities. Now, facing the very real possibility that Protestantism would be throttled in the Netherlands, and with

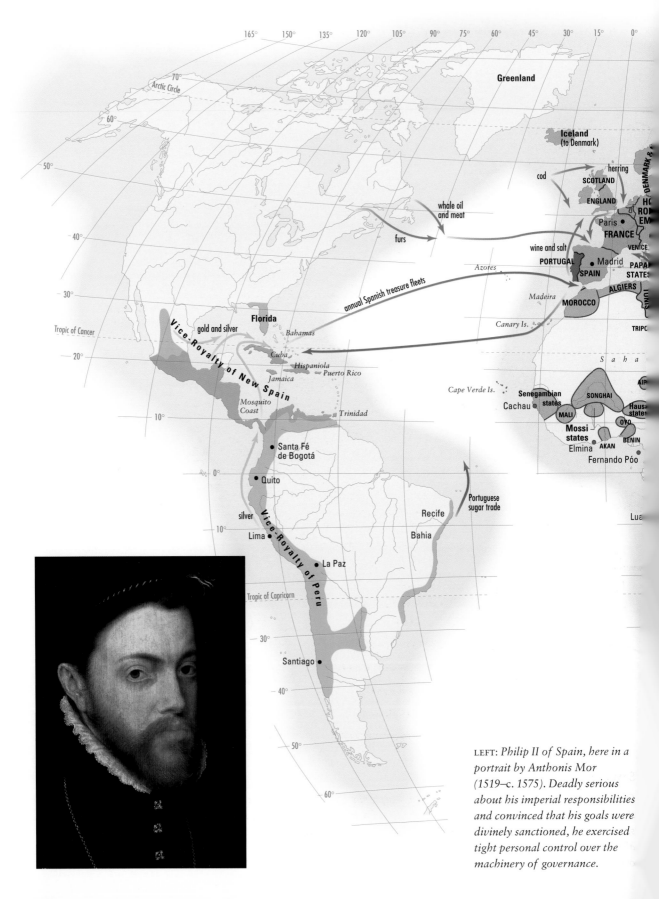

Greenland

Iceland
(to Denmark)

cod
herring
SCOTLAND
ENGLAND
DENMARK &
H O
RO
EM
Paris
FRANCE
VENICE
wine and salt
PORTUGAL
Madrid
PAPAL
SPAIN
STATES
Azores
ALGIERS
Madeira
MOROCCO
TRIPO
Canary Is.
S a h a

whale oil
and meat

furs

annual Spanish treasure fleets

Arctic Circle

Tropic of Cancer

Florida

gold and silver

Bahamas

Cuba

Hispaniola
Jamaica
Puerto Rico

Vice-Royalty of New Spain

Mosquito
Coast

Trinidad

Cape Verde Is.

Senegambian
states
Cachau
MALI
SONGHAI
Mossi
states
AKAN
OYO
BENIN
Elmina
Fernando Póo

AÏR
Hausa
states

Santa Fé
de Bogotá

Quito

silver

Vice-Royalty of Peru

Lima

La Paz

Recife

Bahia

Portuguese
sugar trade

Lua

Tropic of Capricorn

Santiago

LEFT: *Philip II of Spain, here in a portrait by Anthonis Mor (1519–c. 1575). Deadly serious about his imperial responsibilities and convinced that his goals were divinely sanctioned, he exercised tight personal control over the machinery of governance.*

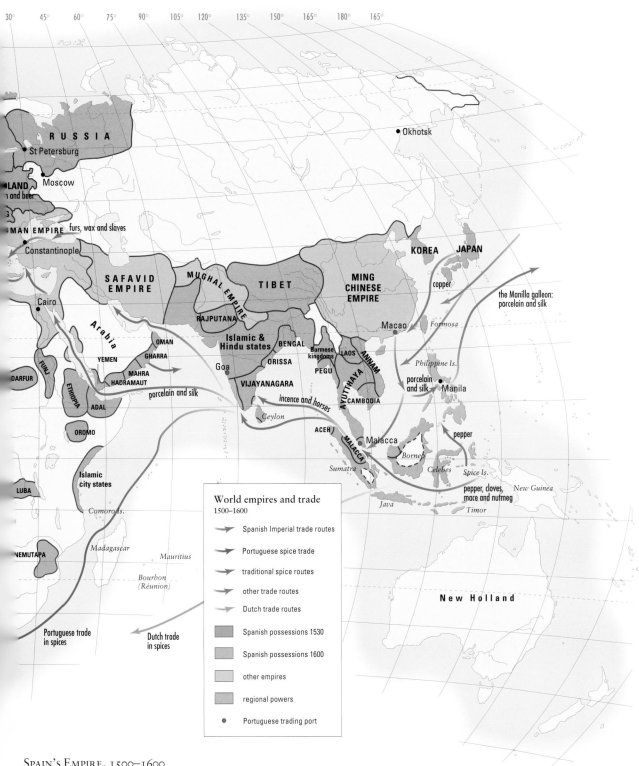

World empires and trade
1500–1600

→ Spanish Imperial trade routes
→ Portuguese spice trade
→ traditional spice routes
→ other trade routes
→ Dutch trade routes
Spanish possessions 1530
Spanish possessions 1600
other empires
regional powers
● Portuguese trading port

SPAIN'S EMPIRE, 1500–1600

Occupying the Philippines in the final decades of the sixteenth century and absorbing Portugal's overseas possessions from 1580 gave Habsburg Spain the largest richest empire in the world. The idea that her rebellious Dutch provinces, barely visible on the map, might not only challenge this behemoth but defeat it militarily and surpass it economically would have seemed incredible to contemporary observers. In fact, by 1607 the Dutch had fought Spain to a standstill, forcing acceptance of the 1609–21 Twelve Years Truce.

England next in line, she reacted aggressively, allying herself with the Dutch, dispatching an expeditionary force to Flanders and sending a fleet under Francis Drake to ravage the Canaries and the Caribbean. That gave Philip the excuse he needed: when Álvaro de Bazán offered to plan an invasion of England he responded positively and asked Parma to do the same.

Bazán, no doubt overstating his requirements out of caution, advocated a massive expedition to be launched from Lisbon. Parma (after an extended delay, for he was unenthusiastic about diverting his forces) proposed a less costly, but more daring, plan: a surprise crossing of the Channel in local shipping. Philip, no doubt recoiling from the cost of Bazán's proposal, settled on a hybrid plan: Bazán would take a fleet into the Channel, rendezvous with Parma and convoy him to England. Orders to that effect were dispatched to Bazán and Parma in July 1586. In terms of tonnage of ships, numbers of troops, quantities of arms, munitions and provisions and distance covered, it would be the most ambitious European naval enterprise to date, ultimately numbering 130 to 140 ships, over 90 of them of 200 tons displacement or more, carrying some 7,000 sailors and 19,000

A dramatic episode in the 1585 siege of Antwerp, the detonation of engineer Federigo Giambelli's 'hellburners,' two ships stuffed with tons of gunpowder confined by layers of masonry, stones and scrap iron. Carried against the Spanish fortified bridge blocking access to the city by the tide, they breached the bridge and killed 800 Spaniards ... ultimately to no avail.

soldiers. Parma would assemble 27,000 troops at their embarkation ports, along with 270 vessels to carry them to England. These things were not done easily.

Galleys aside, the only purpose-built warships available were three Portuguese galleons, survivors of those seized in 1580, and four Neapolitan galleasses. To these we can add 17 galleons, including 10 of Spain's Indies Guard, which were designed to haul bullion and protect treasure convoys. The bulk of the Armada's carrying capacity consisted of impressed merchantmen, armed with whatever could be found, and lightly armed hulks (the generic term for large merchantmen).

A fleet under Drake raided Cádiz in April 1587, destroying twenty-four ships and immense quantities of supplies. Drake's presence put the Indies convoys at risk. Bazán sailed for the Azores to bring them home, and indeed did so, but at considerable cost in terms of wear and tear on both ships and crews. A November storm battered up the Armada in harbour; Bazán died in February 1588.

Bazán's replacement was the Duke of Medina Sidonia, who was short on combat experience afloat, but a superb administrator. Recognizing the enormity of his task, he begged to be excused, but his pleas and subsequent arguments against the wisdom of the enterprise fell on deaf ears, for Philip knew that God approved. Due largely to the duke's competence, the Armada finally cleared the Tagus river on 30 May 1588, but with bad cooperage and putrefying provisions – partly a consequence of Drake's destruction of barrel staves in Cádiz in the previous year. Scattered by a storm while putting into La Coruña (Corunna) for fresh supplies, the Armada was further delayed, finally departing on 21 July. After yet another storm on 27 July that cost it two days and four galleys, the Armada entered the Channel on 30 July. Formed in a deep line abreast, with rearward-

The successful defence of Cádiz against the English in November 1625, by Francisco de Zurbaran (1598–1664) in the Prado, Madrid. The Spanish commander, Don Fernando Giron, at left, is confined to his chair by gout. The operations are amphibious and the Spanish galleys are holding their own; the Spanish were more successful on this occasion than in 1587 or 1596.

OPPOSITE: *An engraving by the Dutch artist Claes Jans Visscher of the English galleon* Griffin *which took part in the Armada campaign. It was drawn long after the event and the details of hull, sails and rigging are problematic.*

curving wings tipped by its most capable warships to discourage attacks from the flanks and rear, it seemed unstoppable.

To face this juggernaut England could muster twenty-three large royal warships, almost all race-built galleons, some thirty large private warships and a host of smaller vessels. High Admiral Lord Howard of Effingham had been persuaded by Drake, his newly appointed vice admiral, to bring the bulk of his force west to Plymouth, leaving a small squadron under Lord Henry Seymour in the Downs, a roadstead off the south-eastern coast of England, to watch Parma.

THE INVINCIBLE ARMADA: THE STRENGTHS OF THE FLEETS, 30 MAY 1588

SPANISH

20 galleons, averaging 600 tons displacement, including 3 former Portuguese royal warships and 10 galleons of the Indies Guard

47 armed merchantmen, averaging 680 tons displacement each

21 hulks, large merchantmen impressed to haul troops and supplies, many of them Mediterranean vessels poorly suited for the Atlantic

4 galleasses, displacing about 1,000 tons each

4 galleys

31 small ships for dispatch vessels and scouts

ENGLISH

23 royal warships, displacing from 250 to 1,500 tons each, the bulk of them race-built galleons

30 private warships, displacing 300 to 600 tons each, the more heavily armed of them equivalent to royal warships of like size

30 private warships, displacing 200 to 250 tons

10 small royal vessels, pinnaces and the like

1 galley

162 small private ships

A contemporary broadside depicting Lord Charles Howard of Effingham, High Admiral of England in 1588, at the time of the Armada.

(1) 30 May: the Armada departs Lisbon numbering 128 ships and 29,453 men, heading north against adverse winds

(2) 14 June: the Armada arrives off Cape Finisterre and waits for supplies to be sent out but nothing appears. Medina Sidonia decides to enter Corunna harbour with 40 ships, the rest to enter the next day. The waiting ships, however, are scattered by a violent storm, some even sailing as far as the Scilly Islands off the Cornish coast. They are found by a Spanish dispatch boat on 30 June and brought back to Corunna

(3) 21 July: the Armada sails from Corunna now numbering, after recovering ships blown off course by the storm and receiving reinforcements, 131 ships and 24,607 men

(4) 25 July: the Armada passes Ushant and makes a heading for England

(5) 29 July: in the afternoon the Armada passes Lizard Point, Cornwall

(6) 30 July: 54 ships of the English fleet sail out of Plymouth, managing during the night to take a position windward of the Spanish fleet. The Spanish are shocked to see eleven more English ships tacking into the wind at what seems incredible speed to join their fleet

(7) 31 July: the English attack and inflict some damage on the Armada with no losses

(8) 2–4 August: the English attack again and harry the Spanish

(9) 6 August: the Spanish fleet anchors some 4 miles off Calais with the English fleet anchoring nearby. Later in the day English reinforcements arrive; the Spanish now face some 230 ships

(10) 6 August: the intended link up with the Duke of Parma's forces in the Spanish Netherlands proves impossible. Parma has effectively deceived the Dutch as to his intentions. They are defending against an attack on Amsterdam. Parma will be ready to link up within 48 hours, but by then it will be too late

(11) 7 August: fireships are sent against the anchored Spanish fleet around midnight on the 7th. The Spanish cut their anchor cables and set sail in disorder

(12) 8 August: at dawn the Spanish fleet is scattered over some 12 miles of ocean. The English attack as the Spanish are reforming and the ensuing battle drags on all day with the English gaining the upper hand. Despite having better ammunition, the Spanish are suffering badly when a sudden squall blows, enabling them to draw away

(13) The Spanish fleet, intending to refit at a Flemish port, is caught by unfavourable winds. Medina Sidonia decides to return to Spain by circling the British Isles. Regaining a close formation they head north, pursued by the English fleet

(14) The English fleet, short of provisions, returns to its home ports

(15) The Armada continues its long journey, battle-damaged and hit by storms, causing terrible hardships. Of the 131 ships that set out, 63 were lost in or as a result of battle or shipwrecked. Of the 34 others lost, their fate was unrecorded or unknown. The remaining 55 ships straggled into Spanish ports during September

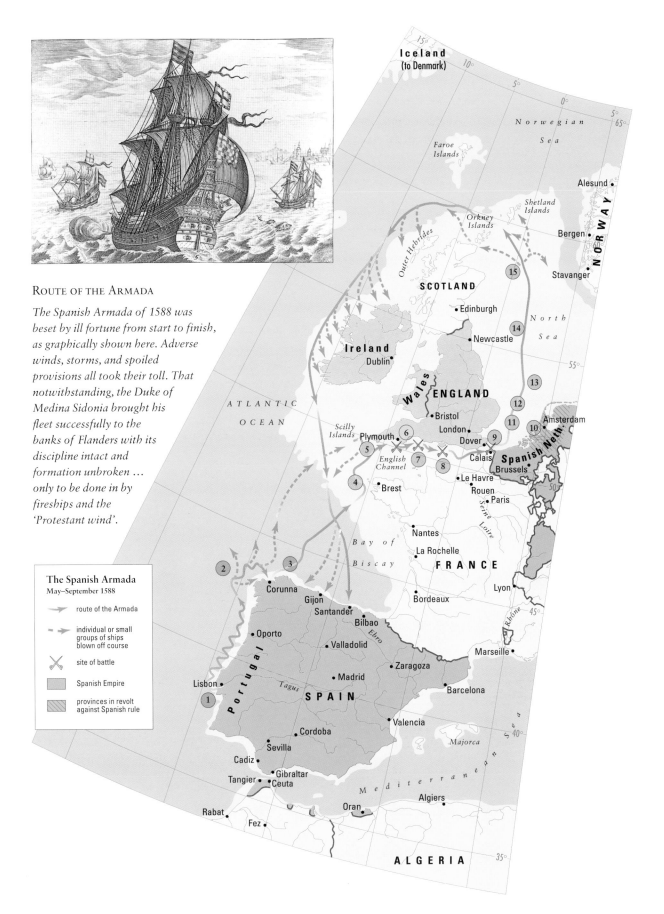

ROUTE OF THE ARMADA

*The Spanish Armada of 1588 was
beset by ill fortune from start to finish,
as graphically shown here. Adverse
winds, storms, and spoiled
provisions all took their toll. That
notwithstanding, the Duke of
Medina Sidonia brought his
fleet successfully to the
banks of Flanders with its
discipline intact and
formation unbroken …
only to be done in by
fireships and the
'Protestant wind'.*

The Spanish Armada
May–September 1588

→ route of the Armada

⇢ individual or small
groups of ships
blown off course

✕ site of battle

Spanish Empire

provinces in revolt
against Spanish rule

The dispatch of fireships against the Armada off Calais shortly after midnight on 7 August 1588, captured on canvas by Hendrik Cornelisz Vroom (1566–1640). The loss of anchors, cut loose in frantic attempts to stay clear of the flames, ultimately did far more harm to the Armada than the fireships.

Informed of the Armada's approach by a watchful pinnace, the English warped out of Plymouth during the night and gained the wind. Medina Sidonia had already missed his first, and probably best, chance of victory two days earlier by rejecting suggestions to sail directly for Plymouth and blockade the English in port rather than wait to assemble his entire fleet.

The Spanish superiority in a boarding fight was evident, as was the English advantage in stand-off gunnery. Indeed, Philip had warned Medina Sidonia in April 1588 that 'the enemy's intention will be to fight at long range on account of his advantage in artillery ... to fire low and sink his opponent's ships', and so it

was, although not as anticipated. The English formed line and passed alongside the Spanish, harrying them with broadsides, but not to any discernible effect. The only advantage came from accidents among the Spanish (a powder explosion and a series of collisions on 31 July) that delivered two ships to the English the next day – one of them the powerful galleon *Nuestra Señora del Rosario* – along with several tons of gunpowder.

On 2 August, the English tried to penetrate the Armada's interior, only to be met by powerful warships that had been detailed by Medina Sidonia to protect the merchantmen and hulks. The wind dropped for a time, enabling the galleasses

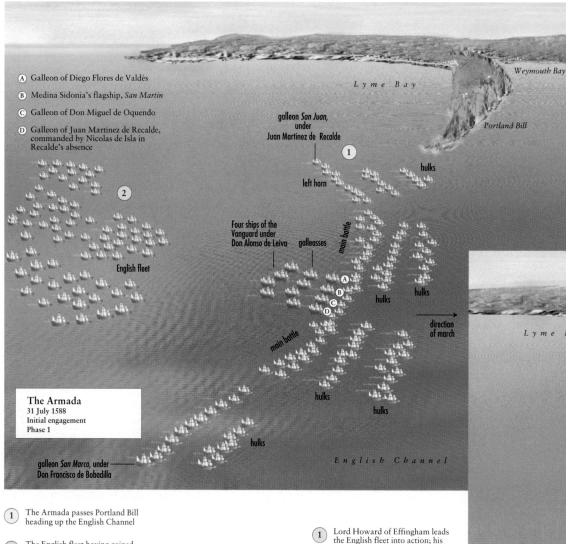

(A) Galleon of Diego Flores de Valdés

(B) Medina Sidonia's flagship, *San Martin*

(C) Galleon of Don Miguel de Oquendo

(D) Galleon of Juan Martinez de Recalde, commanded by Nicolas de Isla in Recalde's absence

Weymouth Bay

L y m e   B a y

Portland Bill

galleon *San Juan*, under Juan Martinez de Recalde

(1)

hulks

left horn

(2)

Four ships of the Vanguard under Don Alonso de Leiva

galleasses

main battle

English fleet

(A) (B) (C) (D)

hulks

hulks

direction of march

main battle

hulks

hulks

The Armada
31 July 1588
Initial engagement
Phase 1

hulks

hulks

galleon *San Marco*, under Don Francisco de Bobadilla

English Channel

L y m e   B a y

**Initial engagement
Phase 2**

(1) The Armada passes Portland Bill heading up the English Channel

(2) The English fleet having gained the windward position begins to close on the Armada

THE ARMADA ENGAGED

In the initial clashes between the Spanish and English off Portland Bill, both sides confronted unforeseen challenges. For the English, the solidity of the Spanish formation was daunting; for their part, the Spanish were surprised and impressed by the superior weatherliness and manoeuvrability of the English ships. As it turned out, the most significant events of the initial encounter were triggered by Spanish accidents: a magazine explosion and an accidental dismasting that left two ships abandoned. The Armada is depicted according to its tactical organization, after Colin Martin and Geoffrey Parker, The Armada.

(1) Lord Howard of Effingham leads the English fleet into action; his squadron attacks the Armada's vanguard

(2) Drake, Frobisher and Hawkins lead their respective squadrons into attack on the Spanish rearguard

(3) By the end of the afternoon the battle was over; the Spanish commander ordered the fleet to reform. In attempting to do so there was a collision in the Andalusian squadron

(4) Late afternoon, *San Salvador*, the flagship of the Vice Admiral and Paymaster General of the Armada suffered a magazine explosion. She was later boarded and captured by the pursuing English and taken to Weymouth

(5) *Nuestra Señora del Rosario*, flagship of Don Pedro de Valdés, is damaged in a series of collisions and loses her foremast. Unmanageable, she is left behind during the night and surrenders the next morning to Francis Drake. Drake's discovery that English gunfire had inflicted only modest damage on *Rosario* may have been behind the subsequent English decision to engage at closer range on 3 and 4 August

Ark Royal, *Lord Howard of Effingham's flagship in the Armada campaign, from a contemporary print.*

Weymouth Bay

Portland Bill

wind direction

English fleet

English Channel

RIGHT: *The Armada under attack in the Channel in a nearly-contemporary anonymous Dutch engraving. Dutch maritime art had not yet attained the levels of accuracy that it would under the baroque masters, but it still conveys important details of ships and events.*

BELOW: *An anonymous Dutch painting of the fireship assault on the Armada, probably painted shortly after the events depicted. In the foreground, an English galleon, second from right, engages a larger Spanish galleon while a second English galleon, left, 'charges' a Spanish galleass. Note the discharge of its right bowchaser.*

to bring their powerful guns briefly to bear, threatening to close and board. Medina Sidonia then reorganized the Armada, placing the hulks and merchant-men in the vanguard, protected by a rearguard of his best warships. On 3 August, the English, newly formed into four squadrons led by Howard, Drake, John Hawkins and Martin Frobisher, blocked the Spanish from the Solent, thereby preventing a descent on the Isle of Wight. By now it was clear that the English could bring their guns to bear at will, but that they were doing little harm.

Several hot actions took place on 3 and 4 August, notably by Drake in his flagship *Revenge*, in which the English closed to substantially shorter ranges than previously, perhaps experimenting to see if they could inflict serious damage. The experiments, if they were that – the convincing hypothesis is Colin Martin's and Geoffrey Parker's, advanced in their seminal work on the Armada – were successful. Having learned that close-in gunnery was effective, the English backed off to conserve powder.

The fleets disengaged on the 5 August, the Armada ploughing stolidly ahead and the English shadowing it, now low on powder and frantically resupplying.

On 6 August, Medina Sidonia, having heard nothing from Parma and fearful of over-shooting his rendezvous, brought the Armada to anchor off Calais, within 25 miles of Parma's embarkation ports. That evening he received his first word from Parma.

Parma had thoroughly outfoxed the Dutch, avoiding the attentions of a blockading squadron under Prince Justin of Nassau, and successfully concealing his intentions, but had held his men back from their ports for reasons of deception. This detail revealed a fatal flaw in Philip's plan: lacking a deep-water port in Flanders or control of the Channel, it required precise co-ordination, something that is exceedingly difficult to achieve with large and heterogeneous forces, both then and now. In fact, Parma ordered embarkation to proceed as soon as he learned that the Armada was at Calais, and within forty-eight hours he was ready, poised to strike.

Meanwhile Lord Howard had anchored within sight of the Armada and was

A near-contemporary depiction by an unknown artist of the Armada under attack. He has effectively conveyed the chaos of battle.

receiving reinforcements by the hour, Seymour among them. A council of war decided to send in fireships, and preparations were made accordingly. Caught in an exposed roadstead, and with an offshore breeze, Medina Sidonia ordered his captains to set a second anchor.

At around midnight on 7 August eight small ships stuffed with combustibles warped in with the tide. Medina Sidonia had posted a screen of small craft as a precaution and their crews managed to tow two of the fireships clear. The rest proceeded on course, their crews taking to the boats; it was perfectly timed and executed. At the sight of the approaching flames, the Spanish panicked, chopping cables and leaving anchors behind. No ship was burned, but the attack succeeded beyond expectations. Dawn found the Armada scattered and the flag galleass aground.

The ensuing battle, named after nearby Gravelines, was intense and confused. Medina Sidonia's flagship, *San Martin,* and four of his best galleons sought to

interpose themselves between the rest of the Armada and the English. They fought with admirable fortitude and were generally successful, but the English, using their agility and firepower to full advantage for the first time, closed and inflicted terrible damage. The wind drove the battle north. One galleon was sunk outright and Medina Sidonia's five stalwarts were mauled. By day's end, the flag galleass had been destroyed and the Armada driven so far to windward that any hope of a rendezvous with Parma was gone. Medina Sidonia gave orders to proceed home the long way round. Most of the galleons made it, a tribute to their design and construction. Many of the rest did not, being driven against the Scottish or Irish coasts and wrecked, their anchors still lying on the bottom off Calais and not available when needed.

It was a close-run thing. Had one of Medina Sidonia's numerous messages to Parma announcing his intentions and progress arrived in time – a real possibility

– Parma could have been ready when the Armada arrived. The English had been unable to stop the Armada and Parma would have had his escort. Had his veterans made it ashore there can be no doubt that they would have made mincemeat of Elizabeth's militia.

It did not happen. England remained Protestant and Elizabeth queen. The Dutch Revolt prospered. The Royal Navy was vindicated as the core of England's defence, but that same navy proved incapable of offensive strategic decision. English raids could be highly destructive – that on Cádiz in 1596 far surpassing Drake's earlier attack – but accomplished little beyond increasing Spanish defence expenditure, including the creation of a navy which, though unable to succeed where the Armada had failed, effectively protected the treasure fleets. The war wore on in inconclusive attrition until Elizabeth's death in 1603 and the truce called by her successor James I in the following year.

A Hendrik Vroom depiction of a sea fight, perhaps the 1596 battle of Cádiz, featuring galleons and galleys locked in combat. If it was indeed intended to show Cádiz, it is a representation of one of the first times in which galleons took on galleys on terms favourable to the latter and won convincingly.

HANSAN STRAIT, 1592

So far our story has been mostly European, for it was Europeans who first took gunpowder to sea with important long-term consequences. There was, however, a singular exception: the Korean repulse of the invasion launched by the Japanese ruler Toyotomi Hideyoshi. The story is a dramatic one of sea power versus land power, perhaps the limiting case. On the Korean side it is also a story of technological innovation harnessed by a gifted leader, Admiral Yi Sun-sin. The background is complex, involving dynastic politics and maritime interactions

among Ming China, Korea and Japan. The three nations' differing technological trajectories were deeply embedded in their cultures and social fabrics, and nowhere was this more striking than in their approaches to gunpowder, war and the sea.

We have already discussed Ming China. Korea's Chosōn dynasty (1392–1910) had close links with the Ming dynasty, whose suzerainty it recognized. The largest single difference among the three nations lay in the political dominance of Japan by a warrior élite, the samurai. Like China and Korea's mandarins, the samurai

were supported by land rents and agricultural taxes in kind and were thus inclined to distrust things commercial and maritime. They were, however, a caste whose members invoked their martial capabilities to justify and enforce their legitimacy. Perhaps in consequence, Japanese culture tolerated a degree of decentralization that was alien to the Confucian ideal of China and Korea. The result was a constant honing of martial skills and a remarkable openness to military innovation, albeit on land.

How and when gunpowder weapons arrived in Japan is uncertain, although the evidence points to the Portuguese and the 1540s. However that may be, the samurai grasped gunpowder's potential and quickly matched, and in some respects surpassed, Europe in the use of individual firearms. As in Europe, mastery of gunpowder weapons facilitated the consolidation of political power, ending a century of constant civil war. In 1575, the *daimyō* (territorial magnate) Oda Nobunaga (family name first, Japanese style) employed massed volleys of arquebus fire to shatter the ranks of the powerful Takeda clan at the battle of Nagashino, paving the way for political unification. The process was interrupted by Nobunaga's assassination in 1582, but his successor, Toyotomi Hideyoshi, carried it to completion. Hideyoshi, who began his rise to power as an ordinary soldier in Nobunaga's ranks, was a man of uncommon ability and boundless ambition. Having unified Japan, he looked elsewhere to leave his mark on history, and settled on China, by way of invasion through Korea.

A sixteenth-century Japanese folding screen, showing in lacquer the arrival of the Portuguese in Japan. The artist has done a creditable job of depicting the unfamiliar details of European sailing ships and their rigging. The most important consequence of these early encounters was the transfer of gunpowder technology.

At first blush, Hideyoshi's plan to conquer the enormity of China seems a pipe dream, but reflection and a look at the map suggest otherwise. The distances involved were no greater than those faced by earlier invading Mongol armies, nor, once ashore in Korea, were the geographic barriers insurmountable. Having honed their tactical and logistical skills in a lifetime of civil war, Hideyoshi's *daimyō* could bring to the battlefield a combination of firepower and shock action that was unrivalled in Asia and, perhaps, the world.

In the summer of 1591, while making diplomatic overtures to the Korean court in Seoul, Hideyoshi ordered preparations for invasion. By the following spring, he had assembled an army of nearly 160,000 men – huge by contemporary Asian or European standards – organized into 9 brigades, plus a fleet of 700 impressed ships manned by 9,200 seamen and commanded by four *daimyō*.

The invasion fleet reached Pusan on 23 May 1592. Finding the defences poorly maintained and the defenders ill-prepared, the Japanese quickly seized the port and drove north, reaching Seoul on 11 June and Pyongyang on 23 July. Estimating that his forces would be in Peking by October, Hideyoshi announced plans to depart from his capital of Kyoto for Korea. As the Japanese went from victory to victory on land, the fleet worked its way along the coast, looting and pillaging as it went, in the best tradition of the Japanese – or at least mostly Japanese – *wakō* pirates of an earlier age, planning to rendezvous with the army on Korea's west coast with supplies and 52,000 fresh troops for the drive on Peking. The Korean king appealed to the Ming for help, but Chinese aid would take time to arrive, if it came at all, and in the meantime the Japanese armies were unstoppable. Only the navy stood between Korea and disaster.

Like the Ming, the Chosōn were thoroughly Confucian and inclined to devalue things martial and maritime. But Korea is a peninsula, with much of the interior readily accessible from the sea, and the Koreans, unlike the Chinese, could not afford to deal with the *wakō* by withdrawing from the coast; their peninsula was too small. Of necessity, they created a standing navy and sent agents to China to bring back the secret of gunpowder. By 1592, the Chosōn dynasty was in decline, undercut by dissent, corruption and incompetence at the top, but the navy consisted of purpose-built warships sailed by professional crews. Moreover, Korean warships were armed with pyrotechnic projectors and cannons, which, if not the equal of heavy European ordnance, were far superior to anything the Japanese possessed. Among the Korean warships were perhaps two dozen oared, cannon-armed vessels with retractable masts and sails, a curved overhead deck protected from fire by thin iron plates festooned with sharpened steel spikes to discourage boarding, and smoke projectors within their dragon-headed prows. These were called turtle ships.

At this point, Admiral Yi Sun-sin comes into our story. Of humble origins, he had advanced by merit through the military hierarchy, observing Confucian protocol, but refusing to suffer fools – including superiors – gladly, and making enemies along the way. When Hideyoshi struck, Yi was commanding the naval

HIDEYOSHI'S INVASION OF KOREA, 1592

The map makes clear the importance of co-operation between Japanese land and naval forces and the critical importance of the Korean navy. Ironically, Hideyoshi's suppression of seaborne piracy among his coastal samurai had the effect of reducing the competence of his naval commanders.

forces of Left, or Eastern, Cholla Province, in the centre of Korea's southern coast. His neighbour to the east, who was responsible for Pusan, was Admiral Wön Kyun, commander of Kyongsang Province. A well-connected poltroon, Wön Kyun withdrew in panic and called for help. Yi marshalled his forces and collected intelligence. On 3 June 1592 his advance guard, probing eastwards, encountered a Japanese squadron off Kyonnaeryang Island, south-west of Pusan, and bloodied it.

Having confirmed his view of the tactical character of the Japanese invasion, Yi now launched his counterstroke. Included in his plans was a newly perfected turtle-ship design that had completed its trials days before the Japanese landing. In a blistering series of combats along Korea's southern coast Yi defeated the Japanese in detail, exploiting his superior knowledge of geography, tides and currents, and helped by the divided Japanese command.

In these fights – there were seven major engagements and numerous lesser ones – the Japanese repeatedly attempted to board under cover of arquebus fire, but Japanese arquebuses and swords, brutally effective on land, were no match for Korean cannon, while the bulk of the Japanese ships were smaller and less

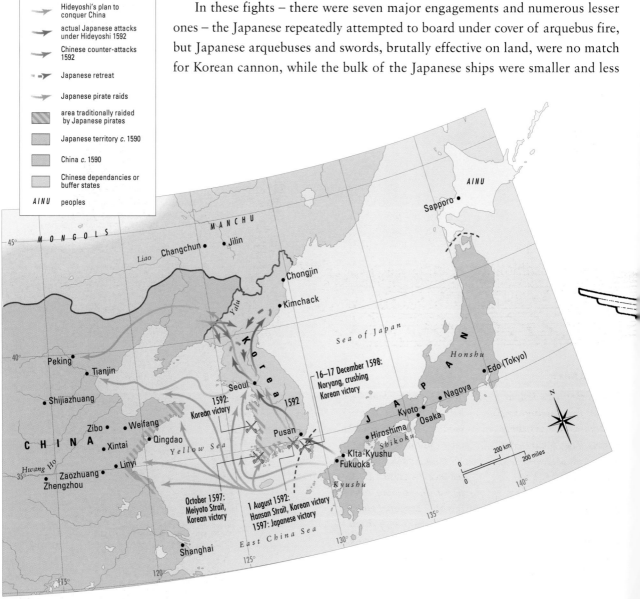

Korea
1592

→ Hideyoshi's plan to conquer China

→ actual Japanese attacks under Hideyoshi 1592

→ Chinese counter-attacks 1592

- ‑ ▸ Japanese retreat

→ Japanese pirate raids

▨ area traditionally raided by Japanese pirates

▨ Japanese territory *c.* 1590

▨ China *c.* 1590

▨ Chinese dependancies or buffer states

AINU peoples

solidly built than the 'superstructure ships' that formed the backbone of the Korean fleet. Turtle ships spearheaded Yi's attacks, belching smoke from their dragons' heads and fire from the cannon in their flanks. Effectively invulnerable to boarding, they shattered the Japanese formations, leaving the few large vessels isolated and the surviving smaller ones to be picked off in detail. Again and again the Japanese retreated ashore, under protection from land-based covering fire. Japanese determination and valour were impressive but insufficient. In an early battle, samurai leaped aboard a turtle ship's back, ripped off iron plates by brute force, chopped their way inside and butchered the crew, a remarkable feat that was not repeated.

Although Yi's victories were incomplete tactically, for he dared not let his men pursue their beaten foes ashore, they were strategically decisive. The turning point came on 1 August in Hansan Strait, when Yi, with 85 ships, perhaps two dozen of them turtles, all but annihilated a Japanese fleet of 70 vessels, 36 of them large and 14 medium sized, ending the last Japanese offensive thrust. On 21 October Yi attacked the Japanese base at Pusan with 74 warships and 18 auxiliaries, destroying 100 of 470 Japanese vessels drawn up along the shore

A modern statue memorializing Admiral Yi Sun-sin, still revered in Korea as a national hero. Yi's enduring popularity as a patriotic symbol presents strong parallels to that of Khaireddin Barbarossa in Turkey and Horatio Nelson in Britain. Like Nelson, Yi died in his moment of triumph, felled by a musket ball.

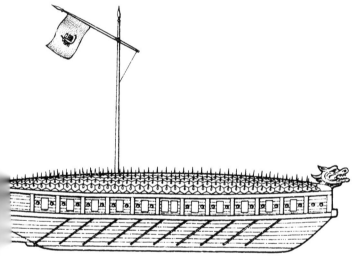

TURTLE BOAT

The turtle boat's design derives from traditional flat-bottomed Korean fishing vessels. They measured about 115 feet from the dragon's chin to the tip of the tail and were about 30 across at the widest part and were armed with ten cannon on the broadside, some of them firing arrow-like projectiles. In action, smoke from a projector in the bows belched from the dragon's mouth. The mast retracted into a slot in the curved, armoured back from whence the vessels got their name. The armour consisted of thin hexagonal plates of iron studded with sharp steel spikes to discourage boarding. On occasion the back was covered with straw to conceal the spikes.

BATTLE OF HANSAN STRAIT, 1592

Admiral Yi Sun-sin's 1592 summer–autumn campaign is one of the great classics of warfare at sea. Taking advantage of Hideyoshi's fragmented command arrangements and the fact that the Japanese were tied to the coast, ravaging as they went, Yi defeated them in detail in a series of blistering engagements. These grew in scale as the Japanese realized the gravity of the threat posed by Yi and his fleet. The climactic battle was Hansan Strait, right. Following defeat, the Japanese went over to the defensive and withdrew to Pusan.

and inflicting heavy losses before superior numbers and Japanese shore batteries forced his withdrawal. Yi pulled back to replenish and refit, leaving the decimated Japanese under blockade.

Korea was a poor country, and the Japanese suffered from a lack of supplies; moreover, their brutality had provoked a bitter guerrilla resistance. A huge Ming army intervened in early 1593 and captured Pyongyang in February. Facing starvation, the Japanese inflicted a sharp defeat on the Chinese to cover their withdrawal, then retreated into the bitter cold of the Korean winter, hurried along by guerrillas. Facing destruction, Hideyoshi's commanders called for a truce and opened negotiations with the Chinese. By October 1593, the Japanese had evacuated Korea, apart from a garrison of 10,000 at Pusan.

The negotiations dragged on as Hideyoshi sought to achieve by diplomacy what he could not gain by arms, while the Ming sought concessions of suzerainty. Conducted through intermediaries, who exploited Sino-Japanese incomprehension to smooth over irreconcilable differences, the negotiations left much unsaid, and the Koreans were caught in the middle. Matters reached a climax in the winter of 1596, when Hideyoshi received Chinese emissaries in Kyoto and for the first time heard the Ming terms accurately translated. Far from proffering a princess in marriage, ceding Korean territory and recognizing his sovereign authority, as Hideyoshi had expected, the Ming offered to install him as king of Japan … a Ming vassal. Flying into a rage, Hideyoshi ordered a renewed invasion. Meanwhile Admiral Yi Sun-sin had been ousted by court intrigue, reduced to the status of a common seaman and replaced by Admiral Wŏn Kyun.

The second Japanese invasion, launched in early 1597 with an army of

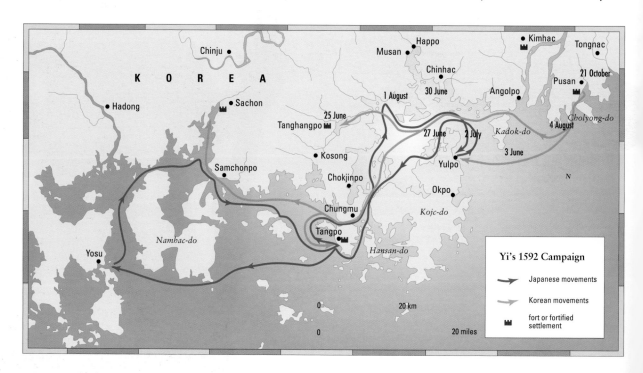

Battle of Hansan Strait
August 1592

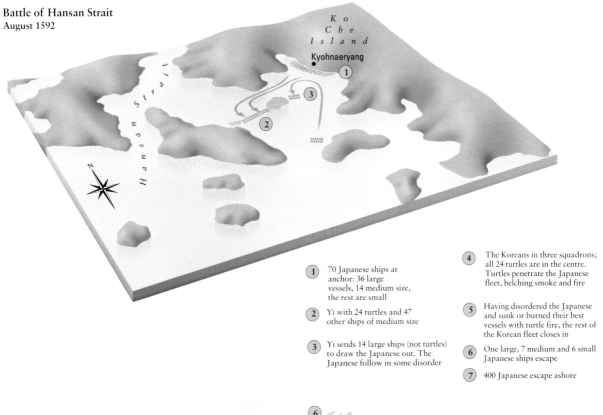

1. 70 Japanese ships at anchor: 36 large vessels, 14 medium size, the rest are small

2. Yi with 24 turtles and 47 other ships of medium size

3. Yi sends 14 large ships (not turtles) to draw the Japanese out. The Japanese follow in some disorder

4. The Koreans in three squadrons; all 24 turtles are in the centre. Turtles penetrate the Japanese fleet, belching smoke and fire

5. Having disordered the Japanese and sunk or burned their best vessels with turtle fire, the rest of the Korean fleet closes in

6. One large, 7 medium and 6 small Japanese ships escape

7. 400 Japanese escape ashore

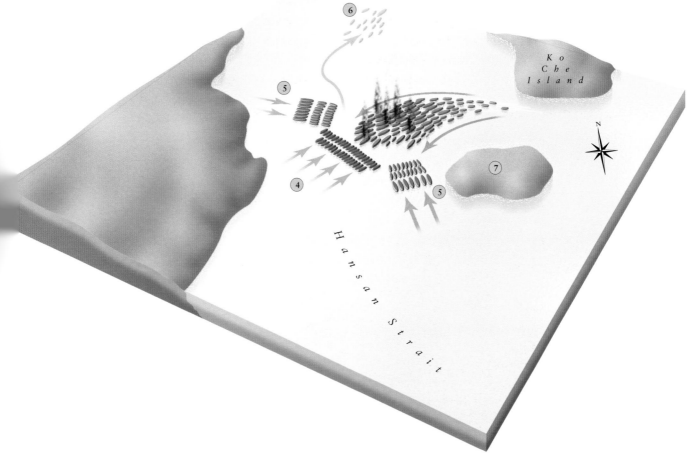

140,000 and an improved fleet, initially encountered little resistance. After consolidating at Pusan, the Japanese struck, and defeating a badly handled Korean fleet in August – Wön Kyun had driven his crews too long and hard, and the Japanese caught them ashore, seeking water. The only Japanese naval victory of the war, it was nevertheless crushing: only twelve Korean ships escaped, apparently all turtle ships. With Japanese armies driving north and naval forces ravaging their way along the southern coast, Korea was on the ropes. The Korean king again sought Ming help and, in desperation, appointed Yi Sun-sin to supreme naval command.

Working to repair the results of Wön Kyun's incompetence, Yi withdrew to Korea's south-western tip. In October, he turned on the Japanese, ambushing with 13 ships a Japanese fleet of 144 in the narrow Meiyoto Strait and annihilating it. Consolidating his resource base, Yi then rebuilt his forces and went over to the attack. A Ming fleet came to his aid, although its overbearing, protocol-conscious admiral gave Yi more problems than assistance. Mixing leadership with diplomacy – Yi gave the Chinese full credit for Korean successes – he once again forced the Japanese back on Pusan and cut off their armies from resupply.

Hideyoshi died in September 1598 and, with his death, Japan sought terms. The diplomats did their work, securing Japanese withdrawal, but in the process snubbing the Koreans, who dug in their heels, insisting on sovereignty and resisting partition. It took time, and as the diplomatic mills ground, war continued in the countryside and along Korea's southern coast. By late 1598, Kyoto and Peking had settled their salient differences, implicitly conceding that Korea should be left alone. On 16 December, the Japanese evacuated in a massive convoy. Whether unconvinced by Japanese sincerity, thirsting for revenge or seeking to make a point, Yi launched his reconstituted fleet against the Japanese, destroying some 200 of an armada of 500 ships off Noryang, in a vicious night engagement. Yi took an arquebus ball and, like Nelson at Trafalgar, died in his moment of triumph. His victories assured that neither Hideyoshi nor his successors would inherit China's imperial throne.

It was a close-run thing. Had Yi fallen in one of his first engagements instead of the last, it is difficult to see how the Japanese could have been stopped. The consequences were huge, for a Toyotomi-ruled China would have been a very different matter to the Ming China that fell to Manchu horse archers in 1644.

The Japanese were among a select handful of peoples who had repelled invasion by the similarly armed and at least equally ruthless and efficient Mongols at the height of their power, the others being the Egyptian Mamelukes in 1260 and the Vietnamese in 1288. Whether the Japanese could have defeated the Mongols in 1274 and 1281 without the famous 'Divine Wind' is debatable. The arquebus-equipped Japanese legions of the 1590s would have had little need of divine assistance.

THE DOWNS, 1639

See gentlemen! The enemy is but small fry; let each one do his best for we have an easy task; the flagship will set a good example.

Don Antonio de Oquendo, Admiral of the Ocean Sea,
upon learning of the Dutch fleet's strength, 15 September 1639

The Armada campaign was a turning point in the Dutch Revolt. Alexander Farnese, the Duke of Parma's invasion preparations gave the rebels a badly needed respite, a respite that was extended when Philip II of Spain ordered Parma to intervene in France's religious wars. Given relief, the Dutch systematically took back most of the places lost to Parma and more. Philip ended the embargo on Dutch shipping in 1590, only to re-impose it in 1595. Nevertheless, by his death in 1598 the Dutch policy of 'trading with the enemy' had produced prosperity. His successor, Philip III, tightened the embargo and ordered Dutch vessels in Spanish ports to be seized. In so doing he sowed the wind, and his empire would reap the whirlwind. Hitherto the Dutch had shown little interest in projecting violence abroad for profit, preferring peaceful commerce instead. The embargo changed that, and in short order: Dutch flotillas invaded Caribbean, South American, African and Indonesian waters, seeking trade and taking it by force, transforming the revolt into a global war. The Dutch, whose warships the English

Amsterdam, in a Dutch engraving of c. 1572. Amsterdam was under Spanish control at the time, but that would change. The constant was Amsterdam's importance as a centre of shipping and commerce, indicated by the shipping clogging the harbour.

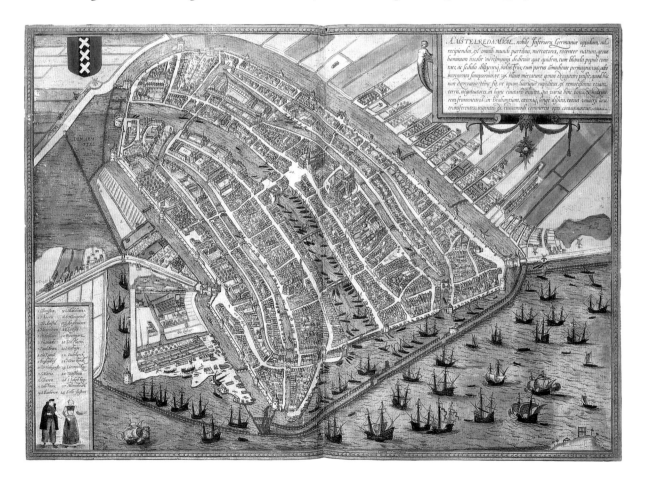

had deemed too small and feeble to help against the Armada, now became the principal exponents of the fighting galleon. Habsburg corsairs would wreak havoc on Dutch commerce – the other side of Philip's maritime strategy – but not enough.

The Dutch seized footholds in the Americas and, sailing directly from the

Engraving of a large Dutch East Indiaman under construction, by Wenzel Hollar (1607–77). By the 1620s and 1630s, large Indiamen were as heavily armed as specialized warships had been only a decade or so earlier. Reaction to Philip III's trade embargo turned the Dutch from peaceful traders by preference to active exponents of armed coercion.

Cape of Good Hope, bypassed Portuguese India and established bases in the Moluccas. Taking spices at the source, they carried them straight home, undercutting Portuguese prices and swelling their coffers. In 1602, the Dutch incorporated the Vereenigde Oost-Indische Compagnie, VOC or Dutch East India Company, and in 1605 seized the spice islands of Amboina, Ternate and Tidore. Between 1606 and 1608 the Dutch blockaded Malacca and established a factory at Pulicat, in India, to tap into the Indian textile trade. Spanish forces from the Philippines retook parts of Ternate and Tidore, but the dispatch of reinforcements from Lisbon served only to underline the vulnerability of large Portuguese carracks to well-armed Dutch galleons.

The war in Flanders ground on, and in the spring of 1607 the Dutch sent a fleet to blockade the Andalusian coast. On 25 April it entered Gibraltar harbour and destroyed the Spanish squadron guarding the straits – just weeks after Spain, facing bankruptcy, had signed a ceasefire in the Netherlands. On 9 April 1609 the ceasefire was extended to a twelve-year truce.

The truce held in the Atlantic, but immediately failed in the East. The Portuguese attacked Pulicat in 1612, the Dutch retaliating by taking two Spanish fortresses on Tidore. In 1615, a Portuguese squadron of four ships lost one of its number, burned by the Muslim Achinese, before being defeated by the Dutch off Malacca. A Dutch squadron of four ships then entered the Pacific through the Straits of Magellan and in July 1615 defeated a Spanish squadron of two at Canete, off the Peruvian coast. The struggle was not entirely one-sided: a Dutch

Portrait of King Philip III of Spain in half armour by Juan Pantoja de la Cruz (1533–1608). Less inclined to intervene in the details of governance than his father, Philip III faced a chronic shortage of resources in the face of growing Dutch strength.

blockade of Manila was broken by Spanish victory at Playa Honda, between 15 and 16 April 1617, and the Spanish hung on tenaciously in the Moluccas. Nevertheless, when the truce expired in 1621 the Dutch were poised for expansion in the East, and that same year chartered the West India Company (WIC) to take the fight to the Habsburgs in the Atlantic, and to turn a profit in so doing.

In 1624 a WIC-organized expedition seized Bahia, the capital of Portuguese Brazil, but the Habsburg lion still had teeth, and in 1625 a major Spanish–Portuguese expedition retook it. Then, in 1628, a WIC fleet under Piet Heyn captured the returning treasure fleet in Matanzas Bay, on Cuba's northern coast. Heyn's feat was never repeated, but the plundered silver financed an expedition in

1630 that took Pernambuco, the heart of Portuguese Brazil's rich sugar-growing region, seriously challenging Habsburg might. Meanwhile the Dutch had consolidated in the East, at first in co-operation with the English, who, in alliance with Shah Abbas of Persia, captured Ormuz, off the south-eastern coast of Persia, in the spring of 1622.

With their power growing, the Dutch expelled the English from the Indies in 1623, established a factory at Zeelandia, in western Taiwan, in 1624, and by 1633–5 had blockaded Malacca and severed the Muslim spice trade with the Red Sea – thereby undoing the work of Affonso d'Albuquerque and the sultans of Aceh.

A celebratory depiction of the return to Amsterdam of the Dutch East India Company fleet in 1599 by Andries van Eertvelt (1590–1652). The three large vessels at left and centre are fluyts, capacious and seaworthy, but heavily armed.

It was in European waters, however, that the decision would be reached. In 1635 Cardinal Richelieu brought France into the Thirty Years War on the Protestant side, and within three years Spain's overland connections with Flanders were severed. Henceforth, Spain could reinforce only by sea.

At first blush, Habsburg prospects seemed reasonable. Spain had built up her navy, and if the Dutch had done the same it was by heavily taxing a small population. The Habsburgs had every advantage in terms of quantity of resources, with the sole and vital exception of seamen, of whom the Netherlands had an abundance, by virtue of its flourishing trade and fisheries. Finally, Spain was helped by England's sympathetic neutrality under Charles I.

In September 1637 and again in December, Spanish squadrons under Don Lope de Hoces reached the northern French port of Dunkirk with reinforcements and bullion, giving the Dutch fleet under Maarten Tromp the slip. Although Tromp drove Hoces back into Dunkirk with losses in February 1638, the wily Spaniard slipped out in March and made his way home.

Meanwhile, the French fleet, under Admiral Henri d'Escoubleau de Sourdis, was threatening Spain's northern coast. King Philip IV of Spain and his ministers, emboldened by Hoces' success, resolved to challenge the French, and to do on a large scale by force what Hoces had accomplished by guile. Before their plans reached fruition, however, a French army supported by de Sourdis' fleet, invaded Spain. Ordered against his better judgement to confront de Sourdis, Hoces

Fluyts getting under way in an anonymous roadstead by Willem van de Velde the Younger. A distinctively Dutch development dating from the end of the sixteenth century, fluyts were the most efficient bulk carriers of their day. With longer hulls relative to their breadth than carracks and with more, smaller, sails, fluyts were easier to handle and required fewer crew members.

was badly defeated at Guetaria on Spain's northern coast on 22 August 1638.

Hoces' defeat notwithstanding, Spanish preparations proceeded, and by June 1639 a strong Neapolitan squadron under Don Antonio de Oquendo, joined by Ragusan and Italian contingents, had reached Cádiz. That month the French army was driven back in a rout and Richelieu ordered de Sourdis into port after an unsuccessful attempt on La Coruña, clearing the board. By August 1639, 50 warships, including Hoces' survivors, were assembled at La Coruña with 20 transports, 8 to 10 of them English, to transport 4 tercios and bullion to Flanders. Instructions from Madrid were vague, and a council of war, convened by the Viceroy of Galicia, offered command to Hoces. Hoces refused, no doubt recalling the disastrous results of his earlier obedience to orders, and de Oquendo became Admiral of the Ocean Sea by default. It was an unfortunate choice: a renowned horseman, with impeccable bloodlines, Oquendo had considerable experience afloat, but – as he had shown at Abrolhos in 1631 – was brave to a fault, impetuous, and viewed combat afloat as a chivalric contest. His flaws would become manifest.

The Armada departed La Coruña on 5 September 1639, with 67 combatant ships, escorting 30 transports with 8,500 reinforcements for the Army of Flanders. Tromp had 28 warships to meet them, 13 cruising the Channel under his command, 10 blockading Dunkirk, and 5 returning from a cruise protecting the North Sea fisheries. To complicate matters, England's King Charles I had

A contemporary sketch of the hull of an armed mid seventeenth-century fluyt, emphasizing the capacious hull and narrow upper works, sharply reduced in size from those of carracks and galleons. The elaborately decorated, and no doubt brightly painted, stern panel is indicative of the contemporary overlap between the aesthetic and the functional.

A near-contemporary Dutch painting of Tromp's fleet before the battle of the Downs. By the time of the Downs, Dutch maritime artists had attained high standards of artistic beauty and – of enormous value to the naval historian – technical accuracy. The ships show the early stages of transition from galleon to the ship-of-the-line.

posted a squadron under Sir John Pennington in the Downs to safeguard English neutrality.

Early on 15 September the Armada fell in with an English ship whose master had encountered Tromp the day before. On learning that Tromp had only thirteen ships in the Channel, the Spanish concluded that victory was as good as won – we have this from Dom Francisco Manuel de Mello, the Portuguese commander of an embarked tercio. Overconfidence was rife. Responding to his captains' requests for instructions, de Oquendo called a meeting of his senior commanders. He issued no orders at all, uttering instead the words quoted above (p. 191).

The Dutch sighted the Spanish in the middle of the afternoon, and Tromp dispatched a ship up the Channel for reinforcements, firing a gun four times every half hour to alert them. He then called a council of war, announced his intention to fight, and instructed his captains to maintain line and hold the Spanish at bay with broadsides. This is according to de Mello, who spoke with Tromp some months later, and if the Portuguese added a rhetorical flourish to Tromp's words – Tromp's journal does not address the point explicitly – it is clear from the next day's events that he was accurate in substance.

Sunrise on 16 September found the Spanish 2 miles north-west of the Dutch, with the wind behind them, and five ships sailing under Tromp's vice admiral, Witte de With, coming up from leeward to join. The Spanish got under way in

considerable disorder, with Oquendo's flagship in the lead heading straight for Tromp. The Dutch formed in a close line-ahead – de Mello says bowsprit to taffrail; Pennington's flag captain, Peter White, says two ship-lengths apart – sailing just close-hauled enough to avoid contact until the Spanish were well strung out, with Oquendo's flagship in the lead. They then luffed up and savaged Oquendo with broadsides. A Dutch ship was destroyed by a magazine explosion on the first discharge, and de With's flagship lost its stern cabin to a gunpowder accident, but the Dutch fought stolidly on. Tromp and de With in turn easily avoided Oquendo's attempts to grapple and board, and the rest of the Dutch let him have it in succession, tacking for a second broadside. Oquendo's flagship was left shrouded in smoke (the words are de Mello's), with flags 'fluttering loose in the air' and shrouds 'hanging like pennants, trembling sadly in the breeze … cut by the chain shot of the enemy'. Others caught up with Oquendo and the battle continued, with the most capable Spanish ships in the lead. The Dutch maintained formation and easily avoided Spanish attempts to grapple, pouring in broadside after broadside. By mid afternoon it seemed that the Spanish might drive the Dutch against the French coast and win by sheer numbers, but Oquendo, his flagship heavily damaged, hove to. At nightfall the wind shifted and the Dutch sailed clear, leaving the Spanish shattered. An English squadron under Sir Henry Mainwaring fell in with them the next day and found them in distress,

Dutch and Spanish galleons duelling ship-to-ship in a painting by Cornelisz Verbeecq (c. 1590–1635) in the National Maritime Museum, Greenwich. The Dutch vessels are less lofty than their Spanish opposites and have closed stern galleries, but are otherwise similar. The early stages of the 1631 battle of Abrolhos must have resembled the action depicted here.

BATTLE OF THE DOWNS

The decisive confrontation referred to as the battle of the Downs in fact consisted of several distinct engagements, the two most important of which are shown here. In the first, the badly outnumbered Dutch, using line-ahead tactics, successfully fended off the Spanish, shredding the most powerful Spanish warships in the process. In the last, fought five weeks later, the heavily reinforced Dutch, attacking under cover of fog, destroyed the Spanish fleet.

'having been shrewdly torn and beaten by only seventeen of the Holland ships in their first encounter'.

The Spanish then worked their way north, hurried along by a daring night attack in the early morning hours of 18 September. Further torn by Dutch gunfire and with Tromp between them and Dunkirk, they anchored in the Downs that afternoon. Tromp, his powder depleted, disengaged.

A period of waiting and reinforcement ensued, with both sides replenishing their gunpowder stores, the Spanish partly by purchase from the English at exorbitant prices. The Spanish were remarkably successful in bringing out supplies and ultimately delivered most of their troops and all of the bullion, using swift frigates to run them into Dunkirk; Tromp received a steady stream of reinforcements. Pennington looked on, with orders to protect the Spanish, but keenly aware of Tromp's growing strength. By 18 October 1639 Tromp had 103 warships, 16 fireships and orders from the States General, the supreme Dutch authority, to destroy the Spanish as soon as weather and tide permitted.

Tromp struck under cover of fog early on 21 October, detaching a squadron under de With to hold off Pennington if necessary. It was not. The Spanish cut

Phase 1

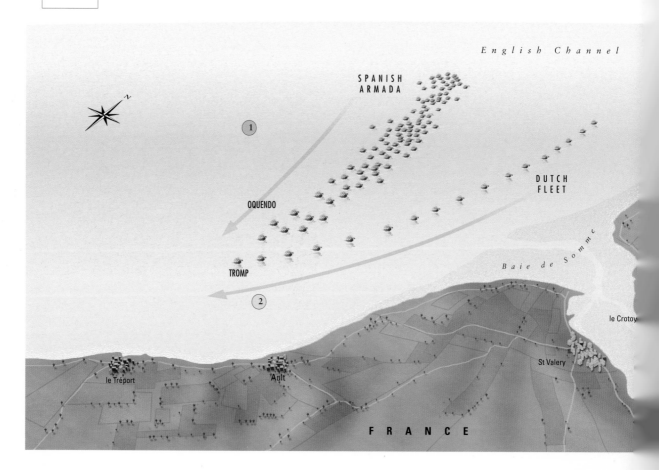

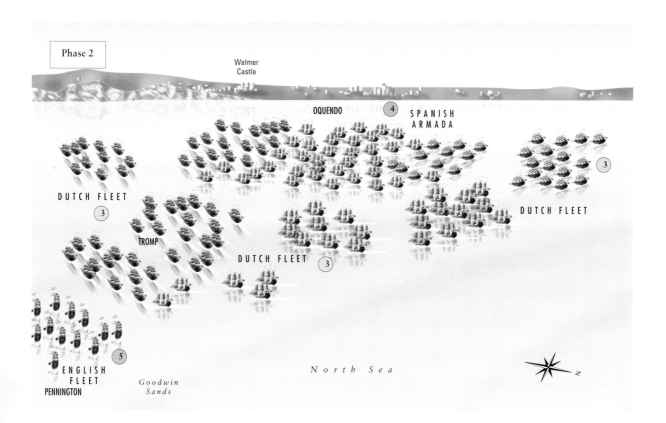

Phase 2

Walmer
Castle

OQUENDO

SPANISH
ARMADA

DUTCH FLEET

3

DUTCH FLEET

3

TROMP

DUTCH FLEET

3

ENGLISH
FLEET
PENNINGTON

Goodwin
Sands

North Sea

5

Berck-Plage

Fort-Mahon-
Plage

1   16 September 1639: Oquendo's
flagship followed by the vice-
flagship and 65 other Spanish
ships headed for Tromp's flagship

2   Tromp with 17 ships maintained
his fleet in line-ahead, with 2 ship
lengths between ships, avoiding
Oquendo's attempts to board and
passing him in line, delivering
multiple broadsides into the
Spanish ships. Tromp loses one
ship which blew up on the first
broadside

3   The 21 October battle was a
three-way engagement between
the Dutch, separated into a
number of squadrons, Spanish
and English fleets

4   The Spanish (now down to
52 ships, a number having slipped
away to Dunkirk during the night
to deliver their cargo of soldiers
and bullion), some cutting their
anchor cables, manoeuvred for
position just off the English coast

5   The English with 25 ships under
Admiral Pennington tried to
interpose themselves between the
Spanish and the Dutch, but failed
in this endeavour

*A contemporary Dutch
impression of the final
stages of the battle of the
Downs. It is unlikely that
things were so neat, but the
ships are beautifully
rendered.*

their cables, many running for the English coast, where they grounded. Quoting Tromp's report to the States General, of the 53 Spanish ships remaining in the Downs, 'about 40 were either stranded, sunk, burnt, or taken, whilst the remainder were harried and scattered' in the running fight that ensued. The Dutch lost a single pinnace that became entangled with Hoces's flagship and shared her fate when she was burned by Dutch fireships. A handful of Spanish ships, Oquendo's flagship among them, reached Dunkirk.

Strategically, the battle of the Downs was decisive, foreshadowing as it did the outbreak of revolt against Spanish rule in Catalonia and Portugal in 1640.

Tactically, it revealed a huge disparity in capability and concept between the Spanish and the Dutch. Tromp's tactics on 16 September – the crucial engagement – have been heralded as the birth of the line-ahead tactics that became dominant during the Anglo-Dutch wars, and remained so until the age of steam. In fact, it was not so simple. Tromp turned to the line-ahead as a defensive expedient in desperate circumstances. For the *coup de grâce* he used fireships and mêlée tactics … as had the English off Gravelines in 1588. His decisions reflected the galleon's growing capabilities and persistent limitations.

Admiral Maarten Tromp's barge entering the Texel in 1645 in a painting done long after the event by British artist Joseph Mallord William Turner (1775–1851). Of considerable artistic merit and technical accuracy, it underlines a historical awareness among British subjects of the Victorian age of Britain's seaborne empire's Dutch antecedents.

THE TWILIGHT OF GALLEY AND GALLEON

A DETAIL FROM HENDRIK CORNELISZ VROOM's rendering of the climactic moment of the battle of Gibraltar, 25 April 1607, showing the Dutch flagship ramming its Spanish opposite, which was blown apart by an exploding powder magazine. The ships are accurately depicted and the force of gunpowder vividly shown. Though it settled nothing – the Spanish and Dutch had concluded a truce in the Netherlands weeks earlier – Gibraltar demonstrated convincingly that Dutch warships, sailors and guns were the equals of any afloat.

THE TWILIGHT OF GALLEY AND GALLEON

THE AGE OF GALLEY and galleon started with a bang: the benchmark was the humiliation of the English fleet in Brest Roads, in April 1513, by Prégent de Bidoux's basilisk-armed galleys. It ended with a drawn-out whimper in the aftermath of the Downs.

The Downs marked the end of a period of transition in warfare at sea – part strategic, part technological and part tactical – that started with Dutch expansion overseas following the Spanish embargo of 1598. The strategic transition is most obvious: until 1598, although the struggle between Spain and Dutch Protestants figured large in the calculations of the major powers, it was confined to the Netherlands both in conduct and consequences. Dutch depredations on Habsburg possessions and commerce in the Americas and East Indies changed that almost overnight, transforming the Revolt of the Netherlands into a global war and placing Spain in a strategic and fiscal vice. The Spanish defeat at Gibraltar in 1607 underlined the Dutch advantage, while the Twelve Years Truce, concluded on terms advantageous to the Dutch, affirmed the magnitude of the change.

The change was most evident in European waters. The Swedish–Danish War of 1643–5 saw several hard-fought engagements, but they were indecisive and involved fleets of no more than forty ships each, some of them no doubt ships-of-the-line, in design if not tactics. With that partial exception, the Downs marked the end of an era as the last decisive engagement between large fleets composed mainly of galleons. That was partly because Spain's deteriorating strategic

position removed it from the board as the dominant European power: *de facto* with the loss of Oquendo's fleet in the Downs; *de jure* in 1648, with the Spanish acceptance of Dutch independence and withdrawal from the Thirty Years War; and definitively in 1659, when the Peace of the Pyrenees ended hostilities with France. It was also partly because, in the years following the Downs, those nations that might have opposed the Dutch bid for world hegemony were hamstrung by rebellion. Catalonia and Portugal rose in revolt against Spanish rule in 1640; England was engulfed in civil war from 1642 until the establishment of the Commonwealth in 1649; and, in 1648, France was plunged into five years of turmoil by the first in a series of tax rebellions called the Fronde. The leaders of the nations in question understandably focused their attention on matters ashore, relegating naval affairs to the margins.

As a result the Dutch remained unchallenged at sea except on a small scale and in distant waters, and there they held the initiative. That situation prevailed until the English Commonwealth began to build up its fleet in anticipation of war with the Dutch. In principle France could have challenged the Dutch at sea – and would later do so under Louis XIV – but was hard-pressed financially by the demands of war with Spain on land. In consequence, naval operations during the Franco-Spanish War were on a comparatively small scale, even before Cardinal Richelieu's death in 1642 deprived his navy of its patron. Thereafter, French naval might swiftly dwindled into insignificance, where it remained until Louis XIV began to rule in his own right in 1661. Not until the First Anglo-Dutch War, at the battle of the Kentish Knock on 8 October 1652, would fleets of sailing warships as large as those that met in the Downs join in battle.

A Cornelis Claesz van Wieringen painting commemorating a visit to Flushing in 1613 by an English squadron transporting Frederick V, Elector of the Palatinate. This wonderfully informative painting, illustrates the early stages of a pivotal transitional period in warship design. Royal Prince *is at centre right, followed by* Red Lion, *commissioned during Queen Elizabeth's reign and rebuilt in 1609.*

165 150 135 120 105 90 75 60 45 30 15 0

Arctic Circle

70

60

50

Greenland

40

30

Tropic of Cancer

20

10

0

10

20

Tropic of Capricorn

30

40

50

60

New France

Acadia

Massachusetts Bay

New Amsterdam

Virginia

• Santa Fe

• El Paso

Florida

Bahama Is.

Cuba

Hispaniola

Puerto Rico

Vice-Royalty of New Spain

Mosquito Coast

Trinidad

Essequibo
Surinam
Cayenne

Santa Fé
de Bogotá •

Quito •

B R A Z I L

Lima •

Bahia

Vice-Royalty of Peru

• La Paz

• La Plata

Rio de Janeiro

• Sacramento

Santiago •

Buenos Aires

Iceland
(to Denmark)

DENMARK & NORW

SCOTLAND

ENGLAND **NETH**

HOL
ROM
EMP

Paris •

FRANCE

VENICE

PORTUGAL

PAPAL
STATES

SPAIN

• Madrid

Algeria

Azores

Madeira

Canary Is.

M O R O C C O

S a h a r a

Cape Verde Is.

St Louis •

Fort James •

TEKRUR

SONGHAI

Hausa
states

MALI

Mossi
states

BOR

Portuguese
Guinea

O'
BEN

Elmina •

AKAN

Fernando Póo

CON

The world in 1650

The changes in the distribution of world power since 1600, the end date of Map 11 (p. 166), are dramatic and largely attributable to the successes of those nations and peoples who most effectively exploited advances in the technology of warfare at sea, though the most important changes are not reflected in political boundaries. The Ottomans and Spain have held their ground, even expanded a bit. Portugal has regained her empire, albeit a diminished one. Russia has filled the vacuum left by the Mongol Khanates. England has established herself as a trans-oceanic Empire. The Netherlands are, however briefly, world hegemon.

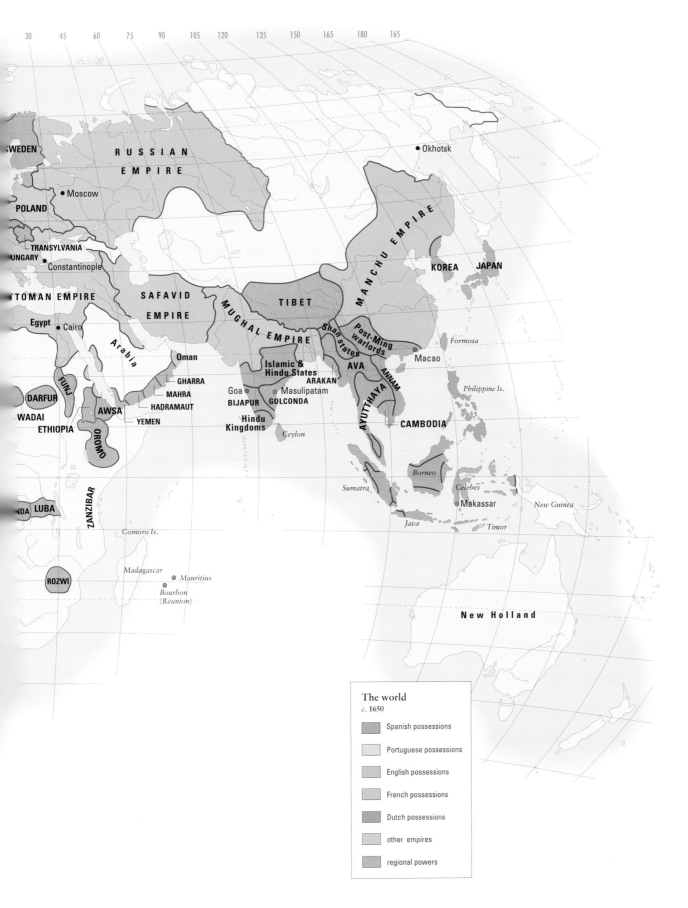

The world
c. 1650

- Spanish possessions
- Portuguese possessions
- English possessions
- French possessions
- Dutch possessions
- other empires
- regional powers

Meanwhile the galleon was giving way to the ship-of-the-line. The transition was gradual and at first applied only in European waters. Larger English warships, in particular, were functionally ships-of-the-line from the 1630s, but captains and admirals were slow to adopt the line-ahead tactics that dependence on broadsides logically entailed. Boarding and entering were the tactics of preference, and the line-ahead was considered a defensive expedient until halfway through the First Anglo-Dutch War (1652–4). Then, at the battle of Portland, from 28 February to 2 March 1653, the English rear, isolated and assailed by the bulk of the Dutch fleet under Tromp, with the advantage of the wind, survived by forming line-ahead and reducing the fight to an artillery duel, thus mirroring Tromp's tactics of fourteen years earlier. By the war's end, first the English and then the Dutch had formally adopted the line-ahead. That marked the beginning of a new era, an era strikingly unlike that of galley and galleon, for ships-of-the-line fighting in linear formation could, unlike galleys and galleons, sustain and protect maritime empires as well as capture bases and disrupt commerce.

Galleons continued to be an important means of power projection in distant waters long after the Downs, although engagements involving as many as a dozen were a rarity. The most important of these galleon wars, as we might term them, were between the Dutch and Portuguese for the East Indies and Brazil. The Dutch won the former, taking Malacca by siege in 1641 after eight years of blockade, conquering most of Ceylon (Sri Lanka) by 1640 and reducing Portugal's eastern empire to Goa, East Timor and Macao. Surprisingly, the Portuguese prevailed in Brazil, by taking a leaf from the Dutch book and pursuing hostilities by means of

A Hendrik Vroom painting of Spanish warships engaging Barbary corsairs from the National Maritime Museum. Such actions would have been far more typical of the day, and in the aggregate nearly as important, as the major sea battles to which we have devoted most of our attention.

a self-supporting corporate entity, the Companhia Geral do Comércio do Brasil (the Brazilian Commerce Company), modelled on the VOC (the Dutch East India Company). Founded in 1648, the Companhia dispatched a fleet to Brazil in late 1649, supported by profits from the tobacco and sugar trades. The West India Company responded in kind, but was strapped for cash: the Dutch sailors, unpaid and mutinous, refused to stay abroad, and by 1650 the Companhia controlled Brazilian waters. Abandoned and isolated, the last Dutch planters surrendered in 1654.

Curiously, the eclipse of the Mediterranean war galley was more gradual than that of the galleon. The galleon was transformed into the ship-of-the-line, but the galley was already pressing its design limits and had nowhere to go but bigger. Tactically dominant in waters where it could operate, it was a prodigious consumer of human and fiscal resources. Having reached the apex of their strategic power at Lepanto in 1571, galley fleets declined abruptly in importance thereafter. Galleys retained their tactical utility, but in increasingly specialized roles and decreasing numbers. As late as 1599 Spain sent a galley squadron from the Mediterranean to Flanders under Federico Spinola. It operated successfully in the Channel; the Dutch built galleys to counter it, but these never numbered more than eight. The galley squadron was destroyed in 1603 by the Dutch and was never replaced. The galleys of the Knights of St John raided freely in Levantine waters throughout the 1640s, for the verdict of Lepanto held; their depredations served mainly as a *casus belli* for the Ottomans against Venice in 1654, for the Knights' galleys took refuge in Venetian ports on occasion.

Entitled 'Shipping in the Bosporus,' this van de Croos painting shows a variety of early to mid seventeenth-century vessels with commendable accuracy.

A bird's-eye view of the Venetian fortress of Retimno at the time of the War of Crete. Such places were critical nodal points of Mediterranean warfare at sea throughout the period of our concern.

Galleys and galleasses played a significant role in the Venetian–Ottoman wars for Crete, from 1654 to 1669, and the Morea (the Peleponnese), from 1694 to 1698, but they were operating in conjunction with sailing warships, mostly purchased from the Dutch. France operated a small galley squadron in the Channel in the wars of Louis XIV, although by then France's galleys were arguably serving mainly as floating prisons and as an outlet for the energies of potentially recalcitrant nobles. Both Sweden and Russia used galleys in the Great Northern War of 1700–21, but this was largely because of the geography of the Baltic's inshore islands and the availability of conscripted soldiers as oarsmen.

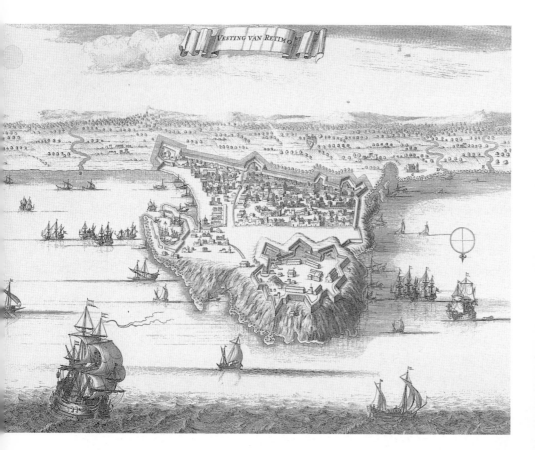

These final conflicts were an afterglow, for by 1650 the age of galley and galleon was effectively at an end. It had been a brilliant epoch, producing major changes in the global allocation of political and economic power. The importance of the ensuing era of warfare at sea, that of the ship-of-the-line, has long been recognized, for it was ships-of-the-line that gave first England, and then Britain, world hegemony. But it is worth remembering that heavy gunpowder ordnance made the ship-of-the-line what it was, and that the considerable problems of harnessing big guns to a floating gun platform were first solved by the designers of the Mediterranean war galley, and later by those of the galleon.

Depiction of a battle between galleons and galleys – in their final days – by Abraham Storck (1635–1710). Here, a powerfully-armed galleon clashes with two galleys.

BIOGRAPHIES

ALBA, FERNANDO ALVAREZ DE TOLEDO, 3RD DUKE OF (1507–82), SPANISH MILITARY LEADER
Emperor Charles V's favourite commander and perhaps the best general of his day, Alba was a brilliant logistician and understood the risks of battle. His ruthless anti-Protestantism as Philip II's Governor General in the Netherlands (1567–73) turned the Dutch revolt into a religious war.

d'ALBUQUERQUE, AFFONSO, PORTUGUESE NAVAL COMMANDER AND GOVERNOR GENERAL OF THE ESTADO DA INDIA (SERVED 1509–15)
The first great naval strategist of the modern era, Albuquerque gave Portugal's eastern empire its definitive form by seizing Goa (1510), Malacca (1511), and Ormuz (1515).

BARBAROSSA, KHAIREDDIN (1483–1546), MUSLIM GHAZI LEADER AND OTTOMAN KAPUDAN PASHA FROM 1533
Originally known as Hizir Re'is, Barbarossa ('Red Beard') was a master of galley tactics and the most successful of the sea ghazis opposing Spain in the western Mediterranean in the early 1500s. After consolidating his hold on Algiers, he travelled to Constantinople in 1533 to take up his appointment as Sultan Süleyman I's high admiral.

BARBARIGO, AGOSTIN (DIED 7 OCTOBER 1571), VENETIAN NAVAL COMMANDER
Barbarigo commanded the Left Wing of the Holy League's fleet in 1571 and replaced Sebastian Venier, his *Capo da Mar*, in councils of war when Venier's antipathy to the Genoese and sharp reaction to Spanish provocation made him *persona non grata*. Barbarigo led his wing to victory and died in battle.

BAYEZID II, OTTOMAN SULTAN (REIGNED 1481–1512)
Bayezid defeated – but failed to capture and execute – his half-brother Cem in the succession struggle following Mehmed II's death and Cem found refuge with the Ottoman state's enemies: the Egyptian Mamelukes, the Knights of St John, and eventually Charles VIII of France. Since both princes' claims to the throne were equally valid by Ottoman law, Bayezid was hamstrung in the west so long as Cem remained alive and able to renew the struggle. Bayezid moved decisively against Venice after Cem's death in 1499.

DON ÁLVARO DE BAZÁN (1526–88), MARQUÉS OF SANTA CRUZ FROM 1569, SPANISH NAVAL COMMANDER
Son of Álvaro de Bazán the Elder, Charles V's Captain General of the Galleys of Spain, he was the most renowned Spanish admiral of his day, commanding the Christian reserve at Lepanto, leading the naval arm of Philip II's invasion of Portugal in 1580, and defeating the French at Punta Delgada in 1582. He died in February 1588 as commander-designate of the Armada.

CHARLES V, HOLY ROMAN EMPEROR AND KING CHARLES I OF SPAIN (RULED 1516–56)
Charles inherited the dual kingdom of Ferdinand of Aragon and Isabella of Castile in 1516 and was elected Holy Roman Emperor in 1519. The accession of Mexico and Peru made his empire the largest on earth and the subsequent discovery of rich silver deposits in both places, particularly Peru, made it the richest. He retired to a monastery in 1556, his strategic designs frustrated by Valois France and evil luck.

CHENG HO, CHINESE ADMIRAL (COMMANDED 1405–35)
A Ming court eunuch, probably of Central Asian origins, Cheng Ho led a series of massive naval expeditions into the Indian Ocean between 1405 and 1435, expanding his imperial masters' suzerainty and influence. The expeditions ceased when mandarin scholar–bureaucrats gained ascendancy over the court eunuchs.

COLONNA, MARC ANTONIO (1535–84), PAPAL CAPTAIN GENERAL AT SEA
A seasoned warrior–diplomat, in 1571 Colonna served as an effective intermediary between Don Juan of Austria and the prickly Venetians in the difficult

process of welding the fleet of the Holy League into an effective fighting force. His lantern galley fought alongside Don Juan's at Lepanto.

DORIA, ANDREA (1466–1560), GENOESE LEADER AND NAVAL CONDOTTIERO
Patriarch of an ancient and wealthy Genoese family, Doria was one of the shrewdest and most capable practitioners of galley warfare. His most notable political act was to switch Genoa's allegiance from France to Spain in 1528. Defeated by Khaireddin Barbarossa at Prevesa in 1538, he nevertheless effectively represented his city and his imperial patron.

DORIA, GIAN ANDREA (1539–1606), GENOESE LEADER AND NAVAL CONDOTTIERO
Andrea Doria's great-nephew and heir, Gian Andrea inherited his forebear's post as Philip II's Captain General of the Sea in the Mediterranean. Defeated by Piali Pasha at Djerba in 1560, he commanded the Christian Right at Lepanto with results that remain controversial to this day.

DORIA, PIERO (DIED 6 JANUARY 1380), GENOESE CAPTAIN GENERAL AT SEA
Doria inherited his post when his predecessor, Luciano Doria, was killed at the battle of Pola, 6 May 1379. He commanded the seizure of Chioggia and was famous for rejecting Venetian entreaties for negotiations. He was killed during the siege by a section of wall brought down by a Venetian cannonball.

DRAKE, SIR FRANCIS (C. 1540–95), ENGLISH CORSAIR AND NAVAL LEADER
A favourite of Queen Elizabeth and one of the most competent seamen and naval tacticians of his age, he was at heart an entrepreneur and freebooter. Knighted in 1581 after his circumnavigation of the globe, he was appointed vice admiral in 1588, serving as Howard of Effingham's second in command for the Armada campaign. His prescient appreciation of the effects of close-range gunfire was probably critical to the defeat of the Armada.

EDWARD III, KING OF ENGLAND (REIGNED 1327–77)
Best known for his land victories over the French in the Hundred Years War, Edward was one of the few European monarchs of his day personally to command at sea. His victory at the battle of Sluys in 1340 preserved England from the threat of French invasion.

ELIZABETH I, QUEEN OF ENGLAND (REIGNED 1558–1603)
Henry VIII's daughter by his second wife, Anne Boleyn, Elizabeth's accession to the throne was highly improbable. Once there, she proved a shrewd and capable leader. Her intelligent use of her nautically-inclined subjects' aptitude for using armed violence for their – and her – enrichment laid the foundations for England's rise to world hegemony.

FARNESE, ALEXANDER, DUKE OF PARMA (1545–92), SPANISH MILITARY COMMANDER
Philip II's best general, Parma was brilliantly successful against the Dutch Protestants, but was repeatedly diverted by Philip's orders to intervene elsewhere just when victory seemed within his grasp. Had Philip heeded Parma's advice, he might well have prevailed in the Netherlands.

DON GARCIA DE TOLEDO, MARQUÉS DE VILLAFRANCA (1514–78), SPANISH NAVAL COMMANDER
A skilled strategist, Don Garcia was the architect of victory at Malta in 1565 as Philip II's Captain General of the Sea in the Mediterranean and viceroy of Sicily. He lived into retirement, and at Philip II's request proffered advice to Don Juan of Austria when the latter was appointed Captain General of the Fleet of the Holy League in 1571.

DON JUAN OF AUSTRIA (1547–78), SPANISH MILITARY COMMANDER AND CAPTAIN GENERAL OF THE FLEET OF THE HOLY LEAGUE (1571–73)
Bastard son of Emperor Charles V and half-brother of Philip II, he was groomed for positions of leadership by his father. His youth and inexperience notwithstanding, and despite the handicap of his illegitimate birth, he proved a gifted diplomat and inspirational leader, defeating the Turks at Lepanto. After the break-up of the Holy League, he was appointed Philip's commander-in-chief in Flanders and died there.

GAMA, VASCO DA (DIED 1542), PORTUGUESE NAVAL COMMANDER

Scion of a noble Portuguese family, Da Gama commanded the first European expedition to reach India by sea and return with a cargo of spices. He returned to lead the Portuguese to victory over the forces of the Zamorin of Calicut of the Malabar Coast in 1503.

HENRY VIII, KING OF ENGLAND (REIGNED 1509–47)

In addition to reforming the Church of England and marrying six wives, Henry strengthened the Royal Navy and – more important over the long haul – supported the development of cannon founding in England.

HEYN, PEITER PIETERSZOON (1577–1629), DUTCH ADMIRAL

Peit Heyn commanded the Dutch West Indies Company fleet that captured the entire home-bound Spanish treasure fleet in Matanzas Bay, Cuba, in 1628. The exploit was never repeated, but the proceeds funded the Dutch assault on Portuguese Brazil for nearly three decades.

HOWARD OF EFFINGHAM, LORD CHARLES, HIGH ADMIRAL OF ENGLAND FROM 1586

Descended from the Howard High Admiral who died at the hands of the French in Brest Roads in 1513, Howard was a naval innovator, administrator and leader of remarkable competence. His reform of the Royal Navy and support of development of the race-built galleon were essential components of victory over the Armada in 1588.

MEDINA SIDONIA, ALONSO PÉREZ DE GUZMÁN, 7TH DUKE OF (1549–1615), COMMANDER OF THE INVINCIBLE ARMADA

A successful commander on land – he organized and led the counter-attack against Drake's 1587 attack on Cádiz – and a competent administrator, his impeccable bloodlines led to his selection by Philip II to command the Armada of 1588.

MEHMET II, 'THE CONQUEROR', OTTOMAN SULTAN (REIGNED 1444–46, 1450–81)

A ruthless and brilliant intellect – he is said to have spoken seven languages including Italian and Hungarian – he was one of the first monarchs to fully appreciate the strategic potential of heavy siege guns. The burden of taxation needed to support his expansive foreign policy helped produce a tumultuous succession struggle following his death in 1481.

MÜEZZENZADE ('SON OF THE CALLER TO PRAYERS') ALI PASHA (DIED 7 OCTOBER 1571), OTTOMAN KAPUDAN PASHA

Sultan Selim I's Kapudan Pasha after Piali Pasha's dismissal, he was defeated by Don Juan of Austria at Lepanto. Brave and capable he was crossed by bad luck … or perhaps by orders from Selim II to fight come what may.

OQUENDO, DON ANTONIO DE (1577–1640), SPANISH ADMIRAL

A grandée with impeccable bloodlines, his reputation was burnished by victory over the Dutch at Abrolhos in 1631. Oquendo was a renowned horseman and devotee of the chivalric ideal … which qualities contributed directly to his defeat at The Downs in 1639.

PHILIP II, KING OF SPAIN (REIGNED 1556–1600)

The most powerful monarch of his day despite the division of his father's inheritance (Austria went to his German cousins), Philip ruled over the first empire on which the sun never set. His insistence on overseeing every detail of governance undercut his strategic designs in several critical instances. He displayed uncommonly good judgement in selecting key subordinates, but often failed to heed their warnings.

PIALI PASHA, OTTOMAN KAPUDAN PASHA (SERVED 1555–71)

A skilled naval commander, Piali's crushing defeat of the Habsburg fleet under Gian Andrea Doria at Djerba in 1560 was the most brilliant galley fleet victory of the early modern era. He was dismissed by Sultan Selim II for failing to prevent a Venetian relief expedition from reaching Famagusta in January 1571.

PISANI, VETTOR, VENETIAN CAPO DI MARE (1377–82)

A popular hero, Pisani was a rare exception to the Venetian patrician ideal of self-effacing – albeit self-aggrandizing – anonymity. He recovered from defeat at Pola (6 May 1379) to lead Venice to victory in the siege of Chioggia (22 December 1379 – 19 June 1380).

SEBASTIAN I, KING OF PORTUGAL (DIED 3 AUGUST 1578)
The last of Portugal's crusading Avis kings, Sebastian led his army to destruction at Alcazarquivir in Morocco, paving the way for Philip II's assumption of the Portuguese throne in 1580 and Spain's absorption of the Portuguese empire.

SELIM II, 'THE SOT', OTTOMAN SULTAN (REIGNED 1566–75)
Placed on the throne by the machinations of his mother, Süleyman I's favourite wife Hurrem who is said to have had his half-brother Mehmet strangled, Selim ruled through his Grand Vizier Sokullu Mehmet Pasha. The sobriquet Sot was more likely a slur applied by opponents of his policies than an accurate commentary on the effects of his penchant for Cypriot wines.

SÜLEYMAN I, 'THE MAGNIFICENT', OTTOMAN SULTAN (REIGNED 1520–66)
Süleyman led his army to the gates of Vienna in 1529, marking the limits of westward Ottoman expansion on land. By the end of his long reign, he had effectively delegated the day-to-day business of governance to his grand viziers, of whom he had only nine. The last, Sokullu Mehmet Pasha, held the post from 1565 until 1579, well into the reign of Süleyman's grandson Murad III.

TOYOTOMI HIDEYOSHI, RULER OF JAPAN (RULED 1583–98)
Inheritor of a Japan united by his predecessor Oda Nobunaga (died 1582), Hideyoshi was a renaissance prince of boundless energy and ambitions. His armies were the largest and – until the Korean navy intervened – the best supplied of their day.

TROMP, MAARTEN HARPERTSZOON (1598–1653), DUTCH ADMIRAL
A masterful mariner and tactician, Tromp served as Peit Heyn's flag captain (the captain of Heyn's flagship), before rising to prominence as the greatest Dutch naval commander of his day. Blunt and

practical, he was a ruthlessly realistic tactician. His use of line-ahead tactics off the French coast on 16 September 1639 accurately forecast the definitive tactics of the ship-of-the-line.

ULUJ ALI PASHA, TURKISH NAVAL COMMANDER AND OTTOMAN KAPUDAN PASHA (1572–87)
Of North African ghazi origins, Uluj Ali may have been the most skilled galley commander of his day. Commanding the Turkish left at Lepanto, he nearly salvaged victory from defeat. At the head of a large but in many respects defective galley fleet the next year he effectively stalemated the Christians and went on to recapture Tunis from the Spanish in 1574.

VASA, GUSTAV I, KING OF SWEDEN (REIGNED 1523–60)
Leader of the Swedish nobility in throwing off Danish rule and founder of the Vasa dynasty, Gustav was also the father of Swedish sea power. His policy of building up a strong, artillery-armed state navy was a harbinger of later developments in England, the Netherlands and France.

VENIER, SEBASTIAN, VENETIAN CAPITANO GENERALE DA MAR (1570–71)
A crusty patrician in his 70s, Venier, commanded the Venetian contingent of the fleet of the Holy League in 1571. A staunch defender of Venetian prerogatives, his distrust of Gian Andrea Doria and the Genoese posed major problems for Don Juan of Austria. He fought with distinction at Lepanto.

YI SUN-SIN, KOREAN ADMIRAL (DIED 1598)
A brilliant naval tactician, he was a sound strategist who used guerrilla forces to shield his logistical base in south-western Korea from Japanese incursions. Dismissed for his unwillingness to suffer incompetent court favourites gladly after his signal victories of 1592, he was reappointed in the aftermath of disastrous defeat in 1597. Like Nelson, he died in his moment of victory.

FURTHER READING AND SOURCES

The literature of warfare at sea between the High Middle Ages and the beginning of the age of sea power is rich and varied, though with large gaps if we limit ourselves to works in English reasonably available to the general reader. Christopher Allmand, *The Hundred Years War: England and France at War, c. 1300–c. 1450* (1988) covers naval operations competently, though *aficionados* with access to a good library will want to consult *The Chronicles of Jean Froissart*, available in many editions, for contemporary impressions. For Ming China's foray into trans-oceanic exploration, 1421–35, and the remarkable voyages of eunuch–admiral Cheng Ho, Joseph Needham *et al.*, *Science and Civilisation in China*, Vol. 4, *Physics and Physical Technology*, Part III: *Civil Engineering and Nautics* (1971), provide a fascinating account, though Needham and his colleagues have badly exaggerated the dimensions of the famous treasure ships by taking their technologically naïve sources at face value.

Ralph Payne-Gallwey, *The Crossbow*, published in 1903 and frequently reprinted, contains an appendix on the Turco-Mongol composite bow and is basic for individual bolt- and arrow-firing weapons. The definitive work on bronze cannon founding, which remained unchanged in its essentials from the late 1400s, is Carel de Beers, ed., *The Art of Gunfounding: The Casting of Bronze Cannon in the late 18th Century* (1991).

Frederic C. Lane, *Venice, A Maritime Republic* (1973), remains the best single volume on the subject … although the reader will have to consult Daniele di Chinazzo's contemporary *Cronica de la Guerra da Veniciani a Zenovesi* – fortunately available in a modern edition (Venice, 1958) -– for a narrative of the Chioggian War. Three excellent surveys that cover most or all of the period with which this book is concerned within their respective spheres are John H. Pryor, *Geography, Technology and War: Studies in the Maritime History of the Mediterranean 649–1571* (1988, second edition 1992); Nicholas A. M. Rodger, *The Safeguard of the Sea: A Naval History of Britain, 660–1649* (1997); and Jan Glete, *Warfare at Sea, 1500–1650: Maritime Conflicts and the Transformation of Europe* (2000). Pryor brilliantly fulfils the promise of his title and is particularly strong on geography and weather. Rodger's work avoids the Anglocentric bias usual in general surveys and competently addresses the evolution of warship design. Glete breaks new ground by incorporating the Baltic – previously *terra incognito* for naval historians, this one included – into the overall picture. His treatment of Portugal's rise and decline and of the Revolt of the Netherlands are particularly valuable.

Two volumes in the *History of the Ship* series by Conway Maritime Press, edited by Robert Gardiner, address the technical and operational aspects of their subjects in remarkable depth... and with appropriate qualifications where the evidence is incomplete or equivocal as it so often is. *The Age of the Galley: Mediterranean Oared Vessels since pre-classical Times* (1995), edited by John Morrison, contains an impressive array of chapters authored by experts in, to cite but a few subjects: the evolution of war galley design, AD 500–1300 by John Pryor; the design of ancient galleys by John Coates; the mechanics of oared propulsion by Mauro Bondioli, René Barlet and André Zysberg; and the logistics of galley warfare by John Dotson. *Cogs, Caravels and Galleons: The Sailing Ship, 1000–1650*, edited by Richard W. Unger, features chapters on the cog as a cargo carrier by Detlev Ellmers; the cog as a warship by Timothy J. Runyan; the carrack and the evolution of the full-rigged ship by Ian Friel; the caravel and galleon by Martin Elbl and Carla Rahn Philips; and guns and gunnery by the author of this volume. William Ledyard Rodgers, *Naval Warfare Under Oars, 4th to 16th Centuries: A Study of Strategy, Tactics and Ship Design*, first published in 1940 and reprinted in 1967, bridges the transition from crossbow to gunpowder and is notable for clarity of technical explanations.

Charles W. C. Oman, *A History of the Art of War in the Sixteenth Century*, published in 1937 and recently reprinted (2000), though dated in its treatment of socio-economic factors, remains basic for European warfare on land. Oman addresses naval matters only in passing… with the important exception of the Ottoman assault on Christendom. His accounts of the great galley fights, Prevesa, Djerba and Lepanto, and of the sieges of Rhodes and Malta, though occasionally superseded in detail by later research are models of analytical clarity. Gregory Hanlon, *The Twilight of a Military Tradition: Italian Aristocrats and European Conflicts, 1560–1800*, contains first-rate accounts of the Habsburg–Ottoman struggle for control of the Mediterranean and the 1645–69 War of Crete. My own *Gunpowder and Galleys: Changing Technology and Mediterranean Warfare at Sea in the Sixteenth Century* (1974), addresses many of the issues and events covered in the present volume in greater detail. Errors detected by reviewers and additional research – the role of the Papal Captain General at Prevesa, the Muslim order of battle at Lepanto and a Turco-Mongol (or English) archer's sustained rate of fire – were corrected in the preceding pages.

No early modern naval campaign has produced more publications than the Invincible Armada of 1588, and of these the best is Colin Martin and Geoffrey Parker, *The Spanish Armada* (1988); the revised second edition (1999) contains important new insights. By contrast, there is almost nothing readily available in English on Toyotomi Hideyoshi's invasion of Korea. Mary Elizabeth Berry, *Hideyoshi* (1982) gives a useful strategic overview; Stephen Turnbull, *Samurai Warriors* (1987), explains the development of Japanese weaponry and methods of warfare. Jonathan J. Israel, *The Dutch Republic and the Hispanic World, 1606–1661* (1982) gives a solid account of the latter stages of the Eighty Years War, but for the 1639 campaign and the Battle of the Downs, one must track down Charles R. Boxer, translator and editor, *The Journal of Maarten Harpertszoon Tromp, Anno 1639*, published in 1930 and not easily found.

Finally, *The Readers Companion to Military History*, edited by Robert W. Cowley and Geoffrey Parker provides a cornucopia of articles addressing in greater depth and detail many of the events, concepts, and persons referred to in the preceding pages.

INDEX

Picture credits

Every effort has been made to contact the copyright holders for images reproduced in this book. The publishers would welcome any errors or omissions being brought to their attention.

Scala Endpapers, pp. 30, 40–41, 43, 56–7, 80–81, 104, 107, 119, 123, 131, 132, 134, 147, 165 (bottom), 166, 167, 168, 193, 213; Sonia Halliday Photographs pp. 6, 16, 32, 129, 135; British Library pp. 14, 17, 23 (top), 59, 88, 111; Bridgeman Art Library: pp. 21, 28, Bibliotheque Nationale, Paris; p. 24, British Library; p. 36 Museo de America, Madrid; pp. 38, 51 Palazzo Ducale, Venice; p. 42 Museo Nazionale di San Martino, Naples; p. 52 Library of Congress Washington, DC; pp. 58, 74–5, 180–81 Private Collection; pp. 109, 122 Museo Storico Navale, Venice; pp. 124–5 Musée du Vieux Port, Marseille; p. 182 Musée Guimet, Paris; p. 191 The Stapleton Collection; pp. 194–5 Johnny van Haeften, London; pp. 202–3 Trustees of Sir John Soane's Museum, London; pp. 206–7 Frans Hals Museum, Haarlem/Index; AKG pp. 86, 89, 130, 140, 142–3, 156, 172–3; Ancient Art & Architecture Collection p. 108 (top); National Maritime Museum, Greenwich pp. 23 (bottom), 70, 91, 163, 176–7, 196, 198, 199, 201, 210, 211; Art Archive pp. 48, 55, 84, 92–3, 94–5, 98, 118, 127, 137, 162, 165 (top) 171, 178–9, 192, 197; Author's Collection pp. 61, 64, 66, 71; Mary Evans Picture Library pp. 108, 110, 176; Museo Storico Navale, Venice pp. 115, 128, 136, 149; Portsmouth City Museums pp. 116–17; Museo Correr, Venice p. 148; Corbis/Bettmann p. 160, 170 Historical Picture Archive, 185 Asian Art & Archeology, Inc, 187 Kevin R. Morris; Rijksmuseum, Amsterdam p. 204. The map of Rethimnon on p. 212 is reproduced from Olfert Dapper's *Zeekaerte van de Archipel en Archipelesche Eylanden*, Amsterdam, 1688 (Dutch text edition).

Drawings on the title page and on pages 25, 33, 96, 97, 103, 111, 112, 159, 161 and 187 are by Peter Smith and Malcolm Swanston of Arcadia Editions Ltd.

Drawings on pages 62, 63, 65, 66, 67, 68 and 69 are by Peter Harper, from originals by the author.

ENDPAPER: *A near contemporary painting of the battle of Lepanto from the Venetian school. While the colours are no doubt brighter than they were in reality, it beautifully depicts the chaos of battle.*